CONTEMPORARY SOCIAL THEORY
General Editor: ANTHONY GIDDENS

This series aims to create a forum for debate between different theoretical and philosophical traditions in the social sciences. As well as covering broad schools of thought, the series will also concentrate upon the work of particular thinkers whose ideas have had a major impact on social science (these books appear under the sub-series title of 'Theoretical Traditions in the Social Sciences'). The series is not limited to abstract theoretical discussion — it will also include more substantive works on contemporary capitalism, the state, politics and other subject areas.

Published Titles

Tony Bilton, Kevin Bonnett, Philip Jones, Ken Sheard, Michelle Stanworth and Andrew Webster, *Introductory Sociology* (2nd edition)
Emile Durkheim, *The Division of Labour in Society* (trans W.D. Halls)
Emile Durkheim, *The Rules of Sociological Method* (ed. Steven Lukes, trans. W.D. Halls)
Boris Frankel, *Beyond the State? Dominant Theories and Socialist Strategies*
Anthony Giddens, *A Contemporary Critique of Historical Materialism*
Anthony Giddens, *Central Problems in Social Theory*
Anthony Giddens, *Profiles and Critiques in Social Theory*
Anthony Giddens and David Held (eds), *Classes, Power and Conflict: Classical and Contemporary Debates*
Geoffrey Ingham, *Capitalism Divided? The City and Industry in British Social Development*
Terry Johnson, Christopher Dandeker and Clive Ashworth, *The Structure of Social Theory*
Douglas Kellner, *Herbert Marcuse and the Crisis of Marxism*
Jorge Larrain, *Marxism and Ideology*
Gerry Rose, *Deciphering Sociological Research*
John Scott, *The Upper Classes: Property and Privilege in Britain*
Steve Taylor, *Durkheim and the Study of Suicide*
John B. Thompson and David Held (eds), *Habermas: Critical Debates*

Forthcoming Titles

Martin Albrow, *Weber and the Construction of Social Theory*
Ali Rattansi and Dominic Strinati, *Marx and the Sociology of Class*

CONTEMPORARY SOCIAL THEORY

General Editor: ANTHONY GIDDENS

Theoretical Traditions in the Social Sciences

This series introduces the work of major figures in social science
to students beyond their immediate specialisms.

Published Titles

Barry Barnes, *T.S. Kuhn and Social Science*
Ted Benton, *The Rise and Fall of Structural Marxism: Althusser and his Influence*
David Bloor, *Wittgenstein: A Social Theory of Knowlege*
Christopher Bryant, *Positivism in Social Theory*
Mark Cousins and Athar Hussain, *Michel Foucault*
Bob Jessop, *Nicos Poulantzas: Marxist Theory and Political Strategy*
William Outhwaite, *New Philosophies of Social Science: Realism, Hermeneutics and
    Critical Theory*
Julian Roberts, *Walter Benjamin*
Rick Roderick, *Habermas and the Foundations of Critical Theory*
James Schmidt, *Maurice Merleau-Ponty: Between Phenomenology and
    Structuralism*
Dennis Smith, *Barrington Moore: Violence, Morality and Political Change*
Dennis Smith, *The Chicago School: A Liberal Critique of Capitalism*
Piotr Sztompka, *Robert K. Merton: An Intellectual Profile*

Forthcoming Titles

Ira Cohen, *Structuration Theory*
John Forrester, *Jacques Lacan*
Robin Williams, *Erving Goffman*

Deciphering Sociological Research

Gerry Rose
London School of Economics and Political Science

M
MACMILLAN
EDUCATION

First published 1982
Reprinted 1985, 1986, 1987, 1988

Published by
MACMILLAN EDUCATION LTD
Houndmills, Basingstoke, Hampshire RG21 2XS
and London
Companies and representatives
throughout the world

Printed in Hong Kong

ISBN 0-333-28558-1

Contents

Preface

This is a book about sociological research methods but with a
distinctive rationale and approach to the topic. The core of the
approach is the systematic analysis, or *deciphering,* of published
research reports in relation to key issues of methodology. Because
of this focus, many aspects of research methods are discussed only
briefly, and I stress that this book is not intended as a comprehensive text. It should be seen as complementary to existing textbooks; there are two reasons – it deals with the important subject
of deciphering research reports (which is not covered adequately
elsewhere) and it gives a fresh perspective on many problems of
research method.

Previous attempts to devise methods for the analysis of research
reports have been rather limited in scope. The most thorough
treatment of the problem is the book by Tripodi *et al.* (1969),
which is intended for social-work students. Riley's book (1963) is
the most comprehensive work in which research reports are used
as examples for the discussion of methodological problems;
however, it consists largely of exegesis, and gives little attention to
the critical evaluation of the studies with which it deals. These two
works, together with a handful of other sources which are reviewed in Chapter 9, contain useful material but none of them
provides a systematic analysis of the problem of deciphering
sociological research comparable with this book.

The book is intended mainly for the sociology student. It can be
used as the central text for a course of (say) one or two terms'
duration at second- or third-year undergraduate level, in combination with other texts as the basis for any course on research
methods, or for individual study. In Part One I develop the central

theme of deciphering sociological research; research based on quantitative data is discussed in Chapters 1 to 6, and research using qualitative data is the subject of Chapters 7 and 8. Exercises for the reader can be found at the end of each chapter. The advantages and limitations of the deciphering approach are considered in Chapter 9. Throughout Part One there is continued reference to the selected research reports which comprise Part Two of the book. These twelve reports, given as Chapters 10 to 21, are edited versions of articles published in sociology journals, and they act as examples for the analysis in Part One.

Although the book is presented in a form suitable for use in undergraduate teaching, I hope that it will attract much wider attention. As I argue in Chapter 9, deciphering research reports is an activity in which one would imagine the professional sociologist to be highly skilled and competent – but, of course, this is not so, as the standard of much published research shows. The approach which is presented in this book should be extremely helpful to authors and journal editors as well as to the professional sociologist as a consumer of the literature.

ACKNOWLEDGEMENTS

I should like to thank the many students at La Trobe University who, between 1970 and 1979, have been exposed to much of the material in this book and whose reactions have been invaluable. Groups of students at Cambridge, Brunel University and the London School of Economics and Political Science have also provided helpful comments. Much advice and encouragement has been given by colleagues and friends – particularly fellow members of the Sociology Department at La Trobe University. I especially wish to thank the following individuals – Frank Lewins, the late Jean I. Martin, Yoshio Sugimoto, Gordon Ternowetsky, Lyn Richards, Andrew Prolisko, Tony Giddens, and also John Winckler of Macmillan.

The consent of authors and publishers to reprint the edited articles included in the book is gratefully acknowledged; specific recognition is given on the first page of each chapter in Part Two.

I am particularly indebted to Kathy Wondga for expert secretarial assistance in the early stages of writing and for the typing of Part Two, and to Jenny Connor for typing Part One.

London   Gerry Rose
April 1981

Part One

Deciphering Sociological Research

Introduction

Much of the sociologist's work involves reading and interpreting the writing of others. The professional sociologist finds it necessary to 'keep up with the literature' in his areas of interest, and for students at all levels it is considered important to read widely within that same literature. A glance at the sociological journals, or at the relevant shelves of a college library, will show that a significant proportion of sociological writing consists of reports based on empirical research. Few sociologists would dispute the assertion that research reports occupy an important and central place in the sociological literature. However, these reports necessarily include certain technical details and are commonly presented in a highly condensed format; consequently, a research report is often rather difficult reading, even for an individual who is familiar with the subject-matter which has been studied.

If we follow this line of reasoning, it seems clear that one of the sociologist's key skills should be a capacity to understand and evaluate, or to *decipher* research reports. Naturally, an individual sociologist or sociology student will, with increasing experience, develop this skill to some degree; the process is, however, usually somewhat haphazard since the matter is only rarely discussed explicitly. This book focuses directly on this problem, by presenting systematic methods for deciphering research reports. To take a simple example – a sociologist with a professional interest in social deviance may consider Becker's research on marijuana users (see Chapter 11) to be important. But, more specifically, he will wish to have a detailed understanding of Becker's research procedures, the evidence which is presented in the article, Becker's theory of becoming a marijuana user, and most importantly, the way in which Becker relates his evidence to his theory. The answers to these questions will add up to a deciphering of this particular study.

Deciphering Sociological Research

It is my experience that both students and professional sociologists tend to be naive in their approach to reading research reports. For example, it is common to read only the introduction and the conclusions, and the author's account of the research procedures and the tables may be given no more than a brief glance; alternatively, a reader may totally reject a report because he finds a defect or limitation in the research. Responses of this sort are not due simply to lack of time, they are due essentially to lack of skill or expertise in the deciphering of research reports. But what does this expertise involve? There are two main factors: first, the reader needs to have a basic grasp of what is normally termed *research methods* or *methodology;* a second, and less obvious, requirement is for an *analytic framework* which is designed specifically for the task of deciphering. These two factors therefore determine both the content and the structure of the forthcoming chapters. The reader will come into contact with most of the major issues of research methods; however, the objectives of the book give an order and coherence to these issues which is rather different from that found in existing textbooks.

The development of the argument in Part One of this book is crucially dependent on using reports of empirical research as examples. These are provided in Part Two, which consists of twelve selected reports; each is an edited version of an article published originally in one of the sociology journals. These reports will be referred to briefly as 'studies'; some are analysed thoroughly in Chapters 1 to 9, whereas others are referred to more briefly but are equally important in providing a range of examples and further exercises for the reader.

The introduction to Part Two gives details of the editing of the reports for publication in this book. The twelve studies have been selected carefully in relation to a number of factors. The research procedures used and rationale for the research are explained reasonably clearly and succinctly. No reports which use complex statistical techniques are included, and the presentation of statistical results is mainly through tables. As a whole, however, the studies illustrate a range of different approaches to research. They are chosen from several major substantive areas of sociology (e.g. deviance, education, stratification) but do not presume background knowledge in these areas; experience at the level of an introductory sociology course should be sufficient.

The selection of only twelve studies as the basis for my analysis would appear to place certain limitations on what can be achieved. This issue will be discussed in Chapter 9 in the context of a more general consideration of the merits and limitations of the deciphering approach. One vitally important point must be stressed before beginning. The reader should check the analysis in Chapters 1 to 9 carefully against the research reports in Part Two; an understanding of the argument in Part One cannot be fully developed unless this point is taken seriously.

Conventions. In presenting certain of the material in Part One I have followed two conventions which are worth stating explicitly. First, in considering the 'typical' research report or research project I have, whenever possible, referred to the author(s) or researcher(s) in a form which avoids the need to specify sex and number. In circumstances where this has proved too clumsy, I have followed the usual convention of referring to an individual author or researcher as 'he'; like Barnes (1979), I found this convention less distracting than any alternative. Second, double quotation marks have been used for quotation from specific sources. Single quotation marks are used for words or phrases which are worthy of note or which should be treated with caution – for example, a concept which is undefined or a term which should not be interpreted literally.

1
Beginnings

We begin by introducing two examples of research reports – those by Dornbusch and Hickman (Chapter 10) and Becker (Chapter 11). As we shall see, these two studies are quite different from one another and provide an illuminating contrast.

Dornbusch and Hickman's study

The aim of Dornbusch and Hickman's research was to test "Riesman's historical theory", which is, briefly, that there had been a historical trend towards other-directedness in American life, i.e. "a general trend in recent years away from a character structure based on internalized goals towards a social character emphasizing throughout life the guiding reactions of others". Their approach was to use the statements made in consumer-goods advertising as indicators of other-directedness. Clearly, it is assumed that tendencies in certain societal values (toward other-directedness, inner-directedness, and so on) will be reflected in advertising; so, by studying advertisements, we indirectly study trends in these societal values.

What aspects of research methods are involved? To answer this question is it helpful to refer to the glossary of terms (see the Appendix, pp. 305–9). Dornbusch and Hickman's general technique was *content analysis,* a particular kind of *unobtrusive method.* Their *sampling* was the selection of advertisements from one particular magazine over the period 1890–1956. There are six *indicators* of the *concept* of other-directedness (Dornbusch and Hickman call them "indices"); each of these six indicators is a *variable,* and time is also a variable. The *unit* of analysis is the individual advertisement.

These observations on Dornbusch and Hickman's study are rather general. It is helpful to identify the aspects of research methods italicised above, but we can go much further by drawing up a summary of the study in the form of five stages:

A THEORY. There has been a historical trend towards other-directedness in American life.

B THEORETICAL PROPOSITIONS. During the first half of the twentieth century there was an increase in the proportion of advertisments for American consumer goods which are other-directed.

C OPERATIONALISATION

Data-collection: content analysis (this involves systematic coding of verbal statements in the advertisements into six categories).

Sampling: decision to study *Ladies' Home Journal* 1890–1956. Choose one issue from each year (giving sixty-seven issues); choose forty-one of the sixty-seven issues. The sample is then *all* advertisements which appear in these forty-one issues of the magazine.

Unit: the individual advertisement.

Variables (1) Six indicators of other-directedness, corresponding to the six categories of statements. (2) Year of publication (note that this is analysed in decades, see Table 10. 2, p. 167).

D FIELD-WORK. Implementation of the decisions made under stage C. Checks on the validity and reliability of the method (checks between raters, etc.).

E RESULTS. Proposition confirmed, but in a modified form (peak of trend in 1930s, then decline). Discussion and interpretation.

The reasons for the use of the ABCDE layout will become more clear in Chapter 2. The main point to be emphasised here is that Dornbusch and Hickman have used a *theory-testing* approach, i.e. they have taken an existing theory (A), developed from it a proposition which is specific enough to be tested (B), devised a scheme for testing this proposition (C), carried through this scheme in practice (D), and drawn up results and discussed conclusions in relation to the original theory (E). Dornbusch and Hickman's conclusion is that Riesman's theory is generally confirmed, since they find a considerable increase in other-directedness in consumer-goods advertising over the period studied; however, the decline which is found after the 1930s leads to problems of interpretation.

Becker's study

Becker's research is on marijuana users. In contrast to the theory-testing approach to research, Becker's object is to *construct a theory* of the process of "becoming a marijuana user"; this is seen as a specific example of the process through which deviant activities develop. Becker has utilised marijuana users' own accounts of the activity as the basis of his study, and has constructed the theory from this data.

If we check the research report against the glossary of terms in the Appendix, it is evident that Becker's technique for data collection was *interviewing* – probably, focused interviewing is the best description. His *sampling* was the selection of fifty interviewees, and the *unit* of analysis is the individual person. It is also possible to pick out the concepts and indicators, but since this aspect of the study is by no means obvious a discussion will be deferred until later (Chapters 7 and 8).

It seems likely that at the outset of the research Becker simply decided to interview a sample of marijuana users, obtained mainly by personal contact. The intention to construct a theory was firmly in mind, but there was little, if any, preconception of the substantive content of the theory. The sample size (fifty) was probably not decided in advance. It is common, in this style of research, to continue sampling by including additional interviewees until the researcher decides that the sample is of adequate size (this will not normally be an arbitrary decision, for reasons to be discussed later). Becker's results are presented under three basic headings; these are the three factors which are 'discovered' in the course of the study, and which describe the process of becoming a marijuana user. They are (1) learning the technique, (2) learning to perceive the effects, and (3) learning to enjoy the effects. Together, these three factors constitute Becker's constructed theory.

CHARACTERISING RESEARCH REPORTS

These two examples have been chosen because they are polar

opposites in their approach to research, and because they highlight two major dimensions which are of crucial importance in characterising research reports. Consider first the distinction between theory-testing (Dornbusch and Hickman), and theory-construction (Becker). This dimension may be termed the *nature of the theory-evidence link*; as we shall see, the distinction between testing and constructing theories is a useful starting-point, but in many studies the theory-evidence link is rather more complex than either of these alternatives would suggest.

The second major dimension is the nature of the data. Dornbusch and Hickman's data are *quantitative* (or statistical); their empirical results are presented mainly in the form of tables, and some additional figures are given in the text. By contrast, Becker's study is based on *qualitative* data; the evidence which Becker presents in the report takes the form of extracts from the interviews. While there are some studies in which both kinds of data are used (for example, see Lacey, Chapter 15), in most cases a study can be characterised as based on either quantitative or qualitative data.

These two dimensions are in principle quite distinct, but in practice they do seem to be related. Thus theory-testing studies usually rely on the more structured techniques of data collection, such as content analysis or (more typically) a social survey with a standardised questionnaire. These techniques require that details of sampling and data collection be tightly planned in advance. In general, the data will be quantified in a manner which is also specified in advance, and in the research report results will be given in tables or by using other statistical means of presentation. By contrast, theory-construction studies more often use participant-observation and interviewing techniques of the less structured kind. Typically, the research procedures will be more loosely formulated at the outset, and some aspects of the research design (for example, certain details of sampling) are decided in the course of the field-work. Generally, the data will be qualitative, and the evidence offered in the research report will be extracts from interviews or statements based on observations.

Of course, this sketch of the two 'types' of research is rather oversimplified. However, I would argue that the two types represent dominant tendencies in the existing sociological literature, i.e. research carried out to test theories tends to use structured techniques and quantitative data, and researchers who use qualitative data tend to be interested mainly in theory-building. (The terms theory-construction and theory-building are used interchangeably.) Studies such as those of Jacobs (see Chapter 22), who tests an existing theory of bureaucracy using participant-observation data, and Goode (Chapter 13), who builds a theory of the multiple drug use of marijuana users from quantitative data, can be seen as 'counter-examples', since each diverges markedly from these types. More generally, as we shall see later, one can characterise any specific study by analysing the degree to which it conforms to either of these two types.

The distinction between these two types is, in fact, vital for this book, as it acts as a springboard for the methods which are developed for deciphering research reports. In Chapters 2 to 6 I shall be concerned principally with research based on quantitative data, and the framework for the deciphering of such studies is developed from a model for theory-testing research. Chapters 7 and 8 take up the question of deciphering studies based on qualitative data, and the notion of theory-building is central to my analysis of this problem.

One important point remains to be made. Theory-testing and theory-building have been presented as the twin poles of a dimension which I have called the nature of the theory-evidence link, and the two examples were selected to illustrate this distinction. Many studies, however, fall between these two extremes, and combine some elements of theory-testing with some elements of theory-construction. Other studies may be carried out for purposes which cannot be regarded as theory-testing or theory-building: for example, to investigate a perceived social problem, to challenge a generally accepted assertion, or simply to describe a phenomenon of interest to the sociologist. Such studies are often undertaken within a theoretical framework, but do not test theory in the strict sense (Rose, 1979: 134–52). Naturally, if one is to decipher a given research report, it is necessary to characterise accurately the nature of the theory–evidence link – and it is therefore helpful to be aware of the wide variety of possibilities which may be encountered. It is sometimes quite a difficult task to work out the nature of the link. Authors present research reports in a variety of styles; in some cases it is stated quite clearly that a theory is being tested or constructed, but in many other studies such information is not offered directly. An obvious suggestion is that the reader search thoroughly for statements of purpose made by the authors. Where such statements of purpose are not given explicitly, they may nevertheless be implicit.

EXERCISES

1.1 Check each of the two analyses given as examples above against the research reports of Dornbusch and Hickman, and Becker (Chapters 10 and 11). Which elements of the analysis have been *inferred*, rather than being directly stated in the reports? Discuss whether these inferences are justified.

1.2 Select two other studies from Part Two. Answer the following questions for each study. What method or methods of data collection were used? Are the data quantitative or qualitative? What is the nature of the theory-evidence link (theory-testing, theory-construction, or some other purpose)? You will find it helpful to use the glossary given in the Appendix for this question.

2

Framework

The two distinctions made in Chapter 1, between theory-testing and theory-construction and between quantitative and qualitative data, are, of course, not the only dimensions along which we may analyse research reports. Even a brief perusal of the sociological journals shows the diverse nature of research; researchers use widely differing methods of data collection, a range of techniques of data analysis, and a variety of styles of reporting and presentation of results. Despite this variety, however, there are two factors which I shall argue are of central importance in virtually all sociological research.

The first, already introduced, is the nature of the *link between theory and empirical evidence*. The author of a research report usually argues that he has made this link successfully. However, as Hughes points out (1976: 55), theory and evidence (data) are, in effect, in two different languages. 'Translation' is never easy. A significant part of the deciphering of a research report is to evaluate the degree to which the author has been successful in moving between the languages of theory and data.

The second is that certain *key components* of the research process are always present, notably

1. A *sample* is taken.
2. Solutions to *concept-indicator* problems are arrived at, and empirical *variables* are defined.
3. Some method of *data analysis* is used.

While it may be easier to visualise these as components in theory-testing studies using quantitative data (e.g. Dornbusch and Hickman), they are in principle equally applicable to research involving theory-construction from qualitative data, though they may be more difficult to analyse.

A MODEL FOR THE RESEARCH PROCESS

I now introduce a model wich will act as a basic framework for the analysis in Chapters 2–6. Essentially this model shows how the key components noted above are systematically related to one another in order to link evidence to theory in a given research study. At this stage it is proposed as a model for *theory-testing* research only; later discussion will show that with some minor changes its range of application is rather wider. The model is shown in Figure 2.1. It is extremely important to keep in mind that it is an 'ideal-type' model, constructed for a specific analytic purpose. It is similar to models used by several authors including Selltiz *et al.* (1976: 13-14) and Worsley *et al.* (1977: 73–8), who point out that, while the ongoing research process often differs from the model quite substantially, the published reports of the same research may nevertheless follow this format. As Worsley *et al.* say, a model of this sort is more like a systematic set of rules used to organise a finished piece of analysis in a way which is understandable; thus a research report is arranged "so as to bring out the connection between the various aspects of the scientific procedure in a clear and logical way" (Worsley *et al.*, 1977: 76).

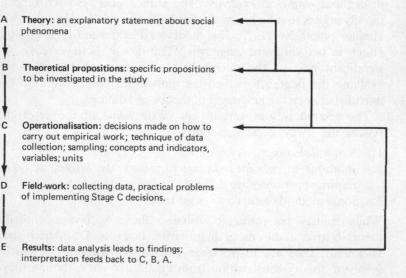

A   **Theory:** an explanatory statement about social phenomena

B   **Theoretical propositions:** specific propositions to be investigated in the study

C   **Operationalisation:** decisions made on how to carry out empirical work; technique of data collection; sampling; concepts and indicators, variables; units

D   **Field-work:** collecting data, practical problems of implementing Stage C decisions.

E   **Results:** data analysis leads to findings; interpretation feeds back to C, B, A.

FIGURE 2.1   *A model for the research process*

A hypothetical example

To illustrate this model suppose we were to carry out a research project to test a theory advanced by Peter Berger (1971: 3–4). The theory is concerned with the relationship of social order and continuity to having children, and provides a convenient example for present purposes as it is succinctly stated in one paragraph:

> The imperative of continuity is closely related to, but not identical with, the imperative of order. I suppose that finally, it is rooted in the simple fact that people have children. If one has children, one feels a necessity to explain the past to them and to relate the present to the past. If one loves one's children (and I take it that this is the case with most people who have them), one will want to project into the future whatever good things one has possessed in one's own life – and there are very few people, even among the most-oppressed, who have possessed nothing good at all. Conversely, if one loves one's parents (the current "generation crisis" notwithstanding, I am inclined to think that this, too, is something of an anthropological constant), one will not finally want to disparage *everything* that constituted the parents' world – especially not if one comes to have children of one's own who not only ask what will become of them but from where they come. *Children are our hostages to history.* Consequently, to be a parent means (however dimly and on whatever level of intellectual sophistication) to have a stake in the continuity of the social order. As a result, there are limits not only to social disorder but to social discontinuity. Enthusiasts for violent change (most of whom, I have noticed, don't have children) fail to recognize this. Successful revolutionaries find out about the limits of disorder, usually to their dismay, as they must settle down to govern the society over which they have gained control. The experiences of the Soviet regime with the institutions of the family and of religion are instructive in this regard.

Let us suppose, further, that the research project has taken the following form:

A THEORY. The continuity of social life is rooted in the simple fact that people have children.

B   THEORETICAL PROPOSITIONS

(i) People who have no children are more likely to be enthusiasts for violent change.

(ii) People who have children feel a necessity to explain society to them, and to explain it as a relatively stable system.

(iii) Attitudes to child-rearing are related to enthusiasm for violent change.

(iv) Enthusiasm for violent change decreases over time when enthusiasts become parents.

(v) People who have children are more likely to have conservative political opinions.

C   OPERATIONALISATION

Data-collection: social survey with interviewer-administered questionnaire.

Sampling: representative sample of 2,000 married females aged between 20 and 30, resident in city *X*, 1980.

Unit: the individual person.

Variables: parental status, attitude to violent change, attitudes to child-rearing, how society is explained to their children, vote in 1979 election. (Decisions must be taken on how to measure these variables; other 'background' variables will also be needed, for example age, occupation, area of residence.)

It is now possible to state five *operational propositions,* of a similar format to B(i) – (v), but framed in terms of the variables now defined and their range of application, i.e. the sample.

D   FIELD-WORK. Organisation of interviewers, problems of quality of data (e.g. what is done about respondents who refuse to co-operate or cannot be located?).

E   RESULTS. What are the findings at the operational level (stage C)? What inferences can be made about stages B and A?

The ABCDE model can now be considered in more detail using this hypothetical project as an example. The arrows from A to B to C (see Figure 2.1) represent the process of 'deducing' specific propositions from a theory and deciding how these propositions are to be operationalised. The statement in A is fairly general; the five propositions in B are much more specific and (unlike A alone) can be seen to be empirically *testable,* though it is still not completely clear how they are to be tested. This is achieved by the next step to stage C. I visualise C as the stage when the researcher has decided exactly what field-work is to be done, i.e. decisions have been made on which data are to be collected, by what means, and from whom.

The point to be emphasised here is that the theory alone does *not* tell you how to get from A to B to C. Berger's original paragraph is an attempt to explain social continuity through people having children, and this general statement is therefore taken as stage A. The paragraph introduces concepts such as parental status and attitudes to violent change, and suggests certain relationships between them, but the five propositions are not stated in exactly the form of stage B; B therefore represents an extension and development of Berger's original ideas. Stage C takes this development much further, as Berger certainly does not say anything about the 20–30-year-old age group, city X, the focus on married females, or how one should measure the variables involved.

To reiterate the point, in order to get to stage C the researcher has to make a series of decisions which are guided by theory but also have a strong element of independence from it. These decisions, which forge the links from A to B to C, are *always* problematic, which is why I have referred to 'deducing'; this is not deduction in the strict sense, for there is no automatic or unambiguous way of getting from stage A to stage C. This is, of course, one aspect of the difficulty of the theory–evidence link introduced above; the progress we have made is to clarify the nature of the link a little. To take the analysis further, some reflections on stages B and C will be helpful.

Theoretical propositions. Stage B will normally consist of several theoretical propositions or hypotheses. (The reader should note that I use the terms 'proposition' and 'hypothesis' interchangeably; in general the former usage is adhered to, especially in Chapters 1–6). The more propositions (there are five in the example), the stronger the test of the theory (Stinchcombe, 1968: 18–20). So we are in a better position to test the theory with five propositions than if we had tested proposition (i) only. And we could be in an even stronger position if we were to test additional propositions derived from Berger's paragraph.

What *is* a theoretical proposition? Further analysis will be given in Chapter 3, but at this stage it may be helpful to say that a proposition makes a *statement* about a relationship which is (in principle) testable. A question like 'Are people who have children likely to be less enthusiastic for violent change than those with no children?' is not a proposition. And the words *"children are our hostages to history"* (Berger, 1971 – see above) do not constitute a proposition, even though they may be considered as an intriguing insight. Homans (1967: 3–21) provides a useful analysis of what is and what is not a proposition, and gives many pertinent sociological examples.

Operationalisation. The move to stage C will be called operationalisation. The specification of stage C is a comprehensive listing of all decisions made about the empirical research. A sample will be specified and methods for data collection stated in detail; in the Berger example this would involve the careful design of a questionnaire to collect data on all the variables. As we shall see in Chapter 3, the variables act as indicators of (theoretical) concepts.

Field-work and results. Decisions of a different kind are involved in stages D and E, for example the ways in which the data are analysed and presented. Although these processes may be difficult technically, the decisions are about empirical matters and are relatively independent of the theory. In the example one would be concerned with problems such as organising interviewers, contacting respondents and trying to get their co-operation, checking and coding the data collected, carrying out analysis by computer, and drawing up tables to show the results.

A crucial distinction

The most important aspect of this analysis is the identification of C as the *pivotal stage* in the research process. This is already evident from my comments on the downward arrows in Figure 2.1, i.e. the movement from stage A through to stage E. It is emphasised again when we consider the process of *inference* from the stage E results. This process is shown by the upward arrows in Figure 2.1. The most fundamental point to be made is that the inferences from E to C are of a different kind from inferences from C to B and to A; they involve different assumptions and have different purposes. Each stage of inference is crucially dependent on the decisions made in the corresponding downward arrows. So the E to C inference is empirical and specific to the piece of research: it entails answering a basic question – to what extent are the operationalised propositions (C) supported by the data?

By contrast, the inferences from C to B and to A are more general – they depend essentially on the logical and theoretical considerations involved in the operationalisation, and *not* on the data as such; so these inferences entail answering a second basic question – what does the answer to the first question imply about the theoretical propositions (B) and the theory (A)?

An example will help to clarify the distinction between the two types of question. Let us return to the hypothetical example, which will be referred to hereafter as 'the Berger example'. Suppose that, as part of the results for this project, we have the figures shown in Table 2.1. As specified in stage C the sample is of size 2,000, and consists of married females only. (The rationale here is to simplify the example; if we also had males and unmarried females in the sample, we would have to separate them out in the analysis because sex and marital status are highly likely to affect the variables being studied. Sex and marital status are, in fact, variables controlled within the sample design, a point which is explained further in Chapters 4 and 5.) The first question is what conclusions should be drawn at the empirical level. As 70 per cent of those who have children voted conservative, compared with only 30 per cent of those who have no children, it seems safe to conclude that there is a relationship between having children and voting. Thus *operationalised* proposition (v) is supported by the data. Note that so far all discussion of the findings is at the empirical (stage C) level – nothing has yet been said about stages B and A.

TABLE 2.1   *Parental status and vote at 1979 election, for a representative sample of 2,000 married females aged 20-30, city X, 1980.* *

Vote in 1979 election	Parental status		Total
	Has children	Has no children	
Conservative	700	300	1,000
Progressive	300	700	1,000
Total	1,000	1,000	2,000
% Conservative vote	70%	30%	50%

*Data hypothetical.

Now consider the second question: what are the implications of the empirical evidence for the theoretical stages B and A? Clearly I, as the hypothetical author of the research report, would argue that the data provide a valid test of theoretical proposition (v), which is, in turn, a test of the general theory A. But these (hypothetical) arguments of mine could be criticised by another sociologist, who might argue that the operationalisation is invalid; naturally this opponent would have to be specific about *why* he thought it to be invalid – he might possibly argue that the vote in 1979 is a poor way to measure political opinion, or that for some reason city X is atypical, so that the relationship between having children and voting would not be found anywhere else. What this illustrates is that, because there are no obvious or unequivocal rules governing operationalisation decisions, the validity of authors' arguments are always, in principle, open to debate. To approach the second question in a more informed way, we need to know more about concept-indicator links and sampling, matters which are discussed in Chapters 3 and 4.

THE APPLICABILITY OF THE ABCDE MODEL

Now, having introduced some of the details, reconsider the nature of the ABCDE model and its uses. As I have pointed out, the model is an ideal type; the process by which research is carried out is by no means as neat and tidy as the diagram might suggest. However, the model is more readily applicable to the 'finished products' of research, that is, to research reports. Why should this be so? Because, as Worsley *et al.* stress (1977: 76–7), in reporting research results an author usually attempts to spell out a convincing argument in the form of the model (or something like it), and we can therefore use the model to assess whether or not the argument *is* convincing, i.e. logically consistent. The applicability of the ABCDE model will be illustrated below by several examples, commencing with Garabedian's study (Chapter 12); it will already be evident that the summary of Dornbusch and Hickman's study, given in Chapter 1, is based on the model.

Thus the application of the ABCDE model to theory-testing research is clear, and indeed the model has been developed with such studies in mind. But how can the model be applied to studies in which theories are constructed, or in which the theory-evidence link takes some other form? Generally, for the deciphering of any study based on quantitative data, it is in fact very helpful to use the model, and to examine closely the extent to which it can be applied. This recommendation can only be fully justified after a wider range of research reports has been examined (see Chapter 6). One general point in support of the recommendation can, however, be made here. A great many studies involve elements of both theory-testing and theory-building; the application of the ABCDE model to such a study helps to separate the theory-testing elements of the research from those of theory-construction. Also, as mentioned briefly in Chapter 1, many research reports have purposes which are, strictly speaking, neither theory-testing nor theory-construction; more generally there is a great deal of variety in the way which evidence is linked to theory (Rose, 1979: 134–52). Thus, as we shall see, most research reports are 'incomplete' in comparison with the ABCDE model, in the sense that steps A and B will not be found in the exact form specified. The attempt to apply the model to a study helps to clarify the author's argument, and to assess the extent of theoretical 'incompleteness'.

For example, consider research to which we might apply the term 'empiricism', i.e. research lacking in theoretical orientation or not making explicit the theory guiding its procedures (Mitchell, 1968: 67). In its most extreme form this kind of research will focus exclusively on stages C, D and E of the model, and there will be no stages A or B. Porterfield and Gibbs's study (Chapter 14), which is analysed in detail later, is an example which is fairly close to empiricism. Porterfield and Gibbs certainly do not state any theory which they want to test, and their attempts at theory-construction are very limited; the article is devoted almost entirely to a description of stages C, D and E. While it is possible to see how this study is linked to theories of suicide, readers have to forge these links themselves (from their knowledge of other literature on suicide).

Two other examples are the reports by Berelson and Salter (see Chapter 22), and Broom and Jones (Chapter 17); these studies are more sophisticated theoretically than that of Porterfield and Gibbs, but again the emphasis in the presentation is on stages C, D and E. In none of these three studies are propositions stated and then tested; in fact, all three can be characterised as *question-*

answering research; certain basic questions are asked which constitute the purpose of the research, for example 'What are the
relationships between occupational position and suicide, and
between occupational mobility and suicide?' (Porterfield and
Gibbs). The three reports differ in (a) the extent to which the
questions are explicitly stated or left implicit, and (b) the extent to
which the theoretical relevance of the questions is explicitly
discussed or left implicit.

Further discussion of incompleteness would be premature here,
for it is necessary to refer to a variety of specific studies before
relevant points can be made. This issue will therefore be deferred
until Chapter 6, except to stress one basic point. 'Incompleteness'
refers only to the theoretical stages of the model. Steps C, D and E
are always present in an empirical research study (they are not
always described adequately in all respects, but that is a separate
problem). It follows that, in deciphering a research report, one can
always make an assessment of the empirical stages of the study,
irrespective of the degree of theoretical incompleteness; the only
impediment to this assessment will be lack of full information in
the report.

Evaluation: the two main questions

In the earlier discussion of how an author would draw conclusions
from research, two kinds of questions were separated. Referring
again to the example based on Table 2.1, we can take the analysis
a little further and make a particularly important point. The
deciphering of a research report can also be undertaken in two
parts, equivalent to the two questions. Thus we first examine the
author's stages C, D and E, and his arguments (e.g. empirical
interpretations of findings) concerning these three stages; by
following through the arguments about the empirical work we are
enabled to evaluate them. Since it is the validity of the author's
arguments at the empirical level which is subject to scrutiny, this
will be called *internal empirical validity* [1] (The Notes section begins
on page 310.)

Second, we turn our attention to stages A and B, and their
relationship to the empirical stages; again the author's arguments
are followed carefully and then evaluated. The validity of the

arguments is scrutinised, this time at the theoretical level, and this will be referred to as *internal theoretical validity*. The distinction between internal empirical validity and internal theoretical validity is not easy to see immediately, nor indeed is the meaning of each term obvious at this stage, but the reader is assured that the full implications will be discussed thoroughly as my analysis is developed; the reasons for the use of the term 'internal' will become clear in due course.

How is this scheme for evaluation to be amended when a research report is 'incomplete' in the sense defined above? In this situation the author will not have answered the two questions exactly as specified, since the ABCDE model will not apply in its exact form. It is, however, always possible to separate out two parts of the research report: *first,* those parts of the author's arguments which are confined to the empirical level, stages C, D and E; and *second,* those parts of the author's arguments which are concerned with the relationship of the evidence to theory (tested or built) or to any other stated purposes of the research. Thus it is always possible to assess internal theoretical validity and internal empirical validity.

As will become clear, this scheme provides the key to a thorough evaluation of all aspects of the argument presented in a research report. The application of the ABCDE model, either in its complete form or (more usually) in an incomplete form appropriate to the particular study, will organize the evaluation in a coherent form. The validity of the author's arguments can then be examined. To see how this approach is put into practice, we now turn to an example.

GARABEDIAN'S STUDY

Garabedian's "Social Roles and Processes of Socialization in the Prison Community" (Chapter 12) will now be analysed in detail. As the title implies, this is a study of the socialization of prison inmates; the focus is on how socialization varies with time in prison. The setting for the research was one prison in the USA; a sample of inmates was selected, and data were collected from them by means of a questionnaire. Garabedian's findings are that there is a distinct pattern of socialization – the degree of conformity to conventional norms follows a "U-shaped" curve during time in prison. This pattern, however, varies when different 'role types' of inmates are considered. Theoretical interpretations are offered to account for these findings. The study can be summarised as follows:

A THEORY. The main theoretical origins of the study are discussed at the beginning of the report, where the theories of Clemmer and Wheeler on socialization patterns over time in prison are contrasted. Other theoretical material on role types is introduced in the section headed "The Inmate Social System".

B THEORETICAL PROPOSITIONS. These are not explicitly stated but it becomes evident from the report as a whole that there is one main proposition (i) and one main question (ii):

(i)   The pattern of socialization over time in prison is "adaptive" (the U-shaped curve).
(ii)   How does the pattern of socialization vary between inmates playing different social roles?

The series of four general questions listed in Garabedian's third paragraph also contribute to our understanding of stage B. Checking these against Garabedian's empirical work, it is possible to add a further question:

(iii) How is the pattern of socialization affected by social processes in the institution?

C OPERATIONALISATION

Data collection: By questionnaire to prison inmates (and staff). It is probable that the questionnaire was self-completed (although it could have been administered by interview).

Sampling: selection of the prison, and of a representative sample of 380 inmates (and 141 staff members).

Unit: the individual inmate.

Variables

1. Socialization is studied through *conformity to staff norms*. This variable is measured from five items on the questionnaire. Each inmate was categorised as conforming or not conforming, through comparing his responses to a 'standard' based on staff norms.

2. *Career phase* was categorised as early, middle, or late, from two items on the questionnaire.

3. *Social role* was measured from fifteen items on the questionnaire. There are five categories – square john, right guy,
politican, outlaw, ding.

4. *Contact with other inmates and staff* was measured from one
questionnaire item. This variable is Garabedian's way of getting at "social processes".

D FIELD WORK. We are not told much about field-work problems, but clearly Garabedian would initially have had a considerable task of collaborating with prison authorities and selecting the
sample. Then, to collect the data, he would have had to organise
the interviews or, if these are self-completed questionnaires,
devise means of distributing the questionnaires and collecting
them so as to minimise non-response.

E RESULTS. Analysis of the data gives Figures 12.1, 12.2 and
Tables 12.1 and 12.2. The section on "The adaptive pattern" deals
with proposition (i) and sections headed "The Inmate Social
System" and "Social Roles and Socialization" explore question
(ii). The final section on "Social Roles and Social Processes" deals
with question (iii), but in the edited version reprinted as Chapter
12 the details of these results have been omitted.

Before proceeding with the analysis of the study, some discussion of this summary is necessary. The application of the model
has enabled a summary to be drawn up in the ABCDE format, but
it is evident that there is some deviation from the ideal-type model
in stages A and B. For example, stage B consists of a mixture of
one proposition and two questions. I stress that this point is *not* a
criticism. It is quite usual to find that a study has a 'general
theoretical orientation', and it is also common to find questions
rather than propositions at stage B; if the questions are precise
enough, they provide just as much guidance for carrying out the
research. What is not provided by questions, of course, is an
expectation that the data will show particular results specified in
advance. For example, Garabedian expects a specific result (U-
shaped curve) to be found for (i), but he is open-minded about
what results he will find for (ii) and (iii).

The major point is that the application of the model has
heightened our understanding of Garabedian's article; it has
reproduced certain essential stages in his argument, and will lead

on to an evaluation. Naturally, continued reference to Chapter 12 will be needed to follow the evaluation as the summary only contains a limited amount of information. As Chapter 12 excludes the results relevant to questions (iii) on "social processes", in the evaluation the focus will be on (i) and (ii) of stage B, i.e. the pattern of socialization and its variation between role types; the data on social processes (variable 4) will be discussed only briefly.

Operationalisation

Consider, first, the definitions of the variables. Remembering that these are Garabedian's solutions to concept-indicator problems, we may raise a series of questions. Variable 1 is conformity to staff norms; is this a good way to judge 'socialization'? Should Garabedian have taken account of the differing *length* of the inmate's prison sentence when measuring variable 2, career phase? And for variable 4, can the degree of contact with other inmates and staff be measured satisfactorily through an item on a self-completed questionnaire? These are not criticisms, they are simply some of the relevant questions which will have to be answered as part of the deciphering of the study.

What about variable 3? The operationalisation of this variable, social role, is particularly interesting. It is derived from the earlier work of Schrag, and it is clear that Garabedian and Schrag have worked closely together.[2] However, it is *not* clear from Schrag's published work (1959, 1961: 347–8) what empirical procedures have been used to identify the five 'role types' – square john, right guy, and so on – in his own research. Apparently, these are the five main ways in which inmates 'type' each other, so one would imagine that observations and interviews would be appropriate data for classifying individual inmates. Garabedian's method, however, is through fifteen items on the questionnaire, each of which is "assumed to reflect a component of the attitudinal organization of a given role type". There is no way for the reader to assess whether this assumption is valid. Presumably, Garabedian and Schrag have compared methods of classifying inmates, and have concluded that the questionnaire method is valid, but this should have been reported or at least referred to. In short, when one reads through the fifteen items, it is not at all clear that they 'get at' the role types which are outlined earlier; thus the measurement of this variable needs much more justification than is given in Garabedian's report.

Garabedian's sampling is in essence quite simple, but it is important to note that it is in two stages. First, one prison has been chosen for the study, and second, a sample of 380 inmates has been selected. The random selection should ensure that the sample is representative of all inmates in this specific prison. But can the findings be generalised to other prisons? This issue will be reconsidered later. A broader point is the general nature of the 'research design'. It is Garabedian's intention to study the *process* of socialization over time in prison. He states that it would have been preferable to use a *longitudinal* (or panel) design, studying the change in conformity of the same group of inmates over their time in prison; in practice, like most researchers, Garabedian settled for a *cross-sectional* design, which is quicker and more economical. The limitations of this design are noted – "firm empirical support of these data must await panel studies".

This analysis of stage C has therefore identified certain potential problems, only one of which has been discussed in any detail (the operationalisation of social roles). I have referred to *potential* problems because, at this stage in the analysis, that is all they are. To show whether an *actual* problem exists, and whether the study is subject to criticism in that respect, one has to spell out exactly why (as I have done in the case of 'social roles'). As we progress with our discussion of this and other studies, we shall see the variety of ways in which analysis of this kind can be developed.

Before continuing with the analysis of Garabedian's study, there are several general points to be made. (1) This study acts as a good first example because most of the details of empirical procedures are clearly presented, and are therefore amenable to analysis; thus many of the problems which are central to the deciphering of a research report can be illustrated very clearly from Garabedian's study. (2) It is important to see how the various questions arise and how they fit together. The model acts as an *organisational* device, which enables one to maintain a grasp of the analysis as a whole while dealing with specific points. (3) Notice particularly how a summary, followed by a consideration of stage C, provides a rich source of ideas for more detailed evaluation. (4) Some of the terminology used above may, at this stage, be foreign to the reader. It will be helpful to refer to the glossary in the Appendix for major terms. Also, in Chapters 3, 4 and 5, the key components of the research process will be explored in more detail; thus terms which are understood only imperfectly now will be clarified later.

Evaluation

The first step in an evaluation is to consider the data analysis and presentation; as we shall see, this is a crucial part of the assessment of *internal empirical validity*. Garabedian's Figure 12.1 is based on 345 inmates, classified as early phase (109), middle (199) and late (37). Presumably the drop from 380 to 345 is because thirty-five questionnaires are incomplete or not returned – this is a relatively small number, which, as Garabedian assures us, would have a negligible influence on the results. Figure 12.1 shows a U-shaped trend, confirming proposition (i).

There are, however, too few inmates in the late phase to permit reliable analysis when they are allocated to the five social roles (e.g. there were only two 'late-phase outlaws'). From the final columns of Table 12.1 the figures in Table 2.2 can be obtained. As a result of these small figures, many of the percentages in Tables 12.1 and 12.2 and Figure 12.2 are extremely unreliable, and Garabedian's extensive discussion of the differences between these percentages is therefore not justified. Quite simply, percentages must be based on considerably more than two, five, seven or nine cases, if they are to be reliable.[3] Even the data analysis based on the early and middle phases is somewhat questionable, for, again, the numbers of inmates in each role category is relatively small (see Table 12.1). For example, "the drop in square john conformists from 67 to 30 per cent between the early and the middle phases does not indicate a stable conformity pattern"; these percentages are based on sample sizes of twelve and twenty respectively.[4] In fact, Garabedian's sample is rather too small to break down into the fifteen categories based on career phase and role type and to compare percentages based on the separate categories.

These comments lead on to the assessment of *internal empirical validity,* which entails examining Garabedian's arguments at stages C, D and E, including inferences from E to C. The crucial point

TABLE 2.2   *Inmates in the late phase (Garabedian's study)**

	No. in sample	Percentage conformists	No. of conformists
Square johns	5	60%	3
Right guys	7	29%	2
Politicians	9	33%	3
Outlaws	2	0%	0
Dings	5	60%	3
Total	28†	39%	11

*All figures derived from Table 12.1
†The 28 omits 9 inmates who were not classifiable into one of the five roles; 28 plus these 9 is equal to the total of 37 late-phase inmates shown in Figure 12.1.

here is whether the statistical analysis and its interpretation is sound. If we examine the data relating to proposition (i), we find the analysis is reasonably good, and that the data do confirm the U-shaped curve suggested. But when we go on to question (ii), the answer must be that the analysis is not sound, simply because the numbers involved are so small and the results are therefore unreliable. In fact, I am not convinced that Garabedian's data show any real differences between the five role types at all; for example, it may well be that the *apparent* differences in his Figure 12.2 are due to random fluctuations which must appear when small numbers are taken as the base for percentages. In general, the data do no more than suggest that certain trends *may* be there.

Note that, for the moment, I have suspended any queries about the *operationalisation* of the study; in brief, to assess internal empirical validity one accepts the author's operational decisions and restricts attention to data analysis and interpretation at the empirical level. Turning now to *internal theoretical validity,* what does the analysis so far imply about stages B and A and other aspects of Garabedian's theoretical conclusions? Even if I were to accept the conclusions Garabedian draws from the data analysis, there are still reservations about the way the research has been operationalised. Apart from the operational definition of 'social role' discussed above, there are other worrying features of the oper-ationalisation. Career phase is measured as follows: early-phase inmates have been in prison less than six months, late-phase inmates have less than six months to go, and middle-phase inmates are the rest. Presumably this means that a prisoner sentenced to nine months would be categorised as 'early' for the first three months, ambiguously as 'early' or 'late' for the second three months, as 'late' for the last three months, and at no stage would be 'middle'. By contrast, an inmate serving a ten-year sentence would spend nine years categorised as 'middle'. So length of sentence clearly has a crucial effect on career phase. However, assume for the moment that all inmates are serving similar length sentences, say eighteen months to two years. There are still problems – why is it that 109 are categorised as 'early' and only 37 as 'late'? Surely, as this is a representative sample, one would expect similar numbers of inmates to be 'early' and 'late'; looked at from another perspective, Garabedian's figures tell us that the rate of *inflow* into the prison – 109 in six months in the sample – exceeds the *outflow* rate of 37 in six months by a ratio of nearly 3 to 1. Surely this is most unlikely. Something may well have gone wrong – either with the sampling, or with the measurement of this variable; possibly career phase cannot be judged accurately from the items on the questionnaire.

What of the two other variables? Conformity to staff norms appears to be measured adequately – certainly there is nothing in the report which would suggest otherwise. Garabedian's account of the scores for staff, and the derivation of a staff 'standard' through which inmates were categorised as conformists or non-conformists, clearly shows the difference between staff and inmates, and the wide spread of scores for inmates. An evaluation of staff and inmate contact will not be undertaken here as Chapter 12 includes only a short note on the results for this variable; a brief analysis can be given, but this is left as an exercise for the reader.

Finally, for internal theoretical validity, we must evaluate Garabedian's *sampling*. This aspect of the operationalisation – the choice of one prison, and a representative sample of inmates from it – is comparatively sound in its design. Note, however, that there is a *non-response* problem. Garabedian's sample is 380 inmates which shrinks to 345 in Figure 12.1, and 245 in Table 12.2. This is a common and in many ways unavoidable situation with question-naire-based research; but the author should recognise that it is likely to introduce bias into the results, and the problem should be discussed. Garabedian did mention the reduction to 345, but not to 245. At a more general level, the broad problem of whether the results from one prison can be generalised to other prisons might also have been considered by Garabedian, as it is a rather important aspect of the study.

On the basis of my analysis, what can one say about Garabedian's study as a whole? It does appear that there is some support for Wheeler's U-shaped adaptation pattern amongst inmates as a whole. We must, however, be sceptical about Garabedian's conclusions that *"the point of heaviest impact* [of prison culture] varies with the different role types", as this statement cannot be made with any reasonable certainty, given the evaluation above.

Comments on the analysis

There are several points to be made about the *method* used for deciphering. First, the strength of using the model has been illustrated here. There are a host of points to be analysed for this study; the model has enabled them to be dealt with separately, but then to be related to one another in a coherent fashion. In other words, the model has helped to *organise* the evaluation. Note, however, that the ABCDE summary does not represent exactly how Garabedian went about the research – it is, rather, a representation of his argument in presenting the research report. The study has been analysed as primarily theory-testing, but there are some aspects which are close to theory-building, particularly questions (ii) and (iii) and Garabedian's subsequent discussion and conclusions about the different patterns of adaptation according to social role. (Because of the reservations expressed above, I have not summarised this aspect of the study or Garabedian's final theoretical discussion.) This is not theory-building in the same sense as Becker, as here the data collection and analysis are tightly structured. It is simply that Garabedian did not start off with any existing theory of which social roles would exhibit which patterns of adaptation. This approach, where an open-ended question (rather than a proposition) is posed as part of stage B, and where the object is development of the theory after the data are analysed, is very frequent in sociology.

The analysis as a whole has illustrated both the use of the ABCDE model, and the way in which the validity of an author's argument can be evaluated. Here, the main point to be made is the distinction between internal empirical validity and internal theoretical validity, which is illustrated in relation to the ABCDE model in Figure 2.2. Some further discussion of these terms may be helpful. The word 'internal' has been used in both cases, since the evaluation as a whole is confined to an assessment of the internal consistency of the argument presented in the report. The relationship of Garabedian's study to the wider literature on prisons or the practical implications of the study have not been discussed. These are 'external' factors, which are ultimately of great importance, but which raise questions which are outside the scope of this book. I would stress, however, that the *external validity* of any study (i.e. its relationship to wider literature and/or its practical implications) should, strictly speaking, be considered *only* after its internal validity has been subject to detailed scrutiny. This point is discussed further in Chapter 6.

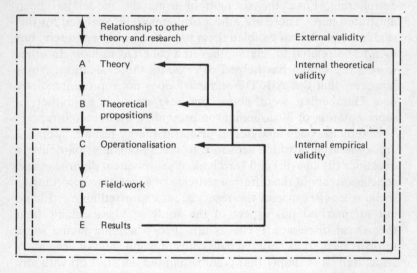

FIGURE 2.2   *The distinction between three different kinds of validity in research reports*

Despite the various flaws in Garabedian's research report, it should not be concluded that this is a 'poor' example. As we shall see, similiar problems emerge in most research reports once they are systematically deciphered, and in terms of 'standards' Garabedian's study is fairly close to average in many respects. It acts as a particularly valuable first example, because the reasoning is so clearly spelled out that the reader is able to analyse most aspects of the study in detail.

EXERCISES

2.1 *The Berger example.* (a) Examine the relationship of the five propositions in stage B to the original extract from Berger. Which propositions (if any) are explicit in the extract, and which have been derived? Are these derivations 'reasonable'? (b) Derive two more propositions from the extract.

2.2 Amend Figure 2.1 so that it represents research characterised as 'empiricisim'. (This is not a trick question – it is very easy.)

2.3 *Garabedian's study* (a) Examine the ABCDE summary; which parts are explicitly stated in Chapter 12 and which parts have been inferred? Are the inferences 'reasonable'? (b) How was variable 4 measured? Analyse briefly whether this variable appears to be a good indicator of the concept of 'social processes'.

2.4 Choose any one case study from Chapters 13–18, and give details of stage C (operationalisation). Be sure to identify the four components – data-collection technique, sample, units, variables.

2.5 Building on the summary given in Chapter 1, *decipher* Dornbusch and Hickman's study.

3

Concepts and Indicators

As we have seen, there are several factors involved in the link between theory and evidence; the most central, however, is the concept-indicator problem. As a first example, reconsider one of the concept-indicator links in Garabedian's study. The theoretical concept of social role was measured by an empirical indicator based on fifteen questionnaire items; in the ABCDE summary the concept was located at stage B and the indicator at stage C. In Chapter 2 the criticism of this part of the study was that Garabedian had not demonstrated this concept-indicator link to be valid. So far, however, several terms – notably concept, indicator and measurement validity – have not been discussed in any depth[1].

What is a *concept?* Let us start by considering it as a 'theoretical idea', for example social role, socialization, other-directedness, deviant identity, social mobility. It will be of interest to look through one of the sociological dictionaries or glossaries of terms (e.g. Mitchell, 1968; Weeks, 1972); these consist largely of catalogues of commonly used sociological concepts, with a discussion of the origins and meanings of them. As we shall see, many concepts have meanings which are difficult to grasp in any immediate sense; we shall come to a more detailed understanding of this problem as this chapter progresses.

One concept introduced in the Berger example (Chapter 2) was 'enthusiasm for violent change'. As the example states, for operationalisation, one would need to develop an indicator for this concept; decisions would be made on how to collect data and construct the indicator from it. Suppose this is done by asking each respondent to state whether he/she agrees or disagrees with the following three statements:

(i)   Violence can be an effective political force in this country.
(ii) The use of violence for political purposes is legitimate.
(iii) There are many aspects of society which should be changed.

The respondent's attitude to violent change could then be measured on a scale of 0, 1, 2, 3 by simply adding up the number of agrees; the higher the score, the more 'enthusiasm for violent change'. For example, a person who agrees with (i) and (iii) but disagrees with (ii) would have a total score of 2; one who disagrees with all three items would have a score of 0. This is simply an illustration, not a serious suggestion for a measurement procedure; in practice, both theoretical and empirical justification is required for any indicator, as we shall see.

For the Berger example, the first proposition in stage B was 'people who have no children are more likely to be enthusiasts for violent change'. In general, *theoretical propositions* (or hypotheses) are stated in terms of *relationships between concepts*. This proposition states a relationship between 'parental status' and 'enthusiasm for violent change'. A proposition also makes an assertion about the direction of the relationship – those with no children will be more enthusiastic. This characteristic distinguishes a proposition from a 'theoretical question'. A theoretical question is often asked in the form of a link between two concepts, such as 'what is the relationship between parental status and attitude to violent change?' – but no assertion is made about what the answer might be.

The equivalent *operationalised proposition* involves defining indicators for both concepts. Thus an indicator is also required for 'parental status'; suppose this is provided by asking each respondent to answer yes or no to one question.

(iv) Are you at present the parent or guardian of one or more childen?

The operationalised propositon is therefore an assertion of a relationship between the two indicators, that is, a statistical relationship between the score based on items (i), (ii) and (iii), and the response to item (iv). Thus, after collecting the data from the 2,000 married females in city *X,* as part of the data analysis one would construct a table relating the two indicators (or variables). The object is to test whether respondents with no children are more likely to have high scores than respondents with children.

The results might be presented in the form of Table 3.1; here, for simplicity in presentation, a 'high' score has been taken as 2 or 3. It is clear from the figures that the operationalised proposition is supported by the (hypothetical) data; if one accepts the validity of the concept-indicator links, the theoretical proposition is therefore also supported.

TABLE 3.1   *Parental status and enthusiasm for violent change for a representative sample of 2,000 married females aged 20–30, city X, 1980**

	Parental status		
Enthusiasm score	Has children	Has no children	Total
Low(0,1)	600	300	900
High (2,3)	400	700	1,100
Total	1,000	1,000	2,000
% high	40%	70%	55%

*Data hypothetical.

At this point it will be helpful to review the terminology discussed so far, in a list which compares terms used on the theoretical and empirical levels. The terms *indicator* and *variable* are equated because they refer to the same entity; the reason for retaining both terms is that 'indicator' is used to discuss linkages with the concept, whereas 'variable' is used when talking about the empirical world only. Note that, as other authors may use these terms differently (especially 'variable'), the reader should be careful in referring to other sources:

Theoretical level	*Empirical level*
Concept	Indicator (variable)
Nominal definition	Operational definition
Theoretical proposition (links two concepts)	Operationalised proposition (links two indicators)
Theory language	Data language

An *operational definition* is a complete definition of a variable; it specifies the procedure used to collect the data and states how the data are analysed to decide the score or category for any individual unit. For example, the three questionnaire items, the construction of a score ranging from 0 to 3, and the categorisation of 0, 1 as low and 2, 3 as high, comprises the operational definition of the variable 'enthusiasm for violent change' shown in Table 3.1. Similarly, Garabedian's account of the measurement of social role in five categories (square john, right guy, and so on) is an operational definition. Each of the quantitative case studies in Part Two provides several further examples (see Exercise 3.1). The term *nominal definition* will be discussed later.

A factor which sometimes leads to confusion is that the title of the concept and its indicator are often identical. For example, enthusiasm for violent change is a concept, but it is also the title of a variable in Table 3.1. If this simple point is not grasped, it often becomes a barrier to the student's understanding of the separation of concept and indicator. But if it is remembered that the concept is a theoretical entity, and the indicator a measurable empirical entity with an operational definition, the distinction between the two should present few problems.

ANALYSING CONCEPT-INDICATOR LINKS

The most fundamental question of this chapter can now be clearly stated – how does one move from a theoretical concept to a valid empirical indictor? How does one justify the validity of the indicator? As we shall see, the nature of the problem seems to preclude exact rules, but nevertheless some progress can be made. First, reconsider the notion of a concept. Concepts may be used at widely differing levels of abstraction; *conceptual analysis* is a crucial part of the process of theorising. Thus concepts are used at stages A and B, but at stage B concepts will be much more specific: for example, other-directedness (A) and other-directedness in consumer-goods advertising (B) in Dornbusch and Hickman's study. Diagrams can be very helpful in analysing the linkages between different levels of concepts, and between concepts and indicators. The *tree-diagram* approach used here follows the general principles discussed in previous work such as Phillips's "ladders of abstraction" (1966: 27–30). As an example, the concept of *alienation* will be considered.

Seeman (1959) analysed alienation from the personal standpoint of the actor (hence the unit of analysis is the individual) as comprising five separate dimensions – powerlessness, meaninglessness, normlessness, isolation, and self-estrangement. Seeman and others later operationalised these five dimensions through the use of questionnaires. Figure 3.1 shows that movement down the tree diagram from concept to indicator is from the more general to the more specific. Theoretical argument first allows the general concept of alienation to be defined in terms of five more specific concepts which are then operationalised through indicators at the emprical level, based on questionnaire items for each.

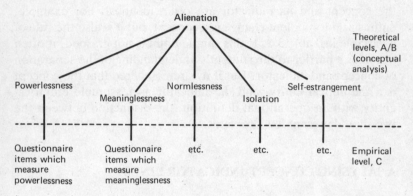

FIGURE 3.1 *Tree diagram for five dimensions of alienation*

To examine this process in more detail, consider powerlessness as an example. According to Mitchell (1968 : 5), Seeman's concept of powerlessness is a "feeling (expectancy) on the part of the individual that he cannot influence the social situation(s) in which he interacts". This is a useful starting-point, but if we refer to Seeman's original article for further clarification we find that there are two other main aspects of the definition. First, powerlessness is not defined in terms of the objective conditions in society (although these are, of course, relevant in studying a person's feelings). Thus

> the individual's expectancy for the control of events is [to be] clearly distinguished from (a) the *objective* situation of powerlessness as some observer sees it, (b) the observer's *judgement* of that situation against some ethical standard, and (c) the individual's sense of a *discrepancy* between his expectations for control and his desire for control (Seeman, 1959: 784)

Second, Seeman does not see *all* expectancies and events as falling within the compass of powerlessness, for he

> would limit the applicability of the concept to . . . the individual's sense of influence over socio-political events (control of the political system, the industrial economy, international affairs and the like) . . . the depiction of man's relation to the larger social order. Whether or not [these] are related to expectancies for control in more intimate need areas (for example, love and affection; status recognition) is a matter for empirical determination (Seeman, 1959: 785).

This theoretical discussion is an example of a *nominal definition*. In general, a nominal definition does not read like a dictionary definition. Indeed, concepts are often discussed in a general theoretical (and empirical) context which helps to define the concept nominally and also helps operationalisation by making suggestions for suitable indicators. Returning to the example of powerlessness, the *operational definition* might be based on five questionnaire items as follows:

1. It is only wishful thinking to believe one can really influence what happens in society at large.
2. More and more, I feel helpless in the face of what's happening in the world today.
3. Persons like myself have little chance of protecting our personal interests when they conflict with those of strong pressure groups.
4. There's little use for me to vote, since one vote doesn't count much anyway.
5. There's very little we can do to bring about a permanent world peace.

Each item would call for a response from several alternatives on an 'agree-disagree' scale, and an individual's powerlessness score would be calculated by combining the five responses. The five items are taken from Neal and Rettig (1967).[2] As we shall see, the nominal definition of a concept is of great importance in assessing the validity of the operational definition (see also Exercise 3.2).

Methodological perspectives

There are many discussions of the concept-indicator problem in the literature on research methodology. Five main sources will be mentioned here; each of these provides a useful perspective on the validity of concept-indicator links.

(1) Phillips (1966: 32-7) lists several desirable attributes of sociological concepts – notably, clarity, scope and systematic import. *Clarity* is the concept's potential for leading to indicators, which depends on the degree to which it implies a chain of lower-level concepts; *scope* is the breadth (or narrowness) of the class of phenomena to which the concept applies; and *systematic import* is the extent to which the concept is used in propositions and theories. Alienation appears to rate highly on scope and systematic import, and perhaps clarity as well. Phillips also cautions against *extreme operationism,* which is a position which argues that clarity and ease of measurement are the most important criteria for concepts. From this position a concept would have no meaning apart from the operations used to measure it empirically, i.e. the nominal definition would be equated with the operational definition. An assertion that the only meaning of the concept of intelligence is 'whatever intelligence tests measure' is an example of extreme operationism.

(2) *Conceptual clarification* (Merton, 1968: 168-71). In the attempt to operationalise a concept we may well clarify it, because the process of measurement may lead to a refined definition of the concept and bring about a greater degree of agreement with the empirical world. This may happen either as a result of research or simply by considering how to carry out research. In the context of this book it is easy to give a general illustration – consider how, once the empirical part of a study has been understood, it also refines one's theoretical understanding of the concepts used in the research. For example, reading Dornbusch and Hickman's study refines our understanding of other-directedness. Note also that conceptual clarification may be achieved 'negatively' if one disagrees with an author's operational definition; in this case we would be arguing that we understand the concept but that the author has not measured it adequately.

(3) *Comparability and precedent.* Most concepts used in research have been operationalised previously by other researchers.

Previous work should not be ignored. Ideally, evaluation of previous measurement techniques should be carried out, and can lead to (a) adoption of some existing technique, (b) refinement, or (c) rejection and development of alternative techniques. It is important to compare different measurement methods, but often this is not done. For example, Garabedian should have shown how his operational definition of social role compared with previous work.

(4) *Multiple indicators*. If we have several different ways of measuring the same concept (rather than only one way), we are in a stronger position. Multiple indicators can be used to check each other or can be combined into a single more reliable measure. Techniques of scale construction rely heavily on this principle. For example, the responses to the five items measuring powerlessness, or to the three items measuring enthusiasm for violent change, would in each case be combined to form a single variable.

(5) *T-concepts and O-concepts*. So far, I have stressed the relatively abstract nature of theoretical, or T-concepts, such as alienation or other-directedness. But consider *time* in Dornbusch and Hickman's study. Time plays an imporant part in the theory to be tested, but is an observational, or O-concept. The distinction between T- and O-concepts is discussed by Abell (1971: 27–8): O-concepts are "given in immediate sense experience but T-concepts are not". As Abell says, this dichotomy is altogether too simplistic, but nevertheless there is an important point to be made. In sociological theory we find many concepts which are very close to observational (or data) language, whereas other concepts are highly abstract or theoretical. The process of operationalisation of a T-concept, moving down a tree diagram, can be seen as a translation into O-concepts. In general, the more theoretical (or abstract) a concept is, the more difficult it will be to operationalise.

Variables from questionnaire items

In giving the examples of concept-indicator links above, I have concentrated on variables which are scales based on series of questionnaire items administered to individual respondents; these have been selected simply as examples which are readily under-

42   *Deciphering Sociological Research*

standable. There are, of course, many other kinds of data from which variables are constructed, and often the unit of analysis is not the individual respondent; Dornbusch and Hickman's study (Chapter 10) is an example. The essential factor to emphasise here is that all aspects of the analysis of the concept-indicator problem in this chapter are of *general applicability*, and are not restricted to the specific situation of questionnaires and scales.

The question of validity

To return to the basic issue, the essential question to ask about any indicator is whether it 'really' measures the concept it is intended to measure, that is, whether it is a *valid* indicator. Unfortunately, there are many problems in answering the question, for, as stated earlier, there are no exact or unambiguous rules for judging validity. Three procedures are, however, commonly discussed (see, for example, Phillips, 1966: 159–62). The first is *face validity*. Here we ask whether 'on the face of it' the indicator measures the concept; to test face validity one systematically compares the operational definition with the nominal definition. Exercise 3.2 is on face validity (and so was exercise 2.3(b)). The second is *criterion validity*. If we have an existing generally accepted indicator of the concept, a new indicator which is proposed can be compared with it as a validity check. The usual method would be to carry out both measures on a test sample. The third is *construct validity*. This depends on testing whether propositions (which are assumed *a priori* to be highly likely) are confirmed when the new indicator is used. For example, one might devise a new measure of occupational status; a test of construct validity would be to take a sample of adults and check whether the new measure is related to education. If there is no relationship, one would doubt the validity of the new measure, as the connection between education and occupational status is well established by previous studies.

Evaluating concept-indicator links in research reports

The perspectives on the concept-indicator link outlined above and the procedures for testing validity are all of potential use in understanding any given author's account and in evaluating the research report. For example, Dornbusch and Hickman have used multiple (six) indicators of other-directedness; to the extent that each indicator shows a similar trend, this will add strength to their findings. Other examples have already been given from Garabedian's study. The question which can be applied most widely concerns face validity; provided sufficient information is given, it is always possible to compare the operational and nominal definitions.

Reliability. So far, I have not discussed the notion of the reliability of an indicator, though, together with validity, it is normally regarded as a key characteristic (Moser and Kalton, 1971: 353–57). Sometimes one can make a limited analysis of the reliability of a variable used in a research report, but more often it is not possible. For example, Dornbusch and Hickman give assurances about the reliability of their six indicators of other-directedness; this analysis cannot be checked from the report itself, but there is no reason for the reader to doubt the account which is given. Similarly, Garabedian's account of the measurement of conformity to staff norms is quite acceptable. However, there are variables for which the data presented by the author can be used to check reliability; for instance, my analysis of Garabedian's data on career phase showed doubts about the measurement of this variable.

In practice, reliability and validity cannot be treated as two separate issues. Clearly, however, in deciphering a research report, one can evaluate concept-indicator links from two different but complementary angles: *first,* by a logical/theoretical analysis which is essentially an assessment of face validity, and *second* (although this cannot be done in all cases), by considering the data presented on the indicator to see whether these can throw fresh light on questions of reliability or validity. It is important to stress this second approach, as it is so often overlooked.

THEORY AND OPERATIONALISATION

Now, consider the implications of the concept-indicator link for the operationalisation problem generally. In terms of the ABCDE model this implies reconsidering the linkage between stages A, B and C. A simple but important point about stage A is that social theories vary greatly in their levels of abstraction or generality. One standard treatment of this issue is that of Mills (1959), who contrasts "grand theory", which is at too high a level of generality to be testable, with "abstracted empiricism", which is research carried out with an absence of theory in any meaningful sense. Mills provides telling criticisms of these tendencies in sociology; his own perspective is that "The capacity to shuttle between levels of abstraction, with ease and with clarity, is a signal mark of imaginative and systematic thinker" (1959: 43). An equally well-known perspective is that of Merton (1968: ch.2), who argues for "theories of the middle range". This is not the place to review the analyses of Mills or Merton; they are referred to here simply to illustrate the point about varying levels of abstraction. Stinchcombe (1968: 48–50), in dealing with this point, distinguishes no less than seven different levels of generality in social theory. Of course, such variation in levels should come as no surprise, given the earlier material in this chapter. As theories are basically composed of relationships between concepts, and concepts are used at widely differing levels of abstraction, the same comment *must* apply to theories. There is, however, an important consequence for the application of the ABCDE model. The level of generality of a theory affects the 'amount of operationalising' to be done; for example, the more abstract the theory at stage A, the more theoretical analysis is needed to 'deduce' specific stage B propositions. This re-emphasises a point introduced in Chapter 2. The process of arguing from A to B to C is virtually never a process of simple deduction; the nature of the theory will determine how closely it approximates to this 'ideal'.

Many sociologists have criticised their colleagues for paying insufficient attention to the logical structure of theory. For example, Denzin (1970: 34), following Homans (1964), discusses the ideal requirements for theory which are, briefly, that "[a] theory is a set of propositions that furnish an explanation by means of a deductive system". His main example is taken from Durkheim's theory of suicide. If one accepts this conception of theory, it minimizes the operationalisation problem, for the deductive system implies that stage B propositions follow from stage A logically and non-problematically. Denzin also says that, given this position, it is clear that "contemporary sociology has few if any theories . . . [there] exist, instead, small attempts at theory, many conceptual frameworks, a few propositional systems without deductive schemes . . . vague explanations" (1970: 35). For example, neither Berger's theory cited in Chapter 2 nor Garabedian's theory would stand up to these ideal requirements. In both cases the movement from A to B to C was problematic, involving clarification and definition of concepts and their relationships.

Characterising the theoretical content of research reports

Although this analysis of theory raises relevant issues, it must be used cautiously. To decipher research reports it is necessary to view the world of social theory as it is, rather than as it might (or might not) be at some unspecified future time.[3] Following my analysis in Chapter 2, testable social theory can be defined as any verbal argument (usually based on relationships between sociological concepts) which contains the germs of testable propositions. This is a loose definition, but it will suffice for present purposes. A glance at the studies in Part Two or any textbook of social theory will show the wide variety of style, presentation and content in such verbal arguments. The theory presented in research reports is often an amalgamation of previous writings (both theory and empirical findings) on the substantive topic investigated, together with the author's original ideas on the subject. The deciphering of a research report therefore entails following the author's theoretical argument in whatever form it is presented, and evaluating it in terms both of the 'logic' of the argument and the concept-indicator links involved. Merton's analysis (1968: chs 4 and 5) of the relationship of theory to evidence provides a useful and realistic perspective on this issue. Merton emphasises how the very process of trying to operationalise a theory leads to reflection, reconsideration and clarification of the theory; these processes may be continued as the research is carried out, the results collated, and a report written. In short, Merton offers an analysis of what happens to theory as the result of research; empirical research can and does play an active role in social theory – it can initiate, reformulate, deflect or clarify theory (Merton, 1968: 157).

Phillips (1966: 42) provides further guidance on different kinds of theory. Following Zetterberg (1963), Phillips distinguishes between four uses of the word theory: first, *sociological classics,* "the important works of early sociologists" (for example, Durkheim's *Suicide*); second, *sociological criticism,* "[tracing] the relationships and continuities amongst sociological ideas from a historical perspective" (for example, Nisbet's *The Sociological Tradition);* third, *sociological taxonomy,* which "refers to an orderly arrangement of sociological ideas into neat categories" (for example, Parsons's writing on action theory); and fourth, *deductive theory,* which corresponds to Denzin's ideal type, discussed above. The important point here is that most social theory falls into the first three categories, and apparently does not *aim* to satisfy the criteria of the fourth category. There are some problems with these distinctions which are clear even from this brief account. For example, many theoretical works may genuinely fall into more than one category; Durkheim's *Suicide* is generally cited as a standard example of deductive theory, yet it is also a sociological classic. The term 'sociological criticism' as a title for the second category seems misleading, and indeed it is uncertain how one could categorise much contemporary critical theory such as the work of the Frankfurt school. Even so, one main point is quite clear. Many social theories will be in a form quite different from deductive theory. Consequently, some theories will need much more reconsideration and clarification than others if they are to be tested out through empirical research. Thus deductive theory should act only as an ideal type against which one can draw contrasts, in order to clarify the analysis of a given research report.

Theorising. When applying the ABCDE model as the basic tool in evaluating a research report, we should therefore remain aware of the wide variety of theory-evidence links, or kinds of *theorising,* which may be encountered. Some basic variations on the ABCDE model have been mentioned in Chapter 2 and we shall return to this topic in Chapter 6; a more detailed analysis of theorising is given by Rose (1979). One important point is that, in most research reports which test theories, the author will normally reconsider the theory after the empirical findings have been described. The *rewriting* of theory (or, at least, parts of the theory) to take account of new findings is the most common result of theory-testing research; this comment applies whether the theory tested is confirmed or refuted. Another kind of theorising occurs when stage B of a research report consists of theoretical questions rather than propositions. In this case the findings will normally lead to the *development* of the theory. Garabedian's study provides an example. It is outside the scope of this book to give a comprehensive analysis of all varieties of theorising – indeed, as far as I know, such an exercise has never been carried to its logical conclusion and there is much opportunity for further work on the topic (Rose, 1979).

The main thrust of this analysis of theory can now be stated very simply. To decipher a given research report, it is necessary to characterise accurately the author's theorising; the material above, together with an awareness of the wide variety of possibilities which may occur, should allow this task to be tackled realistically.

Finally, it should be noted that in some writings, especially those of philosophers of science, the term 'theory' is used in a broader sense than that above. Following Ford (1975), Mullins (1973), Rose (1979) and other sociologists we may use the more specific terms 'metatheory', 'paradigm', 'school of social theory' or 'theory group' when referring to theory in this broad sense; Stinchcombe (1968: 48-50) does not use this terminology, but metatheory would be equivalent to his three highest levels of generality in social theory. The relationship of metatheory or 'schools of social theory' (structural-functionalism, Marxism, symbolic interactionism, and so on) to the conduct of research is, in the main, outside the scope of this book, but the most relevant points are reviewed briefly in Chapter 9.

EXERCISES

3.1 Summarise the *operational definition* of each of the following variables: frequency of marijuana use (Goode, Chapter 13); political knowledge, political interest (Dowse and Hughes, Chapter 16); authority class, class awareness (Lopreato, Chapter 18). For which of these variables are *complete* details given and for which are the operational definitions not fully stated? (Note that any other variables from the quantitative case studies can be used as the basis of this question.)

3.2 (a) In the example of powerlessness (see above), the operational definition is based on five questionnaire items. By comparing the wording of these items with the nominal definition given of powerlessness, assess the *face validity* of the operational defini- tion. (b) Using the nominal definition as your guide, construct five additional questionnaire items intended to measure powerless- ness. The wording of the items should be brief, in reasonably simple language, and such that the respondent can agree or disagree. (With the help of an instructor this question can be taken further by administering the new and the original items to a group of people, and analysing the results, i.e. by conducting a pilot study. For such an exercise the recent literature should be consulted on the measurement of alienation and powerlessness.)

3.3   Assess the validity of the concept-indicator links for each of the variables analysed in Exercise 3.1

3.4   Goode (Chapter 13) argues that marijuana users form a subculture with three components which are (briefly) "association- al", "lifestyle" and "identity". The involvement of an individual in the subculture can be considered under these three headings. Which of Goode's *variables* correspond to each heading? Are there any variables which do not correspond to any of the three? Draw a tree diagram of your results. (Goode's study is analysed in Chapter 6, and the reader may wish to refer to the relevant sections of the analysis, especially the list of variables.)

3.5   In Exercise 1.2 the nature of the theorising in certain case studies was characterised briefly. Reconsider your answers, and re-analyse the theorising in these studies in detail using the methods and materials developed in this chapter. (Other studies may, of course, be substituted if preferred.)

4
Sampling

Sampling, defined in the glossary as 'the selection of units for study', is construed here in the broadest possible sense, to encompass study designs of all kinds including sampling for large-scale social surveys, studies of individuals with specific characteristics and studies which use control groups. The question of *units* will also be discussed. As we shall see, satisfactory solutions to sampling problems involve a combination of theoretical, practical and strategic issues.

REPRESENTATIVE SAMPLING

Since many of the important aspects of sampling stem from the idea of representativeness, it is best to start by discussing representative sampling. This will be done through an example designed to illustrate some of the basic principles. Suppose we are planning research on the relationship between organisational membership and feelings of powerlessness amongst students. The exact purpose of the study will not be considered here – we will be concerned simply with the selection of the sample. Suppose we decide to take a sample of 400 students from the University of X (assume 400 is a restriction imposed by considerations of time and money). What are the obvious alternatives? Eight possibilities are listed below; the number of possibilities and exact nature of each is not the main issue, as there are many other variations and alternatives. The main points to be emphasised are the distinctions between different kinds of representative sampling, and the contrast between representative sampling, in (1) to (4), and the 'approximations' given in (5) to (8).

Population: All enrolled students in (say) 1980 at the University of *X*. Assume the number is 8,000.

Strata: Two basic variables are sex (male or female) and year of enrolment (first, second, third, fourth, graduate). For reasons which will become clear, we shall regard these as *stratified variables* (the term will be explained later).

Representative sampling plans
1.   Simple random sample. A random selection of 400 (from the 8,000), for example by a lottery.
2.   Quasi-random (or systematic) sample. Take every twentieth name from an alphabetic list (the starting point must be selected randomly).
3.   Stratified random sample. First stratify by year and sex (there will be ten categories, first-year male to graduate female). Then either (3a) select one in twenty randomly from each group (proportionate stratified sample), or (3b) select forty randomly from each group (disproportionate stratified sample).
4.   Cluster (or multi-stage) sample. Assume all students at the University of *X* are resident on campus. Select twenty starting addresses (rooms in colleges), and instruct interviewers to start here and work through adjacent addresses (along corridors, etc.) until twenty interviews have been completed from each starting-point. The result would be a cluster sample. In this case it is a two-stage sample: the first stage is the selection of starting addresses; the second stage is the procedure of sampling to complete twenty interviews. [1]

Other sampling plans. The central question is how closely these approximate representativeness:
5.   Accidental sample (or convenience sample). The first 400 students enrolled for 1980 by the university registry.
6.   Judgement sample. If experience has shown that sociology students are a good cross-section of students as a whole, select 400 sociology students.
7.   Snowball sample. A small number of students, who are known by personal contact, are asked to nominate other students who would be prepared to be interviewed for the research; these, in turn, nominate others, and so on. [2]
8.   Quota sample. Assume there are ten interviewers on campus, and each is instructed to find four respondents from each of the ten

age/sex stratification categories defined in (3). Thus we have a total of forty respondents per interviewer.

The eight sampling plans are illustrated further by the figures given in Table 4.1. Even with this additional information, the description given of each sampling plan is deliberately brief, but together with the discussion below it should be sufficient for the purpose of this chapter. There are many thorough accounts of the standard methods of sampling readily available in textbooks. Two of the more easily understood sources are Selltiz *et al.* (1976: appendix A) and Labovitz and Hagedorn (1971: ch. 3). In referring to these and to other sources the reader should note, however, that authors do not all use identical terminology in discussing sampling; for example, the term 'probability sampling' in Selltiz *et al.* (1976 : 516) corresponds to 'representative sampling' in the list above.

The central features and principles of representative sampling can now be discussed using sampling plans (1) to (8) as examples. Representative samples are designed by using random selection as a basic principle. Technically, this means that every member of the *population* (students at the University of *X*) has a known *probability* of being selected. While this probability is usually the same for every member of the population (1, 2 and 3a), this is not necessarily the case (3b). When the probability is the same this means that selection can be thought of as a simple lottery system.

The most important point about a population is that in principle it can be enumerated, i.e. all the members can be listed. This list is termed a *sampling frame*. It is assumed that the university authorities would supply a sample frame, i.e. a list of enrolled students, with details of sex and year. Most representative sampling procedures *require* a sampling frame; the frame must be up to date and reliable. Some representative sampling techniques (particularly cluster samples) do not require the frame to be drawn up – it is enough to know that it exists in principle. For example, in cluster samples the final stage of sampling is implemented by the interviewers and it is not necessary to have a list of every individual in the sample. This kind of procedure is common in large-scale social surveys; for example, see Broom and Jones (Chapter 17).

Strata are basic variables; often they are presumed likely to have

TABLE 4.1 Numbers resulting from eight possible sampling methods: 400 students, University of X

Strata Year Sex	Total Population	(1), (2) Simple and quasi-random	(3a) Proportionate stratified	(3b) Disproportionate stratified	(4) Cluster	(5), (6), (7) Accidental, judgement and snowball	(8) Quota
1 M	1,500	~75	75	40	~75	(?)	(40)
1 F	1,500	~75	75	40	~75	(?)	(40)
2 M	800	~40	40	40	~40	(?)	(40)
2 F	1,000	~50	50	40	~50	(?)	(40)
—	—	—	—	—	—	—	—
—	—	—	—	—	—	—	—
Grad M	100	~5	5	40	~5	(?)	(40)
Grad F	80	~5	4	40	~5	(?)	(40)
Total	8,000	400	400	400	400	(100)	(400)

Notes: (i) ~ denotes 'approximately' (e.g. ~ 40 means approximately 40 students in this category); (ii) figures in brackets denote samples which are not selected by representative sampling methods; (iii) ? denotes unknown figures.

an effect on the phenomena to be investigated, but this need not be so. Operationally they must be known prior to data collection, which means that the information must be available as part of the sampling frame. In the example it is clear that sex and year of enrolment would be known to the university authorities. Proportionate stratified sampling is often used simply to ensure that the sample is 'more' representative. For example, as Table 4.1 shows, (3a) ensures that the numbers in each of the ten categories will be exactly proportionate to the corresponding population figures, whereas (1) and (2) do not.

Sample size is another important issue. How large should a sample be and how small can we allow it to be? This aspect of sampling is commonly misunderstood; in particular, a large sample is in itself no guarantee of representativeness. So, even a snowball sample of size 2,000 would not be a representative sample of students. A more relevant issue in the context of this book is how to judge whether the sample size is adequate in a published study. Garabedian's report provides an example; he had a representative sample but as Chapter 2 makes clear the size proved to be too small to carry out the analysis required. The criterion here was that accurate estimates of percentages must be based on adequately sized groups within the sample. Strictly speaking, exact tests to check whether sample size is adequate for the analysis required can be carried out by using statistical techniques such as significance tests. But in many studies readers who do not have statistical skills can use a more common-sense approach to the problem. So, with Garabedian's study, the question is whether the reader accepts as reliable percentages calculated on two, five or ten cases. The answer is fairly obvious.

The question remains: how does a researcher decide in advance what the sample size should be? In large-scale sampling for social surveys estimates can be made statistically (Moser and Kalton, 1971); in many research projects, however, it must be recognised that time and money limitations are the chief determining factors in sample size. A separate point (often forgotten) is that in some studies it may be possible to use a strategy of "on-going inclusion" (Denzin, 1970: 83; the general principle is also well known to statisticians). To put it simply, the researcher adds more cases to the sample until it becomes evident that the size is large enough. It is probable that Becker used this approach (see Chapter 1). It should be noted, however, that it may not be suited to many kinds of study, notably large-scale social surveys; for example, all the data for public opinion polls generally have to be collected within a short period.

Two important points remain to be mentioned. My comments so far refer to *sampling plans*. Now, one may plan a sample which is perfectly representative, but in practice it will probably fall short of this ideal. This is because of problems at the field-work stage. For example, suppose we obtain from the administration of the University of X a perfect disproportionate stratified random sample (3b). This means we have a *target sample* of 400 names, with a contact address for each. But what will happen when we try to collect the data? Some people will have moved and will not be contactable, others will refuse to co-operate; these are *non-responses*. Thus there is a shortfall between the target sample and the *actual sample*. Within the actual sample some respondents may not be willing or able to answer some questions; for these respondents certain variables cannot be coded, a problem referred to as *partial non-response*. Often the total sample size varies from one table to the next in a research report and partial non-response is usually the reason. Hence a representative sampling plan does not ensure that the sample is perfectly representative in practice. In deciphering a study one should examine problems of non-response and the effect on the representativeness of the sample. Many authors ignore or brush aside non-response problems when writing their reports – sometimes this lack of attention is merited, at other times it is not.

Finally, consider the sampling plans listed as (5) to (8). In each case the sample is designed only as an *approximation* to representativeness, since the plan does not involve random selection from the population. Hence none of the four alternatives could be guaranteed to be typical of students at the University of X, and in fact each plan carries with it fairly obvious biases; for example, the quota method (8) would bias the sample towards the inclusion of those who spend time on campus and against those who live off-campus. None the less, sampling methods of this kind are used very frequently in sociology, as representative sampling may be too costly or time-consuming, or may be impractical; the University of X example does not illustrate these difficulties very well, but the circumstances in which such sampling methods are used will be discussed later in this chapter, and several other examples will be given.

UNITS

The term *unit* has entered into the analysis repeatedly from Chapter 1 onwards but it has not yet been discussed in any detail. The unit is the basic element of analysis, and in much sociological research it is simply 'the individual person'. In many studies the theory clearly entails a specific unit which carries through to the empirical research; for example, in Garabedian's study the theory concerns the socialization process of the individual person in prison, and the empirical unit of analysis is therefore also the individual. In other studies the unit is not obvious from the theory, and is defined only in the course of operationalisation; an example is Dornbusch and Hickman's choice of the advertisement as the unit, for Reisman's theory concerns other-directedness generally and does not specify a particular unit of analysis.

In deciphering a given research report, the important point is to be clear about the unit of analysis. Often, this is a relatively simple aspect of the study, and should involve few problems. If there is some doubt, the reader should scrutinise the tables presented in the report, for these will provide a check on the units. For example, in Table 2.1 a total sample size of 2,000 is shown. If one then asks '2,000 what?' the answer is clearly '2,000 individual persons'; therefore, the unit is the individual person (the fact that these are 20–30-year-old married females is not especially relevant for present purposes). As a second example, consider Garabedian's Table 12.1. No total sample size is given, but there are three pairs of columns based on 86, 131 and 28 respectively; these figures refer to numbers of individual persons, which is therefore (again) the unit of analysis.

Some studies are a little more complex. One fact is that the *sampling* unit may be different from the unit of *analysis*; for example, in Broom and Jones's study (Chapter 17) the sampling unit is the household, whereas the unit of analysis is the individual person (one adult male worker from each household sampled was included). Sometimes, a procedure of this kind has implications for the representativeness of the sample. Another point is that, in some studies, the unit of analysis may vary from one section to another; there are no examples in Chapters 10–21, but see Berelson and Salter (discussed in Chapter 22). Finally, the unit of interpretation may be different from the unit of analysis. This usually occurs where the interpretation hinges on the way the data are *aggregated* in a table; an example is the interpretation of Dornbusch and Hickman's Table 10.2, where the focus is on the changes between decades.

SAMPLING AND GENERALISATION

The specific issue of representative sampling will now be put aside to consider the broader theoretical context. Why the need for sampling? The need stems from the fact that a researcher cannot include in his study *all* the phenomena to which the theory refers (in the example, all students). Thus sampling must be done, and, moreover, it must be done in such a way that one can *generalise* from the sample. This is not just a matter of representative sampling, as we shall see. Sjoberg and Nett (1968: 129–30) make a fundamental distinction between the *general universe,* which is the universe of phenomena to which the theory applies, and the *working universe,* which is the set of all empirical units which the researcher defines as the basis of the study, and from which a sample is selected. Since these terms are used frequently below, in much of the discussion they will be referred to briefly as 'g–u' and 'w–u'. The w–u is an empirical universe, which is located in space and time, whereas the g–u is not normally specified in this way. In the example above the g–u is 'students', whereas the w–u consists of all students at the University of X enrolled in 1980. As another illustration, in the Berger example the g–u is 'people' and the w–u is 20–30-year-old married females in city X in 1980. And in Garabedian's study the g–u was 'prisons', and the w–u was the one prison selected for study over one specific time period.

The working universe refers to the same entity as the term 'population'. While in any given study the two can be equated, both will be retained for use because the term w–u helps us to remember the relationship with the higher-level g–u. The examples given above show the difficulties inherent in generalising from the w–u to the g–u. The w–u is specifically located in space and time, and both these dimensions must be considered as part of the generalisation process. Thus, in the University of X example, one would be concerned both with whether the findings are applicable to students in other universities (space) and whether findings in 1980 will still apply in future years, and if so for how long (time). This carries some further implications for theory. The difficulties which emerge in arguing from the w–u are, in fact, due to the very general nature of the g–u in the three examples. Should not a theory spell out clearly the *conditions* under which it applies? This aspect of theory has received less systematic attention than might be expected in the sociological literature, and the result is that the question of conditions is often left implicit. This is unfortunate, for it is these conditions which should logically lead the researcher to the choice of a working universe (Rose, 1979: 130–2).

But how are working universes selected in practice and what criteria are used? The following list is based on Sjoberg and Nett's review of this problem (1968: 136–44), and incorporates their distinction between logical-theoretical considerations and social-practical factors:

Logical-theoretical reasons

1. Typicality (e.g. try to find a typical suburb for a community study).
2. To confirm a theory (choose a w–u which, *a priori,* seems likely to confirm theory).
3. To disprove or modify a theory (choose a w–u which a *priori* seems likely to be 'deviant').
4. Choose a w–u which has been studied previously (to replicate, assess change, or disprove).
5. Choose a w–u *not* previously studied (e.g. in the hope of discovering new findings).

Social-practical reasons

6. Convenience (e.g. choice of home town)
7. Availability of data (e.g. in studies using official records).
8. Concern for applications (e.g. the w–u may be chosen as a population for which one hopes to be able to suggest policy changes).
9. Need for collaboration or consent to do research (e.g. research in prisons or industrial organisations).

It is probable that other reasons could be added to this list, but it is sufficient for present purposes, and it enables a number of important points to be made. First, except for heading 1, the list is dominated by factors which are 'non-typical'; headings 2–5 show that there may be sound theoretical reasons for the selection of a specific w–u rather than one which is typical in some sense. Second, the social-practical reasons listed are not mutually exclusive, and several of the headings may apply to any given study; for example, Garabedian's choice of the prison was probably in a convenient location (6), certainly involved consent of the authorities (9), and possibly depended on accessibility to prison records (7). In practice, convenience (6) is an important factor in the majority of research projects which involve the collection of new data. Third, in deciphering a research report it is usually much easier to pick out the social-practical reasons than the logical-theoretical reasons. Of course, this indicates the extent to which reasons 6–9 are the important determinants of the selection of the w–u rather than reasons 1–5. As we shall see, the theoretical rationale for choosing a w–u is often unclear in a research report. The basic questions which have to be asked as part of the deciphering of a report are therefore: What is the g–u, i.e. to what extent it is made clear under what conditions the theory should apply? For what reasons (stated or inferred) has the author chosen the particular w–u? More detailed questions can also be raised, but these will be discussed later.

Working universe and sample

Sampling can now be seen as a two-stage process, which is depicted later in this chapter in Figure 4.1. The first stage is the move from g–u to w–u, and the second is the selection of the sample from the w–u or population. Further attention will now be given to this second stage. We have already seen several examples of representative sampling plans, and some possible approximations. One other alternative is that the researcher may decide to study the *whole* of the population. Usually this strategy depends on choosing a population which is of manageable size, as well as being appropriate theoretically. Examples are the studies of Porterfield and Gibbs (Chapter 14) and Breed (see Chapter 22).

In some circumstances one may be able to define the working universe, but it may be impossible to construct a sampling frame. In these cases accidental, snowball or judgement sampling may be used. For example, in Goode's study (Chapter 13) the population is presumably "marijuana users in New York"; obviously there is no list to act as a sampling frame, and Goode uses snowball sampling. This is only one of the many situations in which the aim is to select a sample which is typical of some w–u, but where representativeness is impossible to achieve in the formal sense.

Even in the circumstances which allow a representative sampling plan to be used, as we have seen, the sample is rarely perfectly representative in practice because of problems such as non-response. This implies that representative sampling should be looked on as an ideal-type which, for a variety of reasons, is unlikely to be achieved in the majority of studies. We must look realistically at the samples which researchers have found practicable, and, wherever typicality is the *aim*, we should contrast the real situation with this ideal-type, so that possible biases may be analysed and the problems of generalisation from sample to population can be assessed realistically. For example, in the case of accidental and snowball samples, one has to think through the process of being included in the sample and how closely this process approximates to the random selection of units; and for studies in which representative sampling plans are used, the two kinds of non-response will be important.

Some further sampling procedures

There are many research studies in which, for theoretical reasons, a representative sample is not appropriate. These sampling procedures fall under three headings, the last of which will be discussed in more detail. *First*, when studying a social institution, a social group, or some kind of small 'social system', often the *whole* of a system is crucial theoretically and it is not meaningful to take a sample of the kind described so far. The researcher must study the whole of the social system or select a sample in such a way that the essential aspects of social relationships are preserved. Examples are studies of juries, friendship networks or forms in a high school (see Lacey, Chapter 15). The theories which demand this kind of sampling are often theories about interactions between the indi- viduals in a group; if this is the focus of the inquiry, naturally it is dangerous to leave out any members of the given group. *Second*, in studying events as they happen, there is usually no way of enumerating the population beforehand, and therefore there is no sampling frame. Examples are research on homosexual encounters in public places, and behaviour of customers in restaurants. Denzin (1970: 89–96) discusses both the first and second headings under the general title of *interactive* sampling models and stresses that the researcher should keep in mind considerations of representativeness, in so far as this is possible. For example, an observer of customer behaviour in restaurants might select both the restaurants and the observation periods so as to be typical in some sense. *Third*, there are studies based on control groups and similar approaches, which are approximations to experimental designs. These are called (variously) analytic designs (Oppenheim, 1966), quasi-experimental designs (Campbell and Stanley, 1963) and explanatory surveys (Hyman, 1955), though the three terms cannot be equated exactly. The fundamentals of this approach are now introduced.

COMPARING SIMILAR GROUPS

One of the most basic procedures in analysing sociological data is to make *comparisons* between two or more groups.[3] For example, Garabedian analyses five groups of inmates (square johns, right guys, and so on) separately and then compares them in terms of patterns of socialization, and in Porterfield and Gibbs's study (Chapter 14) a comparison is made between the suicides and a sample of natural deaths. Here, the natural deaths form a *control group* allowing the researchers to judge whether the social mobil- ity of suicides is greater than that of the general population. A third example is that of Breed (see Chapter 22), who compares a sample of suicides in New Orleans with a control group, designed to match the suicide group as closely as possible on a number of specified variables (age, race, sex, area of residence, and so on). The comparisons which are made in these three examples are increasingly sophisticated. Garabedian split a single sample into a number of groups which were then compared, and Porterfield and

Gibbs collected data on two separate samples which were then compared. In Breed's study the samples which were compared were *matched,* i.e. were intended to be alike in certain respects. The idea of 'comparing like with like' takes on increasing importance as we move through the three examples.

There are certain difficulties inherent in making comparisons between groups. To illustrate these, let us reconsider the Berger example. Instead of the sample suggested in Chapter 2 (a representative sample of 2,000 married females) one might decide to contrast two separate samples, say:

(a) 120 married females aged 20–30 *with* children;
(b) 120 married females aged 20–30 *without* children.

Provided that each of the samples is representative of the category from which it is selected, this would appear to be a suitable study design for testing the five propositions. For simplicity, suppose we focus on proposition (i) 'people who have no children are more likely to be enthusiasts for violent change'. Is the study design suitable to test this proposition? Perhaps not, for one might find that the women in sample (a) are generally older than those in sample (b), and that the two samples have different social-class compositions. One would then be faced with the problem of whether differences in enthusiasm for violent change are due to parental status or due to the age or social-class differences between the two samples. The problem is that *uncontrolled variables* (age, social class) are interfering with the analysis. It is helpful to delineate four kinds of variables, as follows:

> Independent variable – parental status
> Dependent variable – enthusiasm for violent change
> Controlled variables – sex, marital status (only married females are considered), age range
> Uncontrolled variables – age (within 20–30), social class (and others)

As the terminology implies, we are concerned mainly with the effect of the independent variable on the dependent variable. But this relationship cannot be studied in isolation, as other variables will affect it. Some of these variables are controlled in the sample design, but other variables are uncontrolled.

In fact, this is a general problem in the analysis of empirical data. The distinction between dependent, independent, controlled

and uncontrolled variables is not peculiar to control group designs
– it applies to the analysis of data, irrespective of the sampling
procedures used. In Chapter 5 data analysis techniques for dealing
with uncontrolled variables will be discussed. But here, let us
return to the example. If we wish to make age and social class
controlled variables, we must choose the samples in such a way
that the two groups are equivalent on these variables. Table 4.2
shows how this might be done; to keep the example simple, class is
categorised simply as 'lower' and 'middle' and age as '20–24' and
'25–30'. The 'before-controlling' figures show a tendency for those
without children to be younger, and more lower class, whereas the
'after-controlling' figures match the two samples on these variables, and give a simple illustration of a matched control group
design.

TABLE 4.2   *The effect of controlling on two variables**

Age and social class	Before controlling		After controlling	
	Children (a)	No children (b)	Children (a)	No children (b)
20–24 Lower	25	35	30	30
20–24 Middle	20	35	30	30
25–30 Lower	40	25	30	30
25–30 Middle	35	25	30	30
Total	120	120	120	120

*The figures shown are the numbers falling into each category of the sample

Control groups

A full discussion of control groups and other kinds of analytic
design is outside the scope of this book, but some brief comments
will be made. First, an account has not been given of the exact
ways in which one might choose individuals to include in the
'after-controlling' samples (a) and (b) in the example above.
Several different approaches are possible, and all involve either
matching pairs of individuals or the two groups as a whole
(Oppenheim, 1966: ch. 1; Riley, 1963: unit 11). Second, it
should be noted that control group designs usually entail samples
that are *unrepresentative;* in the example neither controlled sample
(a) nor (b) would be representative of the category from which is
was selected (at least in any simple sense).

Third, suppose we were to collect the appropriate data from the two samples; the data analysis would test for differences between the two groups in attitudes to violent change, which is the dependent variable. We may call this a *prospective* control group design. By contrast, some studies base two matched groups on categories of the dependent variable and look for variations in the independent variable. For example, one might select a group of delinquents and a group of non-delinquents matched on certain factors and compare their social-class backgrounds; here the independent variable would be social class, and the dependent variable delinquency. Control group designs of this kind may be called *retrospective*. The existing literature tends to emphasise prospective designs (e.g. Campbell and Stanley, 1963, who term them "quasi-experimental") and there is little methodological guidance available on retrospective designs. Here, I can do no more than state the difference between the two, and point out that in sociology the retrospective design is the more frequently used. One example is Breed's study (see Chapter 22); also, although the control group used by Porterfield and Gibbs (Chapter 14) is not matched to the suicide group, the approach is nevertheless retrospective.

To summarise, if we consider the simplest situation, a control group or other analytic design is set up to test a specific proposition (or explore a specified relationship) which itself defines the independent and dependent variables. Several other variables will be controlled. The result will be a sample which is non-representative. The study will test what it is designed to test, but only rarely will it be possible to use the data for any other purpose. This situation may be contrasted with *descriptive designs* (i.e. representative and other kinds of samples aimed at typicality), where the object of studying specific relationships plays no great part in the sampling. In general, analytic designs are appropriate only when the object of the study is to test a single proposition or a set of related propositions.

Controlled variables

The practice of controlling variables in sampling has wide application and is not confined to control group designs. The simplest and most common situation is where variables are controlled as part of the definition of the working universe; these variables are controlled by excluding certain categories, including only certain categories, or holding certain variables constant. For example, Breed (see Chapter 22) controls sex, race, length of residence and age range by studying only white, male, resident suicides aged 20–60 in New Orleans, and Porterfield and Gibbs (Chapter 14) control sex and age range, as only the suicides of adult males are studied. Also, in the Berger example, whichever of the sampling alternatives we consider, sex, marital status and age range have been controlled. In fact, the choice and definition of the working universe will *normally* entail control of one or more variables. It follows that, in deciphering a given research report, one should follow through (and then evaluate) the author's rationale for these controlled variables; for example, do Porterfield and Gibbs justify their control on sex and age range of the sample of suicides?

THE ANALYSIS OF SAMPLING IN RESEARCH REPORTS

Although the application of this chapter to any given study will often be quite clear, it will be helpful to review the use of the material in deciphering a research report. The reader should first summarise the details of sampling in the author's own terms. Second, one should identify the general universe, the working universe and the sample; here, Figure 4.1 will be of assistance. It shows how the theoretical and empirical levels are related to the move from general universe to working universe. The arrows correspond to the rationale for the sampling as a whole (this may or may not be stated explicitly by the author) and the core of the evaluation will be to analyse this rationale. Third, in analysing the lower arrow, one should, of course, use the material above on representative sampling, approximations, other approaches and analytic designs, depending on which kind of sampling has been employed. Fourth, one should analyse the extent to which the sampling plan was successfully put into practice, and the importance of factors such as non-response; one simple procedure, which often clarifies the analysis, is to check the N-sizes (sample sizes) in different tables for consistency. Fifth, the reader should examine the *generalisations* made in the report. Often, the most important generalisations are made as part of the author's theoretical conclusions; in a study which is close to the ABCDE model it is the process of inference from C to B to A which is scrutinised here. It is not uncommon for an author to generalise from a limited working universe to a broad general universe, and the reader has to analyse whether this process is justified.

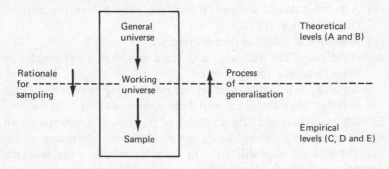

FIGURE 4.1   *Sampling as a two-stage process*

These five stages in the analysis of sampling are not necessarily sequential (for example, a check on *N*-sizes will often refine the reader's understanding of the basic details of sampling), but together they will constitute a thorough evaluation of the problem of sampling and generalisation. The question of *units* must also be considered as part of the evaluation, and the material given earlier in this chapter should give sufficient guidance on this topic. The studies analysed in Chapters 2 and 6 act as examples of how the assessment of sampling, generalisation and units enters into the deciphering of research reports.[4]

EXERCISES

4.1   This exercise is to consist of a five-stage analysis (as above) of the sampling and generalisation involved in several of the quantitative studies from Part Two. It is suggested that the reader

(a) Review the sampling in the two studies by Garabedian, and Dornbusch and Hickman.

(b) Analyse the sampling in two or more other studies.

4.2 *Exercises in sampling design.* Suppose that you have been asked to act as a consultant in research design for the following studies. What would be the main factors involved in sampling? (Both theoretical and practical factors should be discussed.) What are the main elements of the designs you would recommend? There is no need to give exact details of sample size, and so on; the object is simply to work through the logical problems.

(a) A representative sample of children aged 6–8 in the area or city in which you live.
(b) A sample of habitual drunk drivers.
(c) A sample of 200 males, resident in a suburb of a city which you know, who are about to retire.
(d) An analytic design to test for the relationship between absence of father from the home and delinquency of child.

In each case there may be a variety of possibilities; you may wish to discuss one main sampling design and note any alternatives. For (a), (b) and (c) you will wish to consider whether the working universe is defined adequately; also, for these three exercises, if representativeness is not possible formally, you should say *why* it is not possible and how good an approximation you can suggest.

5

Data Analysis

This chapter provides an introduction to some basic issues in the analysis of quantitative data. As a first example, reconsider the relationship between the two variables 'parental status' and 'enthusiasm for violent change' in the Berger example. For the sake of simplicity, suppose we have a small sample of twenty married females chosen by representative methods, with data on the two variables as shown in Table 5.1.

TABLE 5.1

Person No.	Parental status	Enthusiasm score	Person no.	Parental status	Enthusiasm score
1	C	L	11	NC	H
2	C	H	12	NC	H
3	NC	H	13	C	L
4	C	L	14	NC	H
5	NC	L	15	NC	H
6	C	H	16	C	L
7	NC	H	17	C	H
8	C	L	18	NC	H
9	C	L	19	NC	L
10	NC	L	20	C	H

C = has children   L = low score (0, 1)
NC = has no children   H= high score (2, 3)

In analysing these data, one might first consider the dependent variable, enthusiasm score. In the sample there are nine low scores and eleven high scores, and we may therefore construct Table 5.2.

68   *Deciphering Sociological Research*

This is a one-dimensional or *univariate* table, since it is based on one variable only; in statistical terminology it shows the *distribution* of the variable 'enthusiasm for violent change'.

TABLE 5.2   *Enthusiasm for violent change for a sample of twenty married females**

Enthusiasm score	No.	%
Low	9	45
High	11	55
Total	20	100%

*Data hypothetical.

Table 5.2 is, however, of little consequence by itself. This is not because the example and the data are simplistic – it is because the main interest is in the *relationship* of the two variables, rather than either one of them individually. If we consider the two variables together, there are six women with children and low scores, four with children and high scores, three with no children and low scores and seven with no children and high scores. Listing figures in this way shows no obvious pattern, but when they are arranged in Table 5.3 the nature of the relationship emerges. Despite the slightly different format, it is evident that the patterns in Table 5.3 are identical to those of Table 3.1; the difference is that Table 3.1 was based on a (hypothetical) sample of 2,000 rather than 20. Table 5.3 is an example of a *bivariate* table (also referred to as a two-dimensional table, contingency table, or cross-tabulation) showing the relationship between two variables. Although this example is extremely simple, it does illustrate several features of bivariate table construction. The first is the relation of the data to the table. The situation may appear more complex when there are large samples and many variables involved, but in principle one is simply counting *units* into the 'cells' of the table. The process of constructing a bivariate table or cross-tabulation from the data is essentially the same, whether it is done by simple counting, on punch-cards or by computer.

As we progress with this chapter, other features of tables will be

TABLE 5.3 *Parental status and enthusiasm for violent change, for a sample of twenty married females**

Enthusiasm score	Has children		Has no children		Total	
	No.	%	No.	%	No.	%
Low	6	(60)	3	(30)	9	(45)
High	4	(40)	7	(70)	11	(55)
Total	10	(100)	10	(100)	20	(100)

*Data hypothetical.

considered, including the calculation of percentages and the interpretation of tables given in research reports. There are, however, strict limitations on the coverage of data analysis in this book. In particular, statistical techniques as such will not be discussed. This is an extremely important topic (and one which many students find difficult), but it requires a treatment in much more detail than is possible here; some guidance on textbooks is, however, given below. It will be evident from Part Two that I have intentionally selected research reports in which the data analysis and presentation is mainly through tables and percentages; the implications of this selectivity will be considered in Chapter 9. For the moment, the reader should note that, while tables are the simplest form of data analysis, the issues dealt with in this chapter are by no means trivial; also, much of the material presented here has implications for more complex kinds of data analysis.

In restricting the main attention to tabular analysis, it must also be recognised that certain kinds of variables are only rarely considered. To explain this, we must note that there are four different *levels of measurement* of variables as follows:[1]

1. *Dichotomous* variables have two categories. Examples: sex (male, female); parental status (has children, has no children).
2. *Nominal* variables have three or more (non-ordered) categories. Examples: Garabedian – social role (five categories); Broom and Jones – occupation (three – manual, non-manual, farm).
3. *Ordinal* variables have three or more categories but in a definite order. Examples: Garabedian – career phase (three– early, middle, late); Goode – marijuana use (five – every day to less than monthly).

4. *Interval* variables are based on scores (rather than categories) which allow differences of magnitude to be expressed. Examples: Goode – number of other drugs used (0,1,2,3, . . .), so one might say person *A* has used twice as many other drugs as person *B;* suicide rate, where it is possible to say that country *X* has three times as high a suicide rate as country *Y*.

In general, the analysis of dichotomous, nominal and ordinal variables is achieved through tables, whereas for interval variables one uses other methods (such as correlation techniques) which do not involve counting units into cells. In this book the focus is on the first three levels of measurement. The analysis of interval variables is, in the main, outside the scope of the book.

Two further points must be mentioned. First, the four levels are in increasing order of sophistication of measurement. In data analysis it is always possible to 'reduce' the level of sophistication by grouping an interval variable or by amalgamating categories of a nominal or interval variable to form a dichotomy. Such practices are very common, as results can often be presented more simply or more briefly. For example, in Table 3.1 the 'enthusiasm for violent change' score (an ordinal variable – 0,1,2 or 3) was simplified to two categories (a dichotomous variable – high, low). There are several examples in the studies that follow; for instance, Goode shows the number of other drugs used (an interval variable) as 0,1–2, 3 or more (an ordinal variable) in Table 13.7. Generally, the ways in which reductions can be achieved are: interval to ordinal to dichotomy; ordinal to dichotomy; nominal to dichotomy. Thus, in principle, any variable can be reduced to a dichotomy.

Second, it is helpful to introduce the idea of an *average,* which applies most clearly to interval variables. For example, we can consider the average number of other drugs used by Goode's sample; the average would be calculated by adding the relevant figures (number of other drugs used) for each member of the sample, and dividing by the sample size. The result might be (say) 2.6 drugs; in stricter terminology this would be called a *mean value.* Now, consider whether mean values can be calculated for variables on the first three levels of measurement; in fact, variables such as sex, social role and career phase do not (logically) have mean values. It is only when a variable measures magnitude or size that it is possible and sensible to calculate a mean value.[2]

Thus the mean or average value – which, in a sense, *summarises* the values of the variable – is applicable only to interval variables. To summarise a dichotomous, nominal or ordinal variable, one generally uses the percentage distribution; a simple example is Table 5.2. In some studies (e.g. Lacey, Chapter 15) mean values are given for interval variables, but in Part Two no statistics are presented at a more complex level.

Books on statistics

Much of the discussion above will appear simplistic to the reader already familiar with basic statistics. However, the principle aim is to give sufficient material for understanding the data analysis and interpreting the tables presented in the studies in Part Two. To analyse a research report which uses more complex statistics it is, of course, necessary to have an understanding of the relevant techniques. As we shall see in Chapter 9, given this understanding, the deciphering of such a report should be no more difficult than for a study which uses only tabular presentation of results.

There are many excellent textbooks on statistics prepared for the special needs of sociologists, including those of Blalock (1972) and Anderson and Zelditch (1968). Kalton (1966) gives a very brief but useful introduction, including a chapter with examples of simple significance tests. A valuable supplement to the literature on statistics is Silvey's (1975) book on the analysis of social survey data, which includes sections on coding variables and producing tables.

TWO-VARIABLE RELATIONSHIPS

To carry forward the brief discussion of two-variable analysis given above, it is first necessary to distinguish between *asymmetric* and *reciprocal* relationships. Suppose we name the two variables X and Y, and let $\rightarrow$ denote the influence of one variable on the other. Building on the analysis of Rosenberg (1968: ch. 1), we can define:

(1) *Asymmetric relationship* $(X \rightarrow Y)$. The independent variable (X) influences the dependent variable (Y): for example, father's

social class → son's education level.

(2) *Reciprocal relationship (X⇄Y)*. An interacting or mutually reinforcing relationship: for example, husband's hostility to wife ⇄wife's hostility to husband.

An arrow indicates that one variable is seen as having an effect on another; *arrow diagrams* are often a convenient way of depicting relationships between variables and, as will be seen, can be extended to the situation in which several variables are being considered.

There are several important points about this distinction. First, only in the asymmetric case is there a strictly independent–dependent relationship; in reciprocal relationships one cannot distinguish between the dependent and independent variable. Second, authors use a diversity of terms for the influence of one variable on another – for example, "determination" (Rosenberg, 1968) and 'cause' (Selltiz *et al.*, 1976); provided the subject under discussion is statistical relationships between variables, these terms can be equated. Third, in any given circumstance, how are we to decide the direction of influence and, indeed, whether a given relationship is asymmetric or reciprocal? As Rosenberg says (1968: ch. 1), the direction of the arrow depends on two criteria: (a) the time order, and (b) the relative fixity and alterability of the variables. For any two-variable relationship, we may examine these criteria and this will show which is the independent and which the dependent variable; if the criteria do not lead to a definite result, the relationship is reciprocal. It is important to stress that decisions about the nature of two-variable relationships are made on the basis of these two criteria and *not* from the data themselves.

To illustrate the points above, consider some examples from the quantitative case studies. The relationship X, stage of prison sentence → Y, agreement with staff norms, in Garabedian's study, is asymmetric; here X is 'fixed' by length of sentence and time of admission to prison, and Y is 'alterable'. In Porterfield and Gibb's study the final section is concerned with X, crisis → Y, suicide; this is an asymmetric relationship because of time order, as X occurs before Y. In Goode's study, X, buying and selling marijuana, is reciprocally related to Y, use of LSD; neither of these variables determines the other, they simply 'co-vary'. Note that it is often necessary to refer to the operational definition of each variable to clarify whether the relationship is reciprocal or asymmetric. In Goode's study one might be tempted to judge that the relationship between X, marijuana use, and Y, use of other drugs, is asymmetric, as common sense seems to indicate that in most cases X precedes Y; however, as the marijuana-use variable is defined operationally as an average estimated over the past six months, and the 'use of other drugs' variable does not specify the time period, there is no clear time order involved.

Rosenberg (1968: 13–20) analyses asymmetric relationships in considerable detail, and gives a list of several different common kinds, for example stimulus → response (e.g. crisis → suicide) and property → disposition (e.g. parental status → attitude to violent change). These distinctions will not, however, be pursued here, since we shall be concerned with the more general implications of the analysis. Three main themes will be discussed in the remainder of this chapter: the percentaging of two-dimensional tables, the interpretation of such tables, and the extension to the case of three or more variables. The treatment given to each of these topics is necessarily limited, and for further details the reader may refer to Rosenberg (1968) and Silvey (1975). One important point which is not highlighted sufficiently in Rosenberg's book and in the related literature is that this 'survey analysis' approach to constructing and interpreting tables is applicable *only* to studies based on descriptive designs – that is, to samples which are taken to be representative (see Chapter 4). For studies based on matched control groups or other analytic designs, there are certain constraints which must be placed on the data analysis; for example, even the percentaging of a table may not be a matter of choice, for the procedures must be consistent with the nature of analytic design. In this chapter, therefore, attention is confined to tabular analysis based on descriptive designs; since this is, in fact, by far the most common approach to sampling in sociology (see Chapter 4) the procedures outlined will be applicable in most circumstances.

Percentaging

In general, the method of percentaging a bivariate table is determined by which variable is independent and which is dependent. The rule is to take each *category* of the independent variable and use the total figure in that category as the base for percentaging (Rosenberg, 1968: 252). For example, in Table 5.3 parental status is the independent variable. The categories are 'children' and 'no children', with ten cases in each. The percentages of 'high enthusiasm' and 'low enthusiasm' are then calculated out of the two groups of ten. As illustrated in Table 5.3, it is also usual to run percentages in the same way for the total sample. It is important to note that this rule for calculating percentages will apply whatever the *number* of categories of the independent or dependent variables. Also, it is largely a matter of convenience and convention whether the categories of the independent variable form the rows or the columns of a table. Most authors prefer to show the percentages running down the columns; this works well provided the number of categories of the independent variable is not large. However, this is simply a convention, and for many reasons the actual layout of tables will differ from one research report to another.

Why is this method of percentaging normally the most appropriate? Quite simply, in most circumstances the independent–dependent distinction focuses interest on these percentages, because we are concerned with explaining variations in the *dependent* variable. In Table 5.3, 55 per cent of the total sample are highly enthusiastic for violent change. The next question is how the figure varies according to parental status. We then find that 40 per cent high for those with children compares with the 70 per cent high for those without. Our interpretation hinges on a comparison of these two figures with each other and with the total figure. This procedure can be followed in interpreting bivariate tables generally – one simply compares the arrays of percentages for each category of the independent variable with each other and with the total figures. The first question is, in fact, whether there *are* any differences between the percentages. Where the comparison shows that the arrays of percentages are all very similar, one would conclude that the relationship between the two variables is negligible (for the moment we leave aside the problems of sample size and of statistical significance tests).

There are certain circumstances in which it is appropriate to use other methods of percentaging two-dimensional tables; the alternative procedure of taking the categories of the *dependent* variable as the basis for percentaging can be justified if the focus of theoretical interest is in these figures. For example, if the two-variable relationship is education → occupation, a researcher might wish to compare the educational background of the different occupational groups, as in Table 5.4. However, as a general rule, the researcher should use the conventional method outlined above unless there are good reasons for the alternative. For some kinds of asymmetric relationships listed by Rosenberg (e.g. property → disposition), it is difficult to see what could be gained from using the alternative procedure; see Rosenberg (1968: appendix A) and Silvey (1975: ch. 3) on the merits of the conventional method.

TABLE 5.4   *Relationship between occupation and education of the adult male work-force, Australia, 1965**

Education	Occupational division							
	Non-manual		Manual		Farm		Total	
	No.	%	No.	%	No.	%	No.	%
Tertiary	207	30.6	45	4.5	9	3.7	261	13.6
Secondary	392	58.0	609	60.8	107	43.5	1,108	57.6
Primary	77	11.4	348	34.7	130	52.8	555	28.8
Total	676	100%	1,002	100%	246	100%	1,924	100%

*Condensed from Broom, Jones and Zubrzycki (1976: 26, table 2.12). The education variable has been condensed from the four categories shown in Broom *et al.*'s table 2.12 to three by amalgamating the two separate categories referring to secondary education. The data are from a representative sample of the adult male work-force in Australia; this sample is also the basis of Broom and Jones's study (Chapter 17).

So far, we have assumed an asymmetric relationship. In which direction should percentages be run in a table showing a *reciprocal* relationship? In these circumstances factors such as those outlined in the previous paragraph are important, as the nature of the theoretical interest will usually determine which variable is 'taken as independent'. Thus Goode takes marijuana use as 'independent' for the purpose of percentaging in Tables 13.2 to 13.5; this is because marijuana use is the major variable being analysed in the part of the report dealing with this data. Also, the consistency of the use of this variable as 'independent' from one table to the next aids interpretation. In brief, for reciprocal relationships theoretical interest and consistency between tables should determine which variable is taken as 'independent' for the purpose of percentaging.

As a final point, in preparing a table of percentages for publication there are certain common practices which reduce the size of the table and simplify the presentation; two will be mentioned here. First, most of the raw figures may be omitted, and only the percentages presented, together with the N-sizes on which each percentage distribution is based; there are many examples in the quantitative studies, including most of the tables in Goode (Chapter 13) and Broom and Jones (Chapter 17). Second, when the dependent variable is a dichotomy, it is common to present only a percentage referring to one category of the dichotomy for each cell in the table, together with the N-size on which that percentage is based. For example, Garabedian's Table 12.1 shows the percentage of high conformists in fifteen different cells; clearly it is not necessary to show the percentage of low conformists also, as in each case this is simply 100 per cent less the 'high' figure shown. Note that for both of these methods of table presentation, it is a relatively simple matter for the reader to recalculate the raw figures from the percentages if they are needed (see, for example, Table 2.2, which is based on Garabedian's Table 12.1).

Table construction and layout

The purpose of a table is to present results in a form which is clear to the reader. Silvey (1975: ch. 3) gives the five essential components of a table as: title, stub, caption, body, and supplementary notes. Tables 5.2 and 5.3 are rather brief and do not serve as good examples, but see Table 5.4. It has a *title,* the *stub* and *caption* consist of the heading which show the variable names and the categories; the *body* of the table is the figures themselves and there is a *supplementary note.* Silvey's own example (1975: 48) contains substantial supplementary notes, because certain features of the variables have to be explained. This is typical of tables constructed from 'other sources'. In a research report where all tables are based on the same data less explanation is needed;

Davis and Jacobs (1968) give a concise and well-argued account of tabular presentation which is especially applicable to these circumstances, and make many useful suggestions for displaying percentages. Generally, as part of an evaluation of a research report, we have to assess whether the tables are clearly presented; Silvey (1975), Davis and Jacobs (1968), Rosenberg (1968: appendix A) and Broom and Selznick (1968: 10-12) are all helpful sources on this point.

RELATIONSHIPS BETWEEN THREE OR MORE VARIABLES

The case of three or more variables is discussed thoroughly by Rosenberg (1968) and a good shorter treatment is that of Moser and Kalton (1971: 447-51). In the context of this book it is necessary only to outline the material briefly, as in practice authors of research reports rarely analyse more than three variables in any one table; moreover, the procedures of table construction, percentaging and interpretation for more complex tables generally involve similar principles to those described above.

First, reconsider the case of two variables. It is clear from the analysis so far that the nature of the two-variable relationship determines both the way the data are analysed and how they are interpreted. When we are concerned with more than two variables, the general approach is similar. Let us consider the case of three variables. We start by focusing on the relationship between two of these variables, then elaborate on it by introducing the third variable (often referred to as the 'test factor') to see what happens. The test factor is brought into the analysis as a controlled variable, and there are two possible objectives: (a) to see whether the original two-variable relationship is changed (it may, for instance, remain or disappear), or (b) to incorporate the original two variables and the test factor into a three-variable relationship. Thus an approach to the analysis of three-variable relationships begins to take shape. Provided that a given variable has been measured in the research, we are able to test its *impact* upon the relationship being studied; if the impact is significant, we include the new variable by modifying the original relationship. For example, Garabedian starts (in Figure 12.1) by analysing the two-variable relationship career phase → degree of agreement with staff norms. Then he introduces social role as a test factor (in Table 12.1 and Figure 12.2) to see how the two-variable relationship is modified. This is a good illustration of the procedures described by Rosenberg, which are often called 'elaboration'.[3]

There are several examples of tables and graphs analysing three- and four-variable relationships in Dowse and Hughes's study (Chapter 16). Table 16.1 involves three variables, and the focus of the analysis is the joint effect of class and sex (both independent variables) on political knowledge (dependent); in Figure 16.1 there are four variables, of which sex, age and school can be taken as independent and political knowledge is dependent. Later in this chapter we shall return to the study by Dowse and Hughes and extend this brief analysis, but here we use these examples to make a general point.

A table (or other statistical presentation) depicting a three- (or four-) variable relationship normally shows how a single dependent variable is affected by several 'other' variables which are all regarded as independent. Sometimes, however, these 'other' variables may be in an asymmetric relationship to one another, and this in itself may be helpful in the interpretation of the results. It is in these circumstances that Rosenberg's analysis of intervening and antecedent variables (1968: ch. 3) becomes important. This will be illustrated briefly through an example. Suppose that in a study of the process of stratification we consider the relationship of four variables as follows: father's job (Z), son's education (X), son's first job (T) and son's job at age 35 (Y). Because of the time order of these variables, we may depict the relationship as $Z \rightarrow X \rightarrow T \rightarrow Y$. (For the sake of simplicity. I ignore matters such as continuing education after entry into the work-force.) Suppose that the theoretical focus of the study is on the relationship of education (X) to final occupation (Y). We know, however, that Z and T will potentially both have important effects on the relationship of X and Y; both Z and T must therefore be regarded as test factors, but of different kinds. Father's job, Z, is an *antecedent* variable, whereas son's first job, T, is *intervening*. This distinction leads to differences in interpretation of the tables which are produced when the two variables are controlled as test factors. The exact form of the analysis will not be described here, but readers interested in pursuing the matter should consult Rosenberg (1968) or the shorter treatment in Moser and Kalton (1971: 447–51).

ANALYSING TABLES IN RESEARCH REPORTS

In the context of this book the main use of the material in this chapter will be in its application to reading and evaluating the tables presented in a given research report and the interpretations given by the author; this can be conceived as a three-stage process. *First*, characterise the data presented in the study: How many tables are given in the report? Which variables are involved in each table? What additional data (if any) are given in the text? The answers to these questions should therefore cover *all* quantitative data presented in the report, and if some qualitative data are also given, this should be noted. *Second*, focus on each table individually: What was the author's rationale for the inclusion of this table? What variables are involved and which of them are dependent, independent and controlled? What patterns of results are shown by the figures? It is helpful for this analysis if we refer when necessary to the operational definitions of the variables; also, the reader should note any additional information given, such as the results of statistical tests. *Third*, compare the author's interpretation of each table with the table itself: Are the interpretations consistent with the figures? What other points might the author have mentioned? As far as possible, these questions should be confined to interpretations on the *empirical* level (this point will become more clear from Chapter 6).

There are also some special points which are useful in analysing tables. As mentioned in Chapter 4, the N-sizes (total number of units) should be compared for each table in the research report, and checked against the author's account. Apart from identifying any unexplained inconsistencies, this exercise also clarifies certain aspects of the data analysis. For example, are some tables based on a selected group rather than the whole sample, and are some tables based on different units of analysis from others? The question of understanding the results of statistical tests (such as tests of significance) and more advanced statistical techniques is more difficult to handle within this book. Readers are often presented with results such as 'chi-squared $=2.73$' and '$p < .05$' appended to a table, and used as part of the author's interpretation. In these circumstances it is often helpful to refer to a statistics textbook as an aid in following the author's argument; for example, Kalton (1966: ch. 3) gives details of the use of chi-squared tests for contingency tables and some other relatively simple significance tests used quite frequently by sociologists. Here, the problem is best illustrated by considering one study, which is also used as an example of the analysis of tables in research reports; the example is from Dowse and Hughes's study (Chapter 16), and is laid out in the three stages suggested above.

Dowse and Hughes consider two major dependent variables, political knowledge (Figure 16.1 and Table 16.1) and political interest (Figure 16.2 and Tables 16.3, 16.4 and 16.5); Tables 16.6 and 16.7 are concerned with less important variables (party choice and media exposure). The focus on political knowledge and interest, and the way in which the data are presented as a whole, stem from the authors' intention to test the two hypotheses stated early in the report, which imply that political variables will be dependent on age, sex and class. The eight tables and graphs may be summarised as shown in Table 5.5.

TABLE 5.5 *Variables in Dowse and Hughes's study*

	Independent (and controlled) variables	Dependent variable
Figure 16.1	Age, sex, [school type]	Political knowledge
Table 16.1	Sex, class	Political knowledge
Table 16.3	Sex, [school type]	Political interest
Tables 16.4, 16.5,	Sex, class, [school type]	Political interest
Figure 16.2	Age, sex, [school type]	Political interest
Table 16.6	Age, sex	Party choice
Table 16.7	Sex	Media exposure (three variables)

School type (referred to as 'education' in the report) is assumed to be a controlled variable since it is not mentioned in the two hypotheses. Some additional data are given in the text, particularly on political knowledge for certain categories of age, sex, class and school type; here Dowse and Hughes are quoting selected figures from an unpublished table which is more detailed than Figure 16.1 and Table 16.1.

To illustrate the form of the analysis further, let us focus on Figure 16.1 and Table 16.1, which have been referred to earlier as examples of three- and four-variable relationships. (The analysis of the other tables and graph are left as Exercise 5.2(c) for the reader). The use of a graph rather than a table need not confuse us, as in principle it can easily be rewritten as a table (see Exercise 5.2(a)). However, Figure 16.1 omits some important information, for no *N*-sizes are given; for example, we see that about 51 per cent of 11–12-year-old boys at grammar school had high political knowledge scores, but how many of these boys were there in the sample? If we now consider the results, it appears that no clear patterns emerge to confirm the two hypotheses; Figure 16.1 shows that political knowledge increases with age, and that school type makes a great difference, but the hypothesised sex differences are not confirmed.

As Table 16.1 excludes age, it is difficult to see how it can test either hypothesis, and the usefulness of these data is therefore debatable. Nevertheless the table provides us with an illustration of interpreting statistical significance tests. The $p < 0.01$ for the working-class figures means that we can be confident that the difference between boys and girls in political knowledge is not simply due to chance (so it can be regarded as a 'real' difference). The reasoning here centres on the logic of the statistical test, which is as follows:

(a) A 'null hypothesis' is stated, that there is no real difference between the two sexes in the figures for political knowledge, i.e. the apparent difference in the percentages in the first and second lines of the table are no greater than would be expected by chance given two groups of this size.

(b) A chi-squared statistic is then calculated, to allow the null hypothesis to be tested; the value of chi-squared is best described as a standardised measure of the difference between the two sets of percentages.

(c) The chi-squared statistic is compared with a standard table (such a table is usually given as an appendix in a statistics textbook).

(d) The result of the comparison shows that a difference between the two sets of percentages as large as that in Table 16.1 would occur in less than 1 per cent (0.01 as a proportion) of cases by chance alone; thus, of course, the null hypothesis is unlikely to be true.

By a similar logic, when we look at the third and fourth rows of figures in Table 16.1, the $p > 0.10$ implies that there is little evidence for sex differences in political knowledge among the middle class, so this is not to be regarded as a 'real' difference. Here, the probability statement indicates that a difference in percentages as large as that shown between the third and fourth lines in the table would arise in more than 10 per cent of cases simply by chance alone. Readers who wish to follow through the logic of significance testing in more detail than is given above should refer to a basic statistics textbook (e.g. Kalton, 1966: ch. 3). It may be helpful to point out that, for Table 16.1 at least, the results of these more rigorous tests do confirm patterns which can be seen fairly clearly from the percentages, namely that sex differences in political knowledge are much more apparent among working-class children. (The gamma values provide further confirmation, the 0.34 for the working-class group being much higher than the 0.12 for the middle-class group; on gamma, see Freeman, 1965.)

The operational definitions of age, sex and school type are clear, and class is defined simply as manual or non-manual (the respondents are schoolchildren, so this is the father's occupation). The measurement of political knowledge is not specified fully, but is stated to be a score based on twenty-four questions, of which some examples are given. Finally, what are Dowse and Hughes's interpretations of Figure 16.1 and Table 16.1? They argue that both class and sex have an effect on political knowledge, with boys scoring higher than girls and the middle-class scoring higher than the working class. More specifically, they say that hypothesis I was weakly confirmed in secondary modern schools but not in grammar schools, and that hypothesis II is confirmed by Table 16.1. It is difficult to follow all aspects of Dowse and Hughes's argument, and it may be that they have relied on tables more detailed than those presented in the report; these problems will not be discussed further here, but see Exercise 5.2(b).

To return to the methods of analysing tables in research reports, Dowse and Hughes's study allows two additional points to be made. First, the analysis of an individual table will often show that there is one dependent variable and several other variables which are not easily classified as independent or controlled; where there is doubt, it is best to refer to the author's theoretical purpose. Second, one practice which sometimes confuses the beginning student is that a variable may be presented in two or more tables with categories shown differently. Compare Figure 16.1 and Table 16.1: the way in which political knowledge is shown changes from three categories (high, medium and low) to two categories, of which only one is given (high), but this is nevertheless the same variable.

Arrow diagrams. In many research reports arrow diagrams are useful for summarising relationships between variables, and therefore for characterising the general shape of the data analysis in a given study. This is not illustrated easily from Dowse and Hughes's study, but it will become evident when Porterfield and Gibbs's study (Chapter 14) is analysed in the next chapter. As another example, reconsider Garabedian's Table 12.1; an arrow diagram relating career phase, social role and conformity is shown as Figure 5.1. In this case Garabedian argues that career phase has no effect on social role, so both have been taken as independent variables.

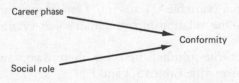

FIGURE 5.1

Small samples. Earlier, Garabedian was criticised for interpreting percentages based on small samples (see Chapter 2); yet one of my examples, Table 5.2, includes similarly sized figures. If this had been a real example, an interpretation of a difference in enthusiasm score for those with and without children would have been quite wrong. However, this is a hypothetical example and figures have been kept small in order to demonstrate the construction of the table from the data. Of course, in a real situation statistical significance tests are the usual method of assessing the extent to whch differences shown in small samples can be regarded as reliable.

Internal empirical validity, as defined in Chapter 2, refers to the assessment of the consistency (or otherwise) of an author's argument at the empirical level. For a research report using quantitative data and where the results are presented as tables, the procedures described above do, in fact, analyse these aspects of the author's argument thoroughly. We have therefore been discussing the content of internal empirical validity in some detail. This point will be taken up again in Chapter 6, when additional examples will be given.

EXERCISES

5.1 *Table construction and interpretation.* Table 5.6 presents some hypothetical data on social mobility; these data can be used as the basis for several exercises. The approach should be similar to that explained for Tables 5.2 and 5.3 (Note, however, that the social mobility data involve three variables and each has three categories.)

(a) Construct three univariate tables (i.e. one for each variable).
(b) Construct two bivariate tables, one showing the relationship of education (variable 2) to job (variable 1) and the other showing the relationship of father's job (variable 3) to job (variable 1).
(c) Interpret the results, first on their own, and second in comparison with Tables 5.4 and 17.1.
(d) Draw up at least one table in a form suitable for publication.

Some further guidance may be useful. Calculation of the appropriate percentages is an integral part of (a) and (b), and also one must be careful to distinguish independent and dependent variables. Second, it may be helpful to consider whether each of the variables is nominal or ordinal. Third, the small size of this sample should not be regarded as crucial for the purpose of this exercise, i.e. the percentages should be interpreted as though they were reliably based on a larger sample (see the note on small samples, above). Finally, since this is intended as a limited exercise in tabular analysis, I have not thought it necessary to state the full operational definitions of the variables, though in a real situation these would be crucial; it is assumed, however, that the definitions are consistent with those used in the Australian survey (see Broom, Jones and Zubrzycki (1976) and Broom and Jones (Chapter 17)).

TABLE 5.6   *Data on social mobility (for Exercise 5.1)**

Person no.	Job (1)	Schooling (2)	Father's job (3)	Person no.	Job (1)	Schooling (2)	Father's job (3)
1	M	P	M	26	F	P	M
2	NM	S	F	27	M	P	F
3	NM	S	M	28	M	S	M
4	M	P	M	29	NM	S	NM
5	NM	S	F	30	NM	P	M
6	NM	S	NM	31	NM	T	M
7	NM	T	NM	32	M	P	M
8	M	S	M	33	M	T	NM
9	F	P	F	34	M	S	M
10	M	P	F	35	NM	S	M
11	NM	P	NM	36	M	S	M
12	NM	S	NM	37	F	S	F
13	M	S	M	38	M	S	F
14	M	S	M	39	M	P	M
15	NM	S	M	40	F	S	NM
16	NM	S	NM	41	NM	T	NM
17	M	S	M	42	M	P	F
18	M	S	M	43	M	S	F
19	M	S	M	44	NM	T	M
20	NM	S	M	45	M	S	NM
21	M	P	NM	46	M	S	NM
22	M	S	M	47	NM	S	M
23	NM	T	M	48	M	P	M
24	NM	T	F	49	F	S	F
25	F	P	F	50	M	P	NM

*This is a hypothetical data-set. The sample is assumed to be fifty adult males selected (on a representative basis) from the Australian work-force and interviewed in 1970. Three variables are shown: (1) is the current occupation of the respondent, coded as non-manual, manual or farm (NM, M and F respectively); (2) is the respondent's educational level, coded as primary, secondary or tertiary (P, S and T respectively); (3) is the occupation of the respondent's father, coded as for variable (1). The coding of the variables is identical with those used in Table 17.1 (Broom and Jones's study) and in Table 5.4, and the example has been constructed so that comparisons can be made with these tables.

5.2

(a) Construct a table presenting the data in Dowse and Hughes's Figure 16.1 (missing *N*-sizes should be noted, but should not deter you from attempting the task; percentages should be measured from the graph, but should also be checked against any figures quoted in the text).

(b) Explore whether Figure 16.1 and Table 16.1 test Dowse and Hughes's two hypotheses. If they do not, what table *is* needed? (Chart the layout for such a table.)

(c) Analyse the remaining tables in Dowse and Hughes's study (including Figure 16.2). Assess the internal empirical validity of the study as a whole.

5.3   Analyse the data presented and assess the internal empirical validity of any of the quantitative studies. (In approaching this exercise be sure to follow the procedures developed in this chapter; the detailed analysis of each individual table, and of its interpretation in the text, is the basic technique.)

6

Techniques for Deciphering

Having reviewed the key components of the research process in Chapters 3–5, we return to the main topic introduced in Chapters 1 and 2, the evaluation of research reports. Porterfield and Gibb's study will first be analysed in detail, then the studies by Lacey and Goode will be considered more briefly. In the last section a general strategy is developed for deciphering research reports which are based on quantitative data.

PORTERFIELD AND GIBBS'S STUDY

This is a study of suicide in New Zealand over the period 1946–51 (see Chapter 14); the focus of interest is the occupations and social mobility of the suicides. The research is based on coroners' records and census data. Porterfield and Gibbs conclude that the suicide rate is relatively high amongst those of higher occupational prestige and amongst the socially mobile. Their evidence also suggests that, in certain circumstances, a crisis may precipitate suicide. The study is summarised below in the format of the ABCDE model:

A.   THEORY. Virtually no reference is made to theory (although, as we shall see later, the study can be related to previous work).

B.   THEORETICAL PROPOSITIONS. There are no explicit propositions; Porterfield and Gibbs's object was to explore three questions.

(i)   What is the relationship between suicide and occupational prestige?

(ii)   What is the relationship between suicide and social mobility from birth to death (i.e. father-to-son occupational mobility)?

(iii) To what extent are pre-suicide crises apparent, and what is the relationship between the existence of crises and social mobility?

It is likely that the authors initiated the project to explore the first two questions and that question (iii) was formulated later, when they discovered data on crises in the coroners' records. Note also that these three questions are not stated in this form in the research report – they are inferred from a reading of the article as a whole.

C   OPERATIONALISATION

Data collection: Analysis of existing official records (coroners' reports); census data are also used.

Sampling: Choice of New Zealand, and time period studied. The main sample is the 955 suicides recorded in 1946–51. A 'control group' of size 321, consisting of a 2 per cent random sample of New Zealand deaths from natural causes in 1948, is also analysed briefly.

Unit: The individual person.

Variables

1. Occupational prestige (Class I: Upper, II: Middle, III: Lower).
2. Occupational prestige of father (Class I, II or III).
3. Occupational mobility (Climber, slider, non-mobile).
4. Existence and kind of crisis (No crisis, career, social, health).

Variables 1, 2 and 3 are based on the Congalton scale, with additional judgements made by Porterfield and Gibbs. Note that in the body of the report the analysis is sometimes based on more detailed categories than those shown in the tables; for example, mobility is rated by several different methods at different points in the text.

D   FIELD-WORK. Obtaining permission to use the records and collaborating with those in charge of them.

E   RESULTS. These are given in three sections, corresponding to (i) to (iii). Data analysis is confined to the 698 *male* suicides, and there is a concentration on those aged 35 or more. Some data are given on the 149 male 'natural deaths' aged 35 or more.

Table 14.1 compares the occupational prestige of all 649 male suicides in the sample with census figures for the male working population. The next two tables make similar comparisons, based on variable 1, between the sample and census figures; Table 14.2 is based on the 348 males who were active workers at the time of their suicide, and Table 14.3 focuses on the 175 male suicides aged 35 or more who were not working. These three tables, together with the discussion in the text, are concerned with question (i).

Table 14.4 shows the father-to-son occupational mobility of the 523 male suicides aged 35 or more through the relationship between variable 1 and variable 2. Some data on the 149 male 'natural deaths' aged 35 or more are given in the text; Table 14.4, plus these data, is concerned with question (ii). In the final section, which explores question (iii), the authors have selected three matched groups of climbers, sliders and non-mobile; there are fifty male suicides in each group. Table 14.5 shows how occupational mobility (variable 3) is related to the existence of crises (variable 4). The reading of the results is helped if we recognise that, unlike many studies (e.g. Garabedian, and Dornbusch and Hickman), the different tables refer to different sections of the sample which the authors choose for specific purposes. This aspect of the study will be discussed below, together with Porterfield and Gibbs's interpretation of the data.

Operationalisation

Porterfield and Gibbs's stage C will now be reviewed in detail. Consider, first, the operational definition of each variable. For variables 1 and 2 occupations are classed as upper, middle or lower class by simply splitting the list of thirty graded occupations (from Congalton, 1953) into three classes of ten; I is from doctor to school teacher, II is from jobbing master builder to bricklayer, III is from shop assistant to road sweeper. This is essentially an arbitrary system, for it is not justified theoretically; for example, there is no theoretical justification for the use of the term 'upper class' to describe category I.

There are several other points to be made about variables 1 and 2. There is no assurance that the coroner, is recording the occupation of deceased persons, used the same definitions as the census, or that the coroner is especially concerned in keeping accurate records of occupations. Also, what happens to non-workers? From Tables 14.2 and 14.3 we see that, of the 523 males aged 35 or more, 348 were working and 175 were "retired, sick, of independent means or unemployed". These 175 are important statistically as they make up one-third of the 523; yet Porterfield and Gibbs do not discuss the meaning of the occupation recorded by the coroner for individuals in this group, nor do they try to justify the assumption about income distribution which is the basis of the census figures given in Table 14.3. The operationalisation of variables 1 and 2 (and consequently, also, variable 3) is therefore somewhat questionable, both on grounds of validity and reliability. I am not arguing that these operational definitions are necessarily wrong; it is simply that Porterfield and Gibbs do not justify them sufficiently or even consider them to be problematic. We shall see later how these points contribute to the evaluation of the article.

The remaining aspects of stage C will be discussed more briefly. For variable 4 one must ask to what extent the existence of a 'crisis' can be judged from coroner's records; this point will be taken up later. The choice of the individual person as the unit of analysis seems justified since this is the 'natural' unit empirically. On sampling, the authors have chosen a working universe (suicides in New Zealand, 1946–51), presumably because of availability of records, and because New Zealand was considered suitable in other respects; all of the working universe has been studied, rather than taking a sample. The 2 per cent control group of natural deaths has been selected by representative methods, and generally the sampling methods are unproblematic; more will be said later about the authors' focus on selected groups within the sample.

Evaluation

First, we consider Porterfield and Gibbs's data analysis and presentation of results. This will enable the *internal empirical validity* of the study to be assessed, by focusing on the authors' argument at the empirical level. Reservations about operationalisation decisions are set aside for the time being.

Tables 14.1–14.3 clearly show more suicides than expected in class I, and less than expected in class III. There are no problems at the empirical level here, except that the presentation of the data is not very clear; the tables would be more easy to interpret if the second and fourth columns were deleted, and one column showing rate of suicides per 1,000 were substituted. For example, in Table 14.2 the rates would be 1.69 (class I), 1.27 (class II) and 1.06 (class III).

Does Table 14.4 'test' question (ii)? Not on its own, for the relationship of occupational mobility to suicide can be seen only if the figures in this table are compared with figures for the male population as a whole. Here, Porterfield and Gibbs should have used their control group; in fact, they do give figures in the text which allow a limited analysis. If we compare the occupational mobility of males aged 35 or more who were suicides (data from Table 14.4) with natural deaths (data on 149 cases in the text), we have the following figures:

	Same class		Mobile up		Mobile down	Total
Suicides	270	(52%)	104	(20%)	149 (28%)	523 (100%)
Controls	93	(62%)	32	(22%)	24 (16%)	149 (100%)

There seems to be more downward mobility amongst suicides, but there is certainly no tendency for more *upward* mobility. Generally, Porterfield and Gibbs go too far in their interpretations on vertical mobility. Indeed, much of this section is simply speculation; it is neither systematic enough nor sufficiently correct empirically to be called theory-construction.

By comparison Table 14.5 is more sound. It clearly does explore question (iii) and it seems that there are differences between the three mobility groups in the incidence of 'crisis'. Of course, it is important to note that the evaluation so far is in empirical terms only.

We now turn to the question of assessing *internal theoretical validity* through an evaluation of the authors' arguments at the theoretical level; a key part of this assessment will be to examine operationalisation decisions in relation to the study as a whole.

In the first part of the report, the data may be misleading. If there are differences between the census and the coroner in recording occupational categories, the figures in Tables 14.1–14.3 will be affected. There is no way of knowing whether the apparent differences in rates between categories I, II and III are 'real' or not; indeed, it may be that the figures *underestimate* the differ-ences – we simply cannot tell. Also Table 14.3 may be suspect on other grounds, because of the procedure used to classify non-workers as I, II or III and to estimate the census figures, as outlined above. Thus the results given in Tables 14.1–14.3 and discussed in the text are by no means conclusive.

It has already been established that Table 14.4 does not answer question (ii), and brief comments have been made on the inter-pretations given in the section on "vertical mobility"; this analysis is extended in Exercise 6.1. To evaluate the last sections of the report, we have to consider the extent to which the existence of a crisis can be judged from official records. The exact procedures used by Porterfield and Gibbs are not clear from the article, and they say it was "not easy". As this variable is the result of a judgement made by the researcher, some check on the reliability of the coding would have been helpful: for example, two people could have been asked to code each case independently and, if possible, without knowing the individual's mobility pattern. However, in comparison with the early sections of the article, this last part is relatively sound, and the interpretations are more closely related to the basic data.

There are two further points as regards internal theoretical validity. How does the arbitrary nature of the occupational classification affect the study? This is an interesting point, for although the classification is theoretically invalid this will not, in itself, completely invalidate the comparisons which are made in the tables. If the coding is applied *reliably,* it should still be possible to see basic patterns in the tables, for the interpretation of the data does not depend crucially on whether the terms upper middle and lower 'really' fit the statistical categories I, II and III. Thus my criticism of the occupational classification is not crucial to the evaluation of the study.

Finally, we must evaluate Porterfield and Gibbs's sampling. As I have implied above, the *selection* of the sample is unproblematic, but several questions arise from the use of specific groups in the sample at different stages in the data analysis. (1) Why are women left out of the analysis? Clearly this is because an analysis of occupation and mobility cannot be carried out adequately for women, most of whom will be recorded as "home duties": remember this is the period 1946–51. (2) Why focus on age 35 or

more? Presumably because the assessment of father-to-son mobility is potentially misleading at an earlier age. (3) Is the 'control
group' really comparable with the suicide group? This is doubtful;
as they are selected from those dying natural deaths, they will
almost certainly be older on average. Given that Porterfield and
Gibbs wanted a control group, they could surely have matched on
age, area of residence, and so on, as outlined in Chapter 4.

Conclusions

As a whole, Porterfield and Gibbs do not present a well-argued
report. It is written in a very brief form, and much of it is difficult
to follow for this reason alone (e.g. the explanation of their use of
the Congalton scale); some important details are omitted entirely
(e.g. reasons for excluding women). On the theoretical level the
purposes of the study and the relationship to theory and previous
research are largely unstated. Altogether, the evaluation of this
article is a fascinating exercise, for one has to do so much 'reading
between the lines'; this ability is needed to some extent for any
study, but here it is crucial.

The lack of an explicit theoretical orientation leads to great
difficulties when the interpretation of results is attempted. Sup-

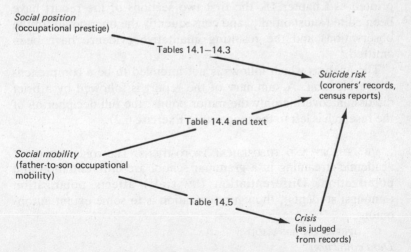

Social position
(occupational prestige)

Tables 14.1–14.3

Suicide risk
(coroners' records,
census reports)

Table 14.4 and text

Social mobility
(father-to-son occupational
mobility)

Table 14.5

Crisis
(as judged
from records)

FIGURE 6.1   *Causal model depicting Porterfield and Gibbs's study*

pose now that we fill in some of this gap in theoretical orientation; some progress can be made by constructing Figure 6.1, which synthesises questions (i), (ii) and (iii). The relationships between the concepts (social position, social mobility, crisis, suicide risk) are depicted by the arrows. The diagram as a whole can be called a *casual model* (or *arrow diagram:* see Chapter 5). The variables, which act as indicators for the concepts, are shown in parentheses in the diagram. The diagram as a whole makes it clear that Porterfield and Gibbs are investigating relationships which are quite common to many theories of suicide (see, for example, Breed, Chapter 22), in the general tradition of Durkheim.[1]

LACEY'S STUDY

Lacey's research focuses on the micro-sociological mechanisms within one English grammar school, especially the processes by which the students become differentiated and sub-cultures are formed. The first-year intake in 1962 (118 boys) was studied, and the report deals with their experience in the first two years. The research is an example of triangulation (see the Glossary), as Lacey used a range of techniques for collecting data, mainly participant observation and questionnaires. For the version re-printed as Chapter 15, the first two sections of the report have been edited substantially, and consequently the finer details of the observations and the resulting qualitative evidence have been omitted.[2]

The analysis which follows is not intended to be a comprehensive evaluation. A summary of the report is followed by a brief discussion covering only the major points; the full deciphering of the research is left to the reader (see Exercise 6.2).

A/B   THEORY AND THEORETICAL PROPOSITIONS. The concomitants of academic streaming in a grammar school are differentiation and polarization. Differentiation (by staff) affects polarization (amongst students), though polarization is to some extent autonomous.

C   OPERATIONALISATION
Data collection
(i)   Participant observation
(ii)   Two questionnaires to boys in the 1962 intake. One at the

end of first year (say, T_1) and the other at the end of second
year (say, T_2).

Sampling
(i) Selection of Hightown Grammar.
(ii) Decision to study the 1962 intake (118 boys) over a period of
time.

Unit: The individual boy.

Variables
  1. First-year class placing (1A, 1B, 1C, 1D – not streamed).
  2. Second-year class placing (2E, 2A, 2B, 2C – streamed).
  3. Friendship choice, T_1 (up to six choices).
  4. Friendship choice, T_2 (up to six choices).
  5. Father's social class (manual/non manual).
  6. Unpopular boys, T_2 (up to six choices).
  7. Expected school-leaving age, T_1.
  8. Expected school-leaving age, T_2.
  9. Position in first-year class, T_1.
 10. Position in second-year class, T_2.

D FIELD-WORK. Initially, Lacey needed permission from the
educational authorities and collaboration from the staff of the
school. Once started, the main problem would have been management of his role as a participant-observer; the collection of
questionnaire data would have been relatively simple.

E RESULTS. Analysis of the questionnaire data gives seven
tables, four of which deal with friendship choices or unpopularity.
Variables 1 and 2 are taken as independent for most of the
analysis, but in Tables 15.5 and 15.7 on friendship and unpopularity the aim is to show the patterns of choice within and between the
different classes.

There are several important points to be made about Lacey's
research. The theory of differentiation and polarization is *developed* during Lacey's time in the school as a participant-observer
and it is then checked by the collection of the questionnaire data.
In effect, there is a blend of theory-building and theory-testing. Of
course, the theory-building aspect of this research cannot be
evaluated from Chapter 15 alone, since the qualitative data
resulting from Lacey's observations has been omitted (here the
interested reader should refer to the original, and to other work

published on the study as cited in Chapter 15). However, one can evaluate the way in which the quantitative data in the seven tables test the theory.

The most crucial questions are about the relationship between the concepts of differentiation and polarization and the ten variables. Which variables act as indicators for which of these concepts? This is not altogether an easy question. The nominal definition of differentiation can be taken as "the process of *separation and ranking* of students . . . largely carried out by *teachers* in the course of their normal duties", and polarization can be nominally defined as "a process taking place *within the student body*, partly as a result of differentiation but . . . with an *autonomy of its own*" (emphases added). If one now considers Tables 15.5 and 15.7, the pattern of friendship and unpopularity choices within and between classes is taken as indicating *polarization,* as it shows the results of the processes which have taken place amongst students. However, these two tables also show that it is *differentiation* which affects polarization, since the placing into the second-year classes is a key act of differentiation.

From this brief analysis and from a review of Lacey's data as a whole it therefore seems that variables 1 and 2 are indicators of differentiation, and variables 3, 4 and 6 of polarization. The other variables are rather less easy to classify under one heading or the other, but it is possible to make two general comments. First, it appears that Lacey often takes the patterns of data (rather than a variable itself) as indicating differentiation or polarization, and therefore the concept-indicator relationships may be more complex than the situation described in Chapter 3. Second, the analysis is made more difficult because Lacey does not provide clear arguments linking concepts and indicators.

The other aspects of Lacey's study are less problematic. Sampling is very straightforward – for example, the strategy of selecting one year's intake to study in detail seems very suitable for the study of processes over time. The data analysis is generally quite simple. One minor point is that in Table 15.8 the closeness of the average age shown may conceal differences between the streams; the percentage in each class wishing to leave at (say) age 16 would probably have illustrated the differences more adequately. Otherwise there are few difficulties with the data presented in Lacey's report, and the *internal empirical validity* of the study appears to be good. The strength (or otherwise) of the concept-indicator links is the crucial question for *internal theoretical validity;* it ought also to be noted that Lacey does not directly address himself to the problem of whether the results for this grammar school (working universe) are applicable to other schools (general universe).

GOODE'S STUDY

This research is on multiple drug use among marijuana smokers. Unlike Becker's study, Goode (Chapter 13) uses quantitative data, and he is concerned to unravel the relationship of marijuana use to the use of other drugs, rather than with the origins of the process of becoming a marijuana user. Goode's data come from interviews with some 200 New York users, and the results suggest that the social context of marijuana smoking is especially important in understanding the use of other drugs.

The study is summarised in the ABCDE format below; the summary is followed by a short discussion dealing with the most important points, but a full deciphering of the research is left to the reader (see Exercise 6.3).

A/B THEORISING. The study has two aims. The first is to throw doubt on simplistic models of drug use which suggest that marijuana smoking inevitably involves high rates of progression to heroin or LSD. The second and *principal* aim is to construct some "tentative generalisations and hypotheses" to account for multiple drug use. The findings are that marijuana use is highly "sociogenic" and that there is a "subcommunity" of users. This subcommunity has positive attitudes to other drugs, and marijuana can be seen as a *lingua franca* in the world of drug-users. The frequent user of marijuana will be highly involved in the subcommunity and is therefore likely to have tried a range of other drugs; the infrequent marijuana smoker is less involved, and consequently the use of the drugs is lower.

C OPERATIONALISATION
Data collection: Personal interview by Goode based on a questionnaire, but probably allowing for more informal questioning as well.

Sampling: Two 'snowball' samples of about 100. Resident New York. The sampling is essentially through personal contact. Total sample size is 204.
Unit: The individual person.
Variables
1. Use of other drugs (thirteen drugs are specified, see Table 13.1 – each is ever/never).
2. Frequency of marijuana use (five categories – "daily" to "less than monthly").
3. Percentage of friends who use marijuana (0–29, 30–59, 60 or more).
4. Buying marijuana (ever/never).
5. Selling marijuana (ever/never).
6. Salience – "first half-dozen things" (Yes/No).
7. Salience – "preferable friends smoke" (Yes/No).
8. Salience – "turn on sibling" (Yes/No).
9. Non-marijuana drug use (marijuana only/1–2 others/3 or more others).
10. Taking LSD (ever/never).

Note that variables 1, 9 and 10 are based on the same data (variables 9 and 10 are in fact developed from the data collected for variable 1).

D FIELD-WORK. Asking initial interviewees to nominate other smokers to be approached and persuading all interviewees to be honest (assurances of confidentiality, and so on).

E RESULTS. Analysis of the data leads to the presentation of ten tables. Goode's object is mainly to show the relationship between the different indicators of involvement with marijuana (variables 2 to 8), or to show how these variables are related to the indicators of other drug use (variables 1, 9 and 10).

On balance the study may be considered as an example of theory-building based on quantitative data. This view is not inconsistent with Goode's modest statements about the tentative nature of his conclusions; the point is that, in terms of procedures, he appears to have constructed these conclusions from the data. Thus the theoretical section on "the social context of marijuana use" is, presumably, one main *result* of the study rather than a *prior* theory which was then tested by the research.[3]

Despite this departure from the ABCDE theory-testing model, Goode's theorising can be analysed using the procedures developed earlier. First, consider the concept-indicator links (previously referred to in Exercise 3.4). Variables 2–8 are indicators of the various kinds of involvement with marijuana use which are described theoretically in the paragraph on subcommunity. We may therefore ask which of these variables act as indicators of Goode's theoretical concepts – association, interaction, life-style, outlook and identity; for example, variable 3 is an indicator of association and interaction. Some of the other variables are, however, more difficult to categorise.

Second, how sound is the data analysis and the internal empirical validity? Are all the percentages shown in the tables based on adequately sized groups, and which of the relationships between variables depicted in the tables are reciprocal and which asymmetric? Are Goode's interpretations consistent with the patterns of data shown in the tables?

Third, consider the internal theoretical validity of the study. Here, we return to the question of concept-indicator links and ask further questions about the strength of these links. Also, the sampling must be analysed. It must be acknowledged that, for a study of an illegal activity such as drug use, there is no chance of obtaining a representative sample. Goode handles this aspect of the study quite well – he discusses the merits of his sampling, is aware of possible biases and is cautious about how widely one can generalise from his findings. Perhaps he is *too* cautious in saying that "the data are probably without application outside the United States", as the results might well apply to other Western-style countries with similar laws to the USA. One point about sampling has escaped him, however. Because the sample is selected by personal contact it is hardly surprising that those in the sample are predominantly sociogenic users; for example, non-sociogenic users or 'loners' are very unlikely to be nominated for the sample. So his results may be characteristic of a section of the marijuana-using population, but not all of that population. In brief, the results are likely to overemphasise the 'sociogencity' of the activity, because the less sociogenic users are less likely to be known to others.

Finally, Goode's study is one of the better-argued reports amongst those considered in this book. The article includes many sections which show an awareness of methodological issues and pitfalls, and in general it is clearly written. One minor point is the style of data presentation and discussion; in the text there are no direct references to the tables and no figures are quoted but it is nevertheless easy to work out which paragraphs refer to each table.

DECIPHERING REPORTS BASED ON QUANTITATIVE DATA

Using the three studies analysed above as examples, it is now possible to make a number of points which are of general applicability in deciphering research reports.

First, how *explicit* is the account? Often there are important details of the study which are not mentioned but are *implicit*, and can be deduced from the report. For example, Goode says little about how he carried out the interviews – did he use a standard questionnaire or not? From the way in which his data analysis is presented, it is almost certain that he used a questionnaire as a basis. Although probably he did not adhere to any set order for the questions, the questions would have been asked using the same wording for each respondent (for example, see the note to Table 13.4). It is also likely that Goode included a more unstructured part of the interview. Another example is Porterfield and Gibbs's exclusion of females from the data analysis; indeed, Porterfield and Gibbs's study illustrates the problem of evaluating research which is reported in a very brief way.

Second, it is often useful to *extend the data analysis* presented in a report. For example, see the re-analysis given above of Porterfield and Gibbs's data on the relationships of suicide to social mobility. Naturally, there are limitations on the re-analysis of data from any given study, depending on the nature and extent of the information given in tables or in the text of the report. Nevertheless, it is worth stressing this technique, since the amount of re-analysis which can be done is often underestimated, and there are circumstances in which it is crucial to the task of deciphering.

Third, a research report produced as a journal article is often simply one of several publications emerging from one study (for example, Lacey); or the research may be part of a wider research programme involving a series of related studies (for example, Garabedian). In these circumstances a knowledge of the context of the research may contribute to the evaluation; for example, it may help in understanding why the author has selected a particular research setting, or why the data presented are restricted to a specific set of variables. For some research reports it may be helpful to refer briefly to other related literature to establish the context of the research (see, for example, note 2 of Chapter 2, on Garabedian's research).

Fourth, the analysis of the links between theory and evidence, already referred to in Chapter 2 and 3, may now be reconsidered. The extent to which theory-testing and theory-building are used in a given study is often quite explicit in the report; but there are cases in which these aspects are somewhat difficult to tease out, and Goode's study is an example. Also, the purposes of a research study are not always theory-testing or theory-building, and some research may lack explicit theoretical orientation. These issues were discussed as 'incompleteness' in Chapter 2. With several more examples now introduced, the problem may be reviewed more thoroughly.

In all of the examples given so far in this book, a crucial part of evaluation has been to apply the ABCDE model. This does *not* imply that the summary of the study is 'forced' into the ABCDE format. The summary must remain true to the original; thus the essential 'shape' of the author's argument will be reproduced in the summary, and divergence from the model will be carefully noted (see, for example, the analyses of Lacey and Goode). Any parts of the summary which are inferred, rather than being explicit in the report, should be noted (see, for example, stage B of the analysis of Porterfield and Gibbs). The list below indicates how the ABCDE model has been applied in each of the six examples, and shows the degree of divergence from the model.

Dornbusch and Hickman's study was chosen as a first example because of the close degree of correspondence with the ABCDE model. Each state of the model is clearly discernible; the authors test (and confirm) the theory and make only a limited attempt to reconsider the theory in the light of the results.

Garabedian's study is reasonably close to the ABCDE model, except that stage A is somewhat vague, and stage B consists of one proposition and two questions. The results are used by Garabedian as a springboard for clarification and development of theory.

Porterfield and Gibbs discuss the purpose of their study only briefly and there is little reference to a theoretical framework. Stages A and B of the ABCDE model can nevertheless be inferred, and this is an important part of the analysis of the study. The authors do make some brief attempts at theory-building, but this aspect of the study is unconvincing. Thus in the report as a whole there is little attention given to theorising, and of the six examples this is the closest to 'empiricism'.

Lacey has constructed a theory based on observational data during the initial period of his study, and then tests it through the collection of questionnaire data. The ABCDE model can be applied to this second part of the research, though it is difficult to separate stages A and B. The questionnaire data confirm the theory, and also allow Lacey to reconsider and develop the theory further.

Goode appears to have constructed a theory from the analysis of his data (although this cannot be judged with certainty). The ABCDE model can, however, be applied with the theory-building aspect of the study noted; as with Lacey's study, it is difficult to separate stages A and B. Although the theory is constructed (rather than tested), it must of course be consistent with the evidence; as Goode's data are quantitative, the ABCDE model still provides a useful framework for evaluating the theory-evidence link.

Becker's study is an example of theory-building from qualitative data. The application of the ABCDE model to the study is uneasy, as the divergence is too great: the main reason (apart from theory-building) is that the research is not based on structured data-collection techniques resulting in quantitative data. The evaluation of research reports of this kind needs a different approach, which will be discussed in Chapters 7 and 8.

The ABCDE model thus provides a framework for the deciphering of a wide range of research reports. If it is used in the manner outlined, the model is very *flexible*. While I am loath to specify exact conditions, in general it will be applicable to research based on structured data-collection techniques and using quantitative data.

The final point to be made at this stage about the analysis of theory–evidence links is that for some studies the application of the ABCDE model may lead to several slightly different but equally acceptable versions summarising the report. This happens when an author is not clear about certain details, especially where the purpose of the study is not explicitly stated. For example, another 'evaluator' using the same techniques might produce a summary of the Porterfield and Gibbs study in which stages A and B differ from the version given above. The acid test of any summary is that it be totally consistent with the actual content of the report, and that any inferences made by the evaluator be explicitly stated.

Analysing the validity of research reports.

Despite the wide variations in research reports, it is evident from the account so far that, for research based on quantitative data, it is normally possible to evaluate the *internal empirical validity* of a study by the methods presented in the last section of Chapter 5. The author's presentation of tables and the author's interpretation of these tables are the main aspects to be assessed for internal empirical validity. In effect, the analysis is confined to the empirical stages C, D and E.

It is not possible to approach *internal theoretical validity* in such a uniform way. For example, for Dornbusch and Hickman's study we must evaluate whether they have (as they assert) *tested* Riesman's theory adequately; by contrast, for Goode's study we must assess whether the theory which is *constructed* is consistent with the empirical evidence. An important point here is that in a wide variety of studies, including both those which test theories and those which simply use a general theoretical orientation, it is common for the authors to present certain sections (often the conclusions) in which some *theorising* is done. Garabedian's study is one example, and there are even a few comments at the end of Dornbusch and Hickman's study where the unexpected peak of other-directed advertising in 1920–39 is discussed briefly. The evaluation of such theorising in relation to the empirical evidence is a vital part of internal theoretical validity. Often it is possible to pick out both specific and general statements made by the author, and to test these against the empirical evidence presented. Many examples can be seen in the analyses given above. Another important aspect of internal theoretical validity is to evaluate the *sampling* and *generalisation* of the study. The sampling design must be assessed in relation to the theorising undertaken in the study, and the implications of practical problems such as non-response must also be considered.

General strategy for deciphering a research report

A general approach can now be presented for analysing research reports based on quantitative data. This six-step procedure is, in fact, a synopsis of the methods developed to this stage. It will be evident that in the evaluation of the examples given so far in this book, this procedure has, in effect, been used throughout.

(1) *Summary* of the study. This should be as far as possible in ABCDE form, but without distorting the author's argument. Divergences from the model should be noted. Any inferences made by the evaluator should be stated explicitly.

(2) *Assessment of operationalisation (stage C)*. First, aim for *exact* details of data-collection techniques, sampling, units, variables (note that the list of variables must be consistent with variables actually presented in tables). Then consider the decisions which were made to arrive at these details – that is, rationale for concept-indicator links, reasons for the sample, and so on.

(3) *Further descriptive details*. While, in principle, it is possible to include all factors relevant for the description of the study within steps 1 and 2, in practice there are normally two areas for which further detail is needed.

(a) *Theory–evidence links*. Further clarification of the author's theorising.

(b) *Data analysis*. A list of tables presented, notes on the problems of data shown in them and on the author's interpretation.

(4) *Internal empirical validity*. Evaluate the empirical part of the study in detail. Internal empirical validity usually involves a close scrutiny of tables and their interpretation at the empirical level (questions about concept-indicator links and sampling are left aside for the time being).

(5) *Internal theoretical validity*. In a study which is strictly theory-testing this involves examining stages A and B in relation to the empirical evidence. More generally, internal theoretical validity will involve examining all theoretical arguments presented by the author both in relation to the evidence presented and in terms

of logical consistency. Sampling must also be evaluated; the crucial questions here are whether the limitations of the sample have been taken account of adequately in the interpretation, and whether the generalisations made by the author are justified.

(6) *A general assessment.* Main conclusions, highlights of the most important points of the evaluation, and any points not covered elsewhere.

Some further comments will be helpful. First, when carrying out an evaluation, one does not simply proceed from (1) to (2) and so on to (6), and finish. Many points which are discovered in the course of the evaluation will cause reflection on earlier work; for example, the summary should certainly be revised after the more detailed work in (2) to (5) has been carried out. Second, it will be evident that the six steps have been stated only briefly, and that for each step it will be necessary to refer to the more detailed material presented earlier before the full implications are seen.

Third, it would in principle be possible to add a seventh stage, 'external validity' (see Figure 2.2) dealing with the relationship of the study to the wider body of sociological literature; for example, for Porterfield and Gibbs's study this would mean considering the implications of the study for theory and research on suicide. Questions of external validity are, of course, ultimately the most important questions which can be asked about any research study, and are indeed the main reason why a sociologist would have any interest in the study in the first place. These questions are, however, outside the bounds of this book since external theoretical validity is not a matter of methodology as such. To return to the example, an assessment of the external validity of Porterfield and Gibbs's study would require a good knowledge of previous writing on the sociology of suicide, in order to see how this new work relates to it (for the moment I ignore matters such as publication date); this would be primarily a theoretical exercise and issues of research method would not contribute directly to the analysis. One important point must, however, be stressed. Strictly speaking, the deciphering of a research report is a necessary prerequisite for considering its external validity; for example, there is little purpose to be served by considering how a recent study on (say) suicide contributes to the existing sociological literature unless one can be sure of the internal validity of the argument presented in the report.

Fourth, the strategy outlined above should be regarded as fairly *flexible*. This flexibility is evident not only in the application of the ABCDE model to a study, but also in the undertaking of the analysis in six steps. For example, it is sometimes difficult to say how much detail should be included in the summary, and how much should be dealt with separately under steps (2) and (3); similarly, it is often difficult to separate questions of internal theoretical validity from those of internal empirical validity. In fact, it is not crucial in either case to maintain a strict distinction between the steps. The importance of the strategy is that it makes the reader aware of what to look for in a study, and provides a skeletal outline for the presentation of the evaluation. It is more important to be sure that all features listed in (1)–(6) are covered in an evaluation than to attempt a strict separation between stages (1) to (3) or between stages (4) and (5). Thus two readers presented with the same article may produce two equally good analyses, incorporating the same points but differing in style of organisation and presentation.

Figure 6.2 indicates the 'flow' of the procedure for deciphering. The links which are shown between individual steps reinforce the points made above about the flexibility of the approach. The procedure allows a concentration upon specific points, while providing a structure through which the relationship can be seen to the whole enterprise of deciphering a research report.

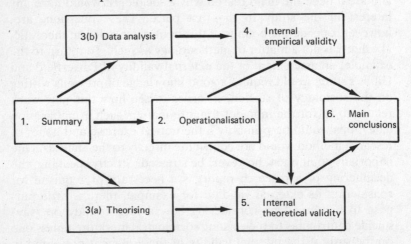

FIGURE 6.2   *Links between stages of the deciphering procedure*

EXERCISES

6.1 Evaluate the interpretations made by Porterfield and Gibbs (Chapter 14) in the "vertical mobility" section, in relation to Table 14.4 and the figures given in the text (be sure to take account of the analysis made above – the purpose of this exercise is to take the analysis further).

6.2 Decipher Lacey's study (Chapter 15) by completing the brief analysis given in this chapter. First, check the summary (step 1), then go on to steps (2) to (6) taking account of the specific points mentioned in the existing analysis of the study.

6.3 Decipher Goode's study (Chapter 13); proceed as for Exercise 6.2.

6.4 Review your earlier analyses of Garabedian's and Dornbusch and Hickman's studies (Exercises 2.3 and 2.5). What extensions or modifications of these analyses are needed in the light of Chapter 6?

6.5 Decipher any other case study from Chapters 16–18. Be sure to take account of any previous analysis given in Chapters 3–5 or carried out in previous exercises.

7

Field-work and Qualitative Data: The Research

In this chapter and the next we turn our attention to research studies which are based on qualitative data collected by participant observation, interviewing and other field-work techniques. This kind of research, which I shall refer to briefly as *field-work* or *field-research*, is rather different from that discussed in Chapters 2 to 6, and normally involves some or all of the following elements: the subject of the study is a social organisation or a more loosely knit social group; there is direct social interaction between the individual researcher (or a small research team) and the organisation or group; the field-work 'evolves' over a period of time; a variety of techniques may be used for data collection, but the most common are participant-observation and unstructured interviewing; the data do not lend themselves easily to quantification, and are collected, analysed and presented in the research report as qualitative data; and there is generally an emphasis on theory-construction (rather than theory-testing).

Systematic attention to the methodology of the field-work approach dates mainly from the late 1960s (for example, McCall and Simmons, 1969), though there is also much of interest in earlier writings (for instance, Becker, 1958). The literature is now fairly extensive, and the key problems of research procedure have been the subject of much debate. We shall analyse this material in due course, but first the studies reprinted in Part Two will be reviewed briefly so that they can be used as examples later.

FIELD-WORK STUDIES

Becker's study of marijuana users (Chapter 11) was introduced earlier, in Chapter 1. The research is based on unstructured but focused interviews with fifty American marijuana users, obtained mainly by personal contact. From the interview material, Becker searches for (and finds) characteristics which are held to be *universally* present in the sample – learning the technique, learning to perceive the effects, and learning to enjoy the effects. Taken together, these describe the *process* of becoming a marijuana user, and elsewhere Becker refers to this type of model as a *sequential* model (1963: 22). Thus he is concerned to establish a universal sequence describing the process. To do this, Becker analysed his data utilising the principle of analytic induction which requires that *every* interview substantiates the hypothesis. I shall reconsider analytic induction later. The main point to be made here is that the three characteristics are discovered in the process of the research and they are effectively new *concepts*. Becker establishes the validity of these new concepts by examples, extracted from his interviews; this is the core of his research report. This process of discovering concepts and how they are linked is the essential feature of theory-construction, irrespective of whether analytic induction is used as a principle.

Birksted's research on adolescent boys (Chapter 19) utilises participant-observation techniques. The sample studied is a group of eight British boys, with whom Birksted spent much time both inside and outside school. Most of the data presented come from interviews or informal conversations involving the author and the boys, which illustrates the centrality of such verbal interactions in participant-observation research. Birksted's results show how school performance is viewed by the eight boys. He finds they are not academically orientated, nor are they anti-school. Academic performance is seen as largely irrelevant to their present life and future plans, and the content of school work is therefore not meaningful to them; for the most part school is simply a time-filler, and their part-time jobs and leisure activities are equally important. Although their school performance is poor by conventional standards, they do not see themselves as failures. In presenting these and other findings Birksted provides a description of how the boys view their situation. It is important to emphasise that, in common with many other studies based on qualitative data, this research has a *descriptive* (rather than a theory-building) objective.

Smith's study, although conducted in an Australian city, is similar to Birksted's in many respects, since Smith uses participant-observation techniques and the subject is an adolescent group (Chapter 20). In this case, however, the group is (loosely speaking) 'delinquent', the research setting is a park which acts as their regular meeting-place, and the focus is on conflict with the police. Much of Smith's data are from interviews and informal conversations which (like Birksted's) were tape-recorded, but Smith also presents data on his observations. The main object of the study is to describe the adolescents' attitudes to the police, which Smith presents as a series of headings – allegations of police violence, allegations of drinking on duty, never trust a copper, state of rivalry, and police are ill-informed; each of these headings is illustrated through examples selected from the data. Smith also discusses the implications of his study for policing, and points out briefly that his findings are consistent with theories of the police as amplifiers of deviance.

Wiener's research (Chapter 21) is on a sample of twenty-one rheumatoid arthritics attending a medical centre in the USA. The data were collected through participant-observation and unstructured interviewing, both at the medical centre and in patients' homes. The study focuses on the coping mechanisms which patients develop for the management of pain, and a key factor is the uncertainty with which the pain comes and goes. Wiener's object is to build a theory, grounded in the data, to describe these coping mechanisms. Her findings are therefore offered as a series of theoretical concepts which show the different mechanisms through which pain is managed. For example, one concept is "pacing", which can be achieved either by "normalization" or by "justifying inaction". In her report Wiener illustrates these concepts through extracts drawn from interviews and observations, and the form of presentation is thus similar to that of Becker, Birksted and Smith. Wiener's study is analysed in more detail in Chapter 8.

Lacey's study (Chapter 15) must also be mentioned, since the first stage was participant-observation in one British grammar school. As I made clear in Chapter 6, it is not appropriate to analyse this stage of Lacey's study in any detail here, since the account of the field-work has been omitted from the edited version reprinted in Part Two; it can, however, be referred to briefly as an example.

In introducing their book on the field-work approach, McCall and Simmonds (1969: 1) provide the following quotation from Dean *et al.* (1967):

> Many people feel that a newspaper reporter is a far cry from a social scientist. Yet many of the data of social science today are gathered by interviewing and observation techniques that resemble those of a skilled newspaper man at work on the study of, say, a union strike or a political convention. It makes little sense for us to belittle these less rigorous methods as "unscientific". We will do better to study them and the techniques they involve so that we can make better use of them in producing scientific information.

What exactly *is* the difference between the informed, insightful, skilled journalist and the sociologist carrying out field-work? In two words – sociological analysis. As McCall and Simmons say (1969: 3), the objective of the sociologist's study is

> an analytic description of a complex social organization (primitive band, gang, occupational group, mental hospital, community or the like). By an analytic description we mean something much more than a journalistic description: an analytic description (1) employs the concepts, propositions, and empirical generalizations of a body of scientific theory as the basic guides in analysis and reporting, (2) employs thorough and systematic collection, classification, and reporting of facts, and (3) generates new emprical generalizations (and perhaps concepts and propositions as well) based on these data.

These quotations help us to begin an analysis of some of the differences between field-work based research reports. The studies by Becker and Wiener provide analytic descriptions through the construction of new theories, for the various elements (concepts, propositions, etc.) listed by McCall and Simmons can be picked out from the reports. The studies of Smith and Birksted can both be seen as involving many of the characteristics of analytic description but also with an element of 'ethnographic' description, as the findings are presented to some extent in the participants' own terms rather than through theoretical concepts. I shall have more to say about this distinction in the next chapter.

The style of each report is fairly similar, and is characteristic of most research based on field-work. The main findings and assertions are highlighted through headings (or, in Wiener's study, also through italics) and are then illustrated through evidence selected from the data. There is an important process at work here, and it will be discussed in more detail in the next chapter. For the moment we turn our attention to the practical problems involved in field-work.

THE PROCESS OF FIELD-WORK

As I have emphasised above, there is now an extensive literature on the conduct of research through field-work; here, I can do no more than provide a brief review of certain practical issues which seems to be central to all field-research. Readers interested in pursuing these issues further can consult several excellent books, including Schatzman and Strauss (1973), McCall and Simmons (1969) and Becker (1970). As we have seen, the field-work approach usually involves an individual researcher or a small team who has close personal contact with the group being studied. The research is undertaken over a period of time during which data are gathered continuously. While observation is often important, unstructured interviews and conversations usually provide particularly valuable data. Even from simple statements such as these, it is possible to see that certain practical problems will be common to most field-work situations: the researcher must negotiate a *role* in relation to the group and *field relations* must be considered both with the group being studied and with other relevant bodies; field-work role and field-relations will vary over the time period of the research (and getting started may be especially difficult); a technique must be used for keeping written records of data (usually termed *field-notes* or *field-diary*) and decisions must be made on if (and when) to use a tape-recorder; from day to day, decisions must be made on what to do next (where to go, what to observe, who to talk to). These problems will now be considered with the help of examples taken from the studies in Part Two.

Field-work roles and field-relations. In a standard treatment of this topic, Gold (following Junker) distinguishes four possible roles: complete participant, participant-as-observer, observer-as-participant, and complete observer (see McCall and Simmons, 1969: 30–9).[1] While these distinctions sensitise us to certain variations in roles, in any one study the range of possible roles is likely to be quite constrained, and the field-worker's main problem will be to establish himself or herself, rather than 'choosing' a role. Thus Birksted first gets to know his boys at the local club before attempting to enter the school setting, and once in the school he also finds it necessary to negotiate a role in relation to the teachers. Naturally this process takes time. Birksted must also be careful to maintain his relationships with the school authorities and teachers without jeopardising the relationship with the boys. The example demonstrates that a field-researcher often has multiple roles which must be handled with care once they are established, lest the 'host' (the school) ceases to collaborate. Smith's role as an observer of the delinquent group raises rather different issues – he has to establish himself with the group by becoming accepted, but not participate in delinquent activities himself. Also, Smith's presence is not known to the police; hence his age and appearance have to be sufficiently similar to the group to pass for one of them when the police appear. To summarise, a field-worker has to establish a role, and to maintain (and adapt) this role for the duration of the research; in the context of this book the most important point is that the reader of a research report must try to characterise accurately the particular role(s) adopted by the researcher and the way in which field-relations have been handled.

Observations, interviews, conversations and documents are the different kinds of data which may be collected by the field-researcher. There are examples in the studies outlined above, except that in none of the four were documents utilised; documents are useful mainly in research on social organisations such as government agencies, where policy documents may be kept and actions are officially recorded (see Chapter 22 on Jacobs's study). In each of the studies of Birksted, Smith and Wiener it appears that the verbal interaction between the resear-

cher and the group ranged from casual conversation to unstructured (but nevertheless formal) interviewing. Schatzman and
Strauss (1973: 70–3) list three "strategies for listening": eavesdropping, in which the researcher plays no part except to listen;
situational conversation, where the researcher asks direct questions at opportune moments; and interviewing as such. It is worth
noting that the total verbal information supplied to a researcher by
any one member of the group may stem from many different
situational conversations. For example, the core members of
Smith's delinquent group will have talked to him on several
occasions, and this is evident in the selections of data which are
presented. For any given research report it is important for the
reader to identify as accurately as possible the different kinds and
sources of data; often, full details are not given directly, but a close
reading of the report will nevertheless allow the data base to be
characterised reasonably well. The data base is often 'triangu-
lated', since more than one kind of data is collected, and sometimes key 'informants' are involved (see Glossary: entry on
'participant-observation').

Field-notes. However rich and interesting the data, they are of
no use unless they are recorded accurately. Thus Schatzman and
Strauss (1973) devote three consecutive chapters to watching
(observation), listening and recording. In some research settings,
for example Wiener's study, it may be quite acceptable for the
researcher to make notes at the time, whereas in others, such as
Smith's study, a note-book might be too intrusive but a small
tape-recorder may be acceptable at opportune times. For some
research projects (especially where the researcher is a covert
participant) neither note-books nor tapes are practicable, and
notes must be made from memory as soon as possible after the
event. The practical aspects of keeping notes in the various
field-situations which may be encountered is dealt with in many
textbooks, and will not be pursued here. The main point to be
made is that the reader of a research report should enquire how
notes were taken and whether tape-recordings were made. Some
authors (Birksted, Smith) are quite clear about these details, but
others do not provide sufficient information. For example, Becker
quotes long interview extracts which would appear to indicate that
the interviews were tape-recorded, but we cannot be certain. (Was
the technology of tape-recording sufficiently advanced at the time
of Becker's research?)

The natural history of a project. Research based on the field-work approach is not tightly structured in advance. Decisions must therefore be made from day to day about the future direction of the project, in the light of the data gathered and the field-work experience so far. The most interesting aspect of Schatzman and Strauss's book is the way in which this situation is explicitly recognised and incorporated into their recommendations for field-work and note-taking. In particular, they suggest notes be organised according to the following scheme (1973: ch. 6):

1. ON *(observational notes)*. Simply notes on what happened with little or no interpretation. "An ON is the Who What When Where and How of human activity" (1973 :100).
2. TN *(theoretical notes)*. Self-conscious, controlled attempts to derive meanings from any one or several ONs. The observer "interprets, infers, hypothesizes, conjectures; he develops new concepts, links these to older ones, or relates any observation to any other" (1973: 101).
3. *MN (methodological notes)*. Mainly reminders and instructions to oneself, for example on the validity of ONs, critique of what one has done, and notes on what to do next.

Field-notes are initially to be kept sequentially (as is usually recommended in textbooks) but are indexed as ON, TN, MN by the researcher at the time. The importance of this scheme is that it helps to monitor the most problematic aspects of an unstructured project, namely 'where have we got to so far' and 'what do we do next'. In addition, the presence of TNs make it clear that data analysis *should* be a continually ongoing process – a point also emphasised by Lofland (1971: 117–18). More will be said about data analysis in Chapter 8.

While the course which any project will take cannot be predicted in advance, it can be seen in retrospect once the research is finalised. Thus each completed project will have a natural history which, according to Becker (1958), constitutes important information which should be included in the research report. A good example is Birksted's study, for he gives an account of starting the project, field-work problems both with the boys and their school, and the reactions of the boys to the research. However, most research reports do not include a full natural history; in these cases the reader should try to piece together as many of the details as possible by an intensive reading of the report.

CHARACTERISING RESEARCH REPORTS

For the reader of a report based on research of the kind introduced in this chapter, the first task will be to come to a good understanding of the field-work process and the data collection; we should now be aware of what particular points to look for in the report. As different authors have different styles of presentation, one may find that certain information is lacking, but it is often possible by a close reading of a report to piece together more than is apparent at first sight. For example, in Becker's study of marijuana users it appears that verbatim transcripts were taken of the interviews, though we do not know whether or not these were tape-recorded. Of course, in the context of this book, the larger task of the reader of a field-work-based research study is to evaluate the report fully; the material in this chapter simply provides a necessary first step, and the topic is pursued to its conclusion in Chapter 8.

EXERCISE

7.1   Review the field-work process and the data collection in each of the studies by Becker, Birksted, Smith and Wiener. If the researcher were a participant-observer, how did he or she manage the role? What were the problems of field-relations? What interviewing was done, what conversations were held and was there any eavesdropping? What was observed? What notes were kept and how, and was tape-recording used? What was the natural history of the research? What important information is *not* given in the report, and how might the author have included this information? (Note that the analysis of these studies is continued as Exercise 8.1.)

8

Field-work and Qualitative Data: The Deciphering

→

The list shown in Table 8.1 presents a simplified comparison between the kind of research analysed in Chapters 1–6 and the field-work approach introduced in Chapter 7. This is a contrast between two ideal-types, and it is essential to remember that most individual studies differ from type I or type II in several respects and that some studies combine certain elements from the two types. The ABCDE model (which is itself an ideal-type) fits type I research exactly but is not applicable to the field-work approach exemplified by type II.

TABLE 8.1   *Comparison of two ideal-type approaches to research*

Components	Type I	Type II
Data	Statistical	Qualitative
Theory–evidence links	Theory-testing	Theory-building
Concepts	Known in advance	Discovered from data
Sampling	Representative	Theoretically directed
Data analysis and presentation	Tables	Author's summaries and illustrations

This comparison allows two main points to be made. First, while types I and II can be considered as polar opposites in their approach to research, there are certain elements in common, which I have listed as the *components* of the research process. As I have continually emphasised in Chapters 1–6, the problems of data, theory–evidence links, concepts (and indicators), sampling and data analysis are *always* part of research method. Second, it is, however, true to say that field-work research has developed certain distinctive approaches to these problems. At the moment the notions of discovering concepts from data and of 'theoretically directed' sampling will not be clear to the reader, but these and other related matters will be discussed below. In this chapter, therefore, I first review the methodological issues which are central to the field-work approach and then consider in detail the procedures for deciphering reports based on such research.

CONCEPTS AND INDICATORS

As I have already asserted, the most distinctive aspect of the field-work approach is the development of new concepts from data. For example, *normalization* is just one of the many concepts developed by Wiener as part of her theory of how rheumatoid arthritics cope with pain. Normalization was not part of Wiener's conceptual scheme of the outset of the project – it is built from the data.

Lofland (1971: ch. 2) gives a host of examples of concepts and indicators developed by field researchers. One of his examples is taken from Sykes and Matza, who developed the concept of 'techniques of neutralization', which are definitions used by delinquents to characterise their actions in such a way that they are favourable to violation of the law. They found five different techniques of neutralization (Sykes and Matza, 1957, as analysed in Lofland, 1971: 29):

1. The denial of one's personal responsibility for the act.
2. The denial of anyone's being injured by the act.
3. The denial of the victim's right to protection, because he is a disreputable person.
4. The denial of the condemnor's rights to condemn the perpetrator, because they are hypocrites and the like.
5. The claim that loyalties to one's friends or other groups supersede loyalty to legal rules.

Lofland's examples make it quite clear that the process of developing concepts and indicators is the core of the analysis of qualitative data. It is through this process that the qualitative researcher describes and analyses the characteristics of social phenemona. Note that there are three closely interrelated parts of the process: (a) identification, discovery or construction of the *concept* (e.g. 'techniques of neutralization'); (b) identification, discovery or construction of the *categories of the concept* (e.g. 1 to 5 in the Sykes and Matza example); and (c) specification of the indicators for (a) and (b) (e.g. fitting the empirical phenomena observed by Sykes and Mataza into their conceptual scheme).[1] This is essentially the same process as that described in the studies by Becker and Wiener. The value of Lofland's account is that the process is clarified by having so many examples brought together; Lofland's distinctions between static and phase analysis and so on is not, however, important for present purposes.

Because the data are qualitative, the nature of the concept-indicator link is rather different from the account given in Chapter 3. From the four studies it appears that concepts are linked to their indicators largely through illustration, i.e. the concept and its categories are presented, and several incidents, observations or interview extracts are given as examples. Becker's study of marijuana users is a clear illustration of this technique. In this case not only are the concepts handled in this way but also the linkages between concepts are illustrated similarly, by interview material.

An important distinction is between *participant concepts* and *theoretical concepts*. One example of using participant concepts is from Garabedian (although this is a statistical study); the five social roles – square john, right guy, and so on – are the terms used by the prison inmates themselves. Another example is Smith's concept of "never trust a copper". Participant concepts are couched in the terminology used by the group under study. By contrast, Wiener's "normalization" and Becker's "learning to perceive the effects" are theoretical concepts, since they would not be immediately recognised by the participants as part of their terminology. Sykes and Matza's "techniques of neutralization" is another example of a theoretical concept. Some authors (for example, Schatzman and Strauss, 1973) argue that theoretical concepts and categories can (and generally should) be based on participant concepts and categories.

In any one research report we may find that a mixture of theoretical and participant concepts is used – an example is Smith's study of a delinquent group. The term *ethnographic description* is often used to refer to a description given entirely in terms of participant concepts and categories, i.e. an 'insider's' view of what a particular social world (prison, bureaucracy, gang, college, taxi-driving) is like. Birksted's report is the best example in the four studies, though Birksted also includes some theoretical material which goes further than ethnographic description.

The implications of this analysis for deciphering research reports are fairly clear. The reader must identify the concepts used by the author, their categories where applicable, and the way in which the data are used to provide indicators. In some studies this process will be fairly easy to follow, but in others it will be more difficult. Three complications are worth mentioning. First, some concepts have no categories as such, for example Becker's 'learning to perceive the effects'. Second, the distinction between concepts and categories may sometimes be difficult to judge. For example, Wiener's concept 'normalization' can be seen as having two categories, 'covering up' and 'keeping up'; alternatively, these can be seen as two lower-level concepts. Provided the logical link is noted between 'covering up' and 'keeping up' and the higher-level concept of 'normalization', the alternative analysis is quite acceptable. Third, for some studies the term 'concept' may seem to fit rather uneasily unless it is interpreted in a relatively broad sense. For example, Smith's heading 'state of rivalry' should be treated in the same way as a concept in this analysis, since Smith presents data as a direct illustration of the rivalry between the delinquents and the police. As a result of these factors, it is often the case that two readers of the same research report will decipher the concept-indicator links slightly differently. In my experience, however, these differences are, in themselves, unlikely to affect the main aim of the analysis, which is of course to assess the *validity* of the author's argument.

SAMPLING

What kind of sampling is usually involved in studies based on field-work? Glaser and Strauss (1967) use the term *theoretical sampling*. In this approach samples are not selected in advance, and decisions on what to do next are made as part of the on-going field-work process (as exemplified by Schatzman and

Strauss's methodological notes – see Chapter 7). While the general ideas of theoretical sampling can be applied quite widely in field-research, it is evident that Glaser and Strauss have in mind research in particular kinds of organizations (e.g. hospitals, factories, prisons,) i.e. social organisations having a specific physical location, and with fairly stable personnel. The problems of sampling may be rather different in research on other kinds of organisations (e.g. political parties, unions, sports clubs) and in investigating what Wiseman and Aron (1970) call "small worlds" (e.g. taxi-drivers, marijuana users, dance musicians). For these looser-knit social systems field-researchers tend to use samples which are approximations to representativeness – an approach to sampling which was discussed in Chapter 5.

To what extent are the sampling and generalisation problems of field-work research different from those dealt with earlier? As we shall see, there are some genuine differences in emphasis, though much of the analysis in Chapter 4 can usefully be applied to studies based on field-work. In particular, the distinctions between general universe, working universe and sample are of crucial importance. For example, in Wiener's study the working universe was all rheumatoid-arthritis patients in one clinic, and the sample was twenty-one of these; from Wiener's account it is not, in fact, clear how these twenty-one were selected (indeed, they *could* have been all those attending the clinic at the time). In order to generalise from the sample, one should consider, first, whether the twenty-one are typical of the clinic population, and second, whether one can argue that the results are applicable to those who suffer from rheumatoid arthritis in other places and at other times. The general universe might therefore simply be 'rheumatoid-arthritis sufferers'. Thus we have characterised Wiener's sampling procedures; the evaluation of this aspect of the study will be discussed later in this chapter.

In some studies it is not possible to identify a definite working universe. Birksted selects eight boys who constitute a friendship group as his sample; the working universe is not all boys in the school they attend, since we know the eight are atypical. Problems of generalisation are left aside in this study since Birksted seems concerned only to establish that the boys' views of school performance are one possible reaction, and the conditions under which this reaction occurs are not discussed. In Becker's study of marijuana users the working universe cannot be defined exactly, but it could be argued to be all regular users in the Chicago area; this definitional problem is, however, no different from that of Goode (Chapter 13). In principle, therefore, the problems of generalising from Becker's sample and from Goode's sample are virtually identical, despite the fact that these are respectively examples of qualitative and quantitative approaches to research.[2] Thus studies of both kinds may involve indefinite working universes.

Smith's study presents sampling problems of a different order. The working universe here is a delinquent group, the membership of which fluctuates from one day to the next; this, however, is a subsidiary problem, and there are two main points to be made. First, the 'sample' taken from the group is not of definable size, nor are the data collected from any one member of this 'sample' comparable in any simple sense with that collected from another member. Indeed, the participant-observation technique used by Smith necessarily entails collecting different amounts and kinds of data for different members of the group; for example, there is little doubt that Smith had much more contact with the core members of the group than with others, since they were present more often and were presumably more vocal. This situation is, of course, typical of most studies which use participant-observation. The second point is that Smith's sampling is to a large extent outside his control, since it is constrained by factors such as who turns up on a particular night, what contact there is with the police, who is prepared to talk, and so on. Thus, while we might expect the material on theoretical sampling to act as a guide to a participant-observer such as Smith, the situations to which he is exposed are only partly within his control and the net result is a sample which is to a greater or lesser extent *accidental*. Theoretical sampling is therefore best seen as an attempt to make systematic the inevitable non-representative or accidental aspects of sampling inherent in participant-observation. In most studies, including that of Jacobs and Becker's research on dance musicians (see Chapter 22), the participant-observer ends up with a mixture of theoretical and accidental sampling.

For reading and deciphering any particular research report, the implications of the material above can now be summarised. The reader should identify the general universe and working universe, in so far as these can be defined, and analyse how the sample was chosen (from the working universe or by other criteria). Where participant-observation techniques have been used, the reader is likely to find a blend of theoretical and accidental sampling. Samples such as this are rarely documented in any detail in research reports, but it is usually feasible to work out some of the other factors involved, and where a natural history of the research is given this should help. Whatever the approach to sampling, there will be problems of generalisation; the reader must, of course, analyse the author's solutions to these problems.

DATA ANALYSIS

So far, I have mentioned only briefly the difficulties of relating qualitative data to conclusions about it (concepts, propositions, theories). As we have seen, the statistical summaries readily drawn up for quantitative data have no analogue, and in writing a report the researcher has, instead, to rely on illustrations, and must try to convince the reader that they are typical. This comment, however, refers only to research reports, i.e. the situation after the final data analysis. What form, then, does data analysis itself take? What is the process by which field-notes are analysed and results drawn out? From the material introduced earlier it is evident that much preliminary analysis can and should be carried out during the course of the field-work (Schatzman and Strauss, 1973; Becker, 1958). However, there comes a time when the field-work is ended, all the data are collected, and the final data analysis is to be undertaken. Most of the data-analysis methods suggested in existing textbooks refer to this stage, though, as might be expected, the main ideas can be employed at the earlier preliminary stages as well.

Schatzman and Strauss (1973), Lofland (1971), Becker (1958), Glaser and Strauss (1967) and several other authors all make recommendations on methods of data analysis, and in some cases insist that their method is quite distinctive. Each of these sources has its merits and certainly provides useful tips. In essence there are two aspects of method involved. First, what system should be used for filing field-notes, cross-referencing, and so on? Earlier, I referred to Schatzman and Strauss's prescription (ONs, TNs and MNs), but there are several other approaches, including that of

Lofland (1971). Second, how can a systematic and practical method then be devised for combing through the field-notes to discover and test hypotheses, concepts and other kinds of results, and what general strategy should guide this process? Let us now focus on this question. In much of the existing writing, strategy is discussed but the practical implications for data analysis are not clear. For example, Glaser and Strauss (1967) argue that their "constant comparative method" is superior to other approaches, but it is far from obvious what consequences the method has for the handling of data. These matters will be pursued further in the next section, since the question of alternative strategies is closely related to the researcher's conception of theory. Here, I want to make one main point – whatever strategy is adopted, the *practical* problems of data analysis will be fairly similar. The researcher is always involved in the cyclical process shown in Figure 8.1.

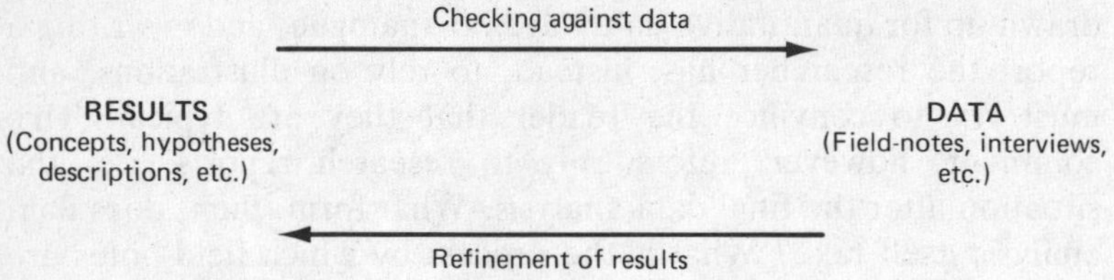

Checking against data

RESULTS
(Concepts, hypotheses, descriptions, etc.)

DATA
(Field-notes, interviews, etc.)

Refinement of results

FIGURE 8.1

At the start of the data analysis the 'results' are often no more than hunches. These tentative results are then progressively revised by repeated checking, which takes the form of combing through field-notes and other data. As part of this process, the researcher should take special account of data which do *not* fit the existing version of the results, since these provide the most crucial test. In brief, the process of data analysis is one of progressive refinement or revision of results until they are consistent with the data; this may seem simple enough in principle, but it is often laborious in practice since the data are complex and varied. The process is reported only rarely, but one good example is Cressey's study on trust violators (see Chapter 22); a thorough account is given of the analysis of the interview data, and revision of the hypotheses into a final version. Cressey was using analytic induction as a general principle, and this shows the researcher when the process of analysis should stop (see also Becker, Chapter 11). In other cases it is more difficult to decide when the data analysis is to be regarded as complete, though some guidance can be obtained from Schatzman and Strauss (1973), Lofland (1971), and others.

For the reader of a research report the main problem, then, is that much of the process of data analysis is typically hidden from view. In fact, there are good reasons to argue that the *natural history* of a research project should not only include details of field-work, data collection and methods for keeping field-notes but also an account of the process of data analysis. However, it must be recognised that these details are usually not given in full, and the process of data analysis is therefore particularly difficult to evaluate in most reports. Thus, as I have mentioned earlier, the reader must focus on the final results presented by the author and the supporting data which are given; the points raised earlier in the section 'Concepts and Indicators' are especially relevant here.[3]

THEORIES AND LINKS WITH EVIDENCE

As we have already seen, the objective of the field-work approach is not always theory-building – for example, description or theory-testing may be the aim of some studies. Glaser and Strauss (1967) show how the objectives of research may be related to strategies for data analysis; Table 8.2, which follows Glaser and Strauss's

TABLE 8.2 *Strategies for the analysis of qualitative data**

| Theory-building | Theory-testing | |
	Yes	No
Yes	1. Inspection for concepts, hypotheses, etc., then checking against data	4. Inspection for concepts, hypotheses, etc.
	2. Analytic induction	5. Constant comparative method
No	3. Test prior hypotheses against data	6. Ethnographic description

*Following Glaser and Strauss (1967: 105, table 1).

reasoning, provides a useful summary, but it is also evident that some studies do not fit into the table easily. For example, both Smith and Birksted aim to provide descriptions but involve some elements of theory; also, in some cases strategies for data analysis may be far less explicit and more informal than any of the six possibilities listed.

For the moment, however, let us focus on the problem of theory-building. What strategies are available for analysing data? We have already encountered analytic induction in the studies of Becker (Chapter 11) and Cressey (see Chapter 22); a discussion is given in McCall and Simmons (1969: ch. 5 – see the articles by Robinson and Turner). Whatever the logical problems of this approach it is clear that it can be applied only to a narrow range of empirical phenomena; in common with most researchers Wiener, Smith and Birksted are not studying 'universal processes', and analytic induction is therefore not a useful strategy. The first strategy listed in Table 8.2 does not have a distinctive title, but I think it captures the spirit of data analysis outlined in the previous section, and it is consistent with suggestions made by Becker (1958, 1970: ch. 3). Theory-building takes place through a process of initial inspection, testing against the data and refinement. As I have said earlier, this process is rarely reported, but in many studies it is fairly certain that it has been used even though one cannot be sure of the details.

The constant comparative method introduced by Glaser and Strauss is intended as a radical alternative, by which *grounded theory* is constructed. As Table 8.2 makes clear, theory-testing is seen as unnecessary if this method is used since "Theory based on data can usually not be completely refuted by more data or replaced by another theory. Since it is too intimately linked to data, it is destined to last despite its inevitable modification and reformulation" (Glaser and Strauss, 1967: 4). This extreme view has, however, been criticised by later authors, for example Ford (1975: 136, 320), who insists that theory-construction inevitably entails an initial act of the imagination which is then carefully checked by testing whether the theory is consistent with the evidence. This is not the place for a discussion on the problem of induction analysed by Ford, but it is relevant to ask whether the constant comparative method really avoids all elements of theory-testing. Certainly, Glaser and Strauss state their case in such a way that the testing or refinement of hypotheses appears to be excluded; however, I think most sociologists would regard it as impossible to analyse a complex qualitative data set without at any stage having to revise some of one's ideas and discard certain tentative hypotheses. It is, in fact, unfortunate that many valuable points made by Glaser and Strauss have been obscured by the debate over whether 'pure' grounded theory is possible.

Having discussed the main strategies of theory-construction, let us now consider the theory itself. The conceptions of the nature of theory held by Becker (1958, 1970) and Schatzman and Strauss (1973) are surprisingly close to the kind of theory discussed in Chapter 3 – that is, a set of systematically related sociological propositions. These sources, then, suggest that theory-building at its simplest consists of developing concepts and relationships between concepts, and such a perspective is, in fact, common to most authors who have written on this subject. An additional factor introduced by Glaser and Strauss (1967: ch. 10) is that theory should be useful and practical – it should be understandable to laymen, and should allow control over the situations it describes. This is an unusual perspective, and I am at a loss to understand why these should be requirements, even in relation to Glaser and Strauss's own research. Glaser and Strauss do, however, make two distinctions between kinds of theory which are of interest here. The first is between *substantive theory* and *formal theory* (1967: ch. 4). Substantive theory refers simply to one substantive area (e.g. juvenile delinquency), whereas formal theory refers to a whole range of substantive areas (e.g. labelling theory as applied to the sociology of deviance). This, then, is really a matter of levels of abstraction in the theory (see Chapter 3). The second distinction is between *propositional* theory, as defined above, and *discussional* theory (Glaser and Strauss, 1967: 115); discussional theory seems to be a useful title for theories such as that of Wiener (Chapter 21) which presents concepts and categories but not propositions as such. Thus Wiener's theory can be characterised as a substantive discussional theory, grounded in the data.

How should this material be used in the deciphering of any given research report? The reader should first characterise the author's objectives, in particular the extent to which theory-building is or is not the aim of the research. Where theory-building is involved, is the theory substantive or formal, propositional or discussional? If the author's aim is descriptive, what kind of description is involved, and is any kind of theoretical perspective used? Second, consider the links between the theory which is built (or other results or conclusions) and the evidence. Since the most fundamental questions are normally about concept-indicator links, we must assess each link by the methods outlined earlier in this chapter. The author may also present certain selected propositions or a fully developed propositional theory. In these cases data should be given in the report as examples and illustrations of the relationships which are asserted; again, we may analyse the strength of the author's argument by assessing the links with this evidence.

ADVANTAGES AND LIMITATIONS

In assessing the merits of the field-work approach it is important to separate three main issues, the first two of which have attracted much critical attention (see, for example, Brown, 1973; Ford, 1975). First, which kinds of social phenomena are most amenable to field-research? In Brown's view the main classes of suitable phenomena are relatively short-term social processes, sequences of behaviour that are directly observable and behaviour with a repetitive character (1973: 8). As Brown argues, there are many phenomena which are important sociologically but for which the field-work approach does not seem to be appropriate; as an example, Brown cites his own research on schizophrenia, for which data are needed on processes of interaction in the family over a period of years. It is evident that much of Brown's critique is concerned specifically with participant-observation and he successfully points out some of the limitations of this technique. However, as we have seen there are many studies in which theories are built from qualitative data based solely on interviews; clearly, there are limits on the range of phenomena for which this technique is appropriate, but these will be different from the limitations of participant-observation. Thus, if the field-work approach is defined broadly to include these two categories of research as well as others, the range of applicability is rather wider than may at first appear.

As we have seen earlier, the major successes of the approach seem to be in research on social organisations and on looser-knit social groups, where the focus of the inquiry is the 'here and now' of group dynamics, the ideology or world-view of the group, or a specific process or experience. To be sure, all these topics have also been investigated by researchers using more structured methods. In many cases, therefore, the choice of an approach will be a matter of personal preference and style, taking account of practical possibilities and restrictions, available resources, and the objectives of the research. For example, Wiener could probably have collected data from rheumatoid arthritics by using a structured questionnaire, but her preferred approach was to use field-work and the guidelines of grounded theory. By contrast, given that Smith's main objective was to describe the delinquent group's attitudes to the police, it is doubtful whether he could have carried out the research by using other methods; here, the restrictions of setting and topic demand the field-work approach.

If we now consider some of the earlier chapters in Part Two, the limitations of field-research become apparent. It is difficult to see how topics such as historical trends in other-directedness (Dornbusch and Hickman, Chapter 10) or national patterns of work-force mobility (Broom and Jones, Chapter 17) could be studied effectively by participant-observation or unstructured interviewing; the field-work approach is comparatively unsuitable for studies of large widespread populations or studies of long-term trends, and research on these phenomena normally employs more structured methods. In some cases the sheer size of the project or topic may be the factor which determines whether or not field-work is a possible approach. Field-research is characteristically done by an individual or a small number of researchers, and it is difficult to see how the approach could be utilised effectively by a large research team. For example, Broom and Jones's interviewers could have been asked to carry out unstructured interviews on occupational histories for the 1,925 male adults in their sample, but with little standardisation in the interview procedure the resulting data would have been impossible to analyse.

The second issue concerns Glaser and Strauss's grounded-theory approach to theory-building. To what extent can it plausibly be argued that this method is 'pure' induction, involving no preconceptions and no testing of the theory which is built? A related point, made by Brown (1973) in his critique of Glaser and Strauss, is that it is very dangerous to abandon the idea of testing theories, and it can also be highly inefficient in terms of research effort. My own view on these matters, as outlined earlier, is that Glaser and Strauss, along with other "inductivists" (Ford, 1975), have misunderstood the nature of their own research procedures on this point, as theory-building inevitably involves some element of theory-testing. The usefulness of Glaser and Strauss's work lies not in their advocacy of pure theory-building, but in their valuable suggestions for research strategies and procedures, many of which have been developed further and presented in a more coherent form in Schatzman and Strauss's book on field-work (1973).

The third point concerns a question which is rather naive in the light of the analysis so far, but it should nevertheless be mentioned – is theory-construction inextricably linked to participant-observation and qualitative data? Clearly not. In practice, there is an empirical link, as most participant-observers have collected qualitative data and constructed theories rather than testing existing theories, but it is not a logically necessary link. Thus Glaser and Strauss (1967: ch. 8) discuss grounding theory in quantitative data; for example, it would be possible to take data from official records like police files on incidents of criminal violence, and construct theories about the occurrence of violence from such data (without doing a participant-observation study). Another example is Jacobs's study (see Chapter 22) which is theory-testing using qualitative data.

DECIPHERING FIELD-RESEARCH

We now consider the aspect of field-research which is the most important for this book – how to decipher research reports based on field-work and qualitative data. The strategy given below is a parallel to that developed in Chapter 6 for reports based on quantitative data, and involves a summary followed by an evaluation.

Summary of the research report. Five main stages should be considered; each is formulated as a series of questions.

1. What was the *natural history* of the research? Outline the original purposes of the research, how the research developed over time, field-work role, field relations, and so on.
2. What *data* were collected and by what methods (observations, interviews and conversations, documents, etc.)? How were notes kept, and was any tape-recording done?
3. How was the *sampling* done? To what extent was it accidental, theoretical and so on? What was the working universe?
4. How was the *data analysis* done? How are the data summarised and presented in the report (illustrations, extracts from interviews, etc.), and how have these data been selected for presentation?
5. What *results* are presented? Here, one must identify the author's objective in the report (theory-building, description of some kind, etc.). What concepts and categories are presented? Which of these are discovered from the data, and which were pre-existing? Which are participant concepts and which are theoretical concepts? What theories or hypotheses are built?

Evaluation. The fundamental question is whether the author's *results* (description, theory, etc.) are consistent with the *data*; the form of the evaluation will therefore be closely dependent on the summary and particularly on question 5. Three separate stages, as below, make up the evaluation; these stages should be followed only as far as is justified by the kind of results given in the report. A fourth, final, stage concludes the analysis of the study.

6. Evaluate the validity of the concept-indicator links. Take *each* concept (and its categories, where these exist) and examine the relationship with the data; exactly what data are taken as indicators of the concept (and its categories)? How well does the author argue the case for the validity of the concept-indicator link?
7. Assess the validity of the theory or hypotheses. As these will generally be stated in terms of relationships between concepts, this question will consist of checking that empirical evidence is given for these relationships.

8. Sampling and generalisation. Examine the effect of the sampling on the validity of the author's argument. When theorising, has the author kept to the limits imposed by his sample selection? If generalisation has been attempted, is it justified?
9. Conclusions. Review the points made in stages 6, 7 and 8, consider any additional factors, and draw general conclusions.

As a whole this strategy should enable a thorough analysis to be undertaken of any field-work based study, but it will be helpful to mention three further points. First, the nine stages have been dealt with briefly since in each case certain sections of Chapters 7 and 8 have been devoted to the problem; the reader should refer back to these sections for more details. Second, the most common problem in applying the procedure will be lack of information in the research report; different authors have different styles – some may omit details of the natural history of the project, others may say nothing about data analysis, and so on. I have made some suggestions on how judgements may be made on details which are not stated explicitly, but in many studies there will be no solution to this problem except to identify it and to note how the information should have been presented in the report. In making criticisms about lack of information it should be borne in mind that, as Becker (1958), says the reporting of a field-work based study in a fully detailed form is no easy task.

Third, the nine stages should be regarded as providing a flexible strategy, rather than as a rigorous step-by-step procedure. The questions listed provide the essential ingredients for deciphering any given research report, but these ingredients may be fitted together in different ways depending on the different circumstances. Thus, for example, how the data are collected and analysed, the concepts and indicators, and the sampling, are always important, but these aspects have to be considered in a way which is appropriate to the objective of the study and how the research report is organised.

Wiener's study

As an example of applying the strategy outlined above, Wiener's research on rheumatoid arthritics will be deciphered. A brief summary of the study has been given in Chapter 7, and subsequently various aspects of Wiener's methods have been referred to. It is assumed that the reader is familiar with this material, and it must also be stressed that repeated reference to Chapter 21 is needed if the analysis below is to be fully understood.

(1) *Natural history*. Wiener's objective is the "collection and analysis of data [on] the sociological aspects of pain management". This involves constructing a *theory* – one which can be used in teaching health professionals about patient care. It is not clear whether this objective was stated in this form at the outset of the research, but is seems likely. Wiener does not state how the field-work was organised or how it developed over time (see below) except to say a grounded-theory approach was used; she is a co-worker of Glaser and Strauss, and exemplifies their research methods (see below). A natural history is not really given; for example, we are not told how the research originated, what problems there were in initiating the field-work or continuing it, or what the reactions of the respondents were. In fact, it is unlikely that there were any significant problems of field-work role or field relations, since a researcher in Wiener's position would be seen in a 'caring' capacity, given the objectives of the study, and patients would be more than willing to talk; the relationship with the medical centre's staff was presumably cleared before the project was started.

(2) *Data collection* was mainly by interview, but some observations were also involved. *Interviews* were presumably unstructured but focused on the topic of pain management; we are told little about interview procedure, where the interviews were held (in the medical centre or in patients' homes), whether or not they were tape-recorded (although this is likely, as verbatim extracts are given) and whether Wiener interviewed any one respondent on just one or on several occasions. *Observations* of "action[s], episode[s] and event[s]" could have been in the medical centre, patients' homes or both. Wiener does not say how field-notes were kept, but it is likely that an approach similar to that outlined by Schatzman and Strauss (1973; and see above) was used.

(3) *Sampling*. The main sample was twenty-one patients suffering from rheumatoid arthritis; all were out-patients at the same clinic, which was part of a major medical centre. Wiener gives no further

details of sample selection. Were these twenty-one *all* those currently attending the clinic, or a sample? If they were a sample, how were they selected? Were they representatively sampled, or is this an accidental sample or perhaps one composed of volunteers? Are the more serious sufferers excluded? How many are female and how many males? The lack of information here would seem to raise problems, and this issue will be discussed later. Wiener also has a sample of observations, and again the basis of the sampling is unclear; however, this is typical of participant-observation as a technique, and we may assume that the observations result from a combination of accidental and theoretical sampling. One aspect which is clear is that the working universe is rheumatoid arthritics attending this one clinic, which is probably in California; the question of a general universe will be discussed later.

(4) *Data analysis.* Since Wiener is using the grounded-theory approach, her strategy of data analysis is the *constant comparative method* (although she does not refer to it in these terms). Her account of discovering concepts and categories (see her first section on research methodology) parallels Glaser and Strauss exactly, as she acknowledges. The actual details of how the field-notes and interviews were sorted and categorised are no clearer in Wiener's report that in Glaser and Strauss's book (although this is a process which is only rarely discussed in research reports generally, as I have already noted).

The data presented in the report are mainly extracts from interviews; in only a few instances is there any reference to data based on observations. The interview extracts are not identified directly, so there is no way of judging whether the material is spread equally over all of the twenty-one patients; this point is discussed further below.

(5) *Results.* The theory which is constructed is quite complex, and is stated in terms of relationships between concepts. As we can see from Figure 8.2, which is an attempt to summarise Wiener's theory and to clarify certain aspects of it, the relationships between different concepts are of three different types: (a) conceptual connections (of a kind analysed in the tree diagrams in Chapter 3), (b) connections indicating that, over time, one physical/psychological state (concept) *leads to* another state (concept), and (c) a relationship in which two or more physical/psychological

states are balanced against each other, in the sense that they are alternatives. The theory, and the evidence which is presented in support of it, will now be discussed in some detail with the help of the diagram.

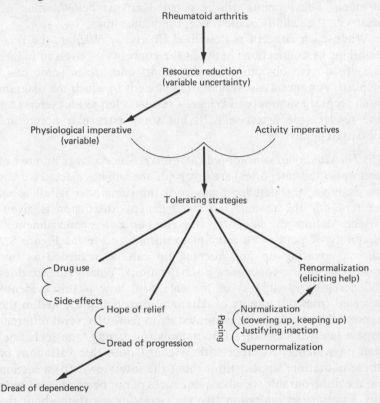

Note: Symbols are as follows: conceptual connections are shown as plain lines, 'leads to' is shown by arrows, and 'balancing of options' by ⌣.
(See the text for further details.)

FIGURE 8.2   *Wiener's theory of pain management*

In common with many other reports, Wiener's style of presentation is to introduce each concept (or category) and then to give illustrations to support the validity of it. The concepts are introduced one by one in an order which approximates that of the diagram, reading from top to bottom. Except for 'rheumatoid arthritis', all the terms used in the diagram are concepts or categories, and all are discovered or invented from the data. None are participant concepts, but they are grounded in participants' terminology and do not refer to highly abstract theoretical phenomena. These points will be pursued further below, when we deal with the validity of the concept-indicator links.

While each concept is described clearly by Wiener, the relationships or connections between the concepts as given in Figure 8.2 are not so obvious from the report and are in some cases implicit. A general assessment of the extent to which the diagram is an accurate summary of Wiener's results is left as an exercise for the reader (see Exercise 8.2), but some particular points are discussed below.

(6) *The validity of concept-indicator links.* Since a large number of concepts (and categories) are involved, one will be selected here as an example; the detailed analysis of the remainder is left as an exercise for the reader, but some general discussion is given. Wiener defines the category of *covering up* as the concealment of disability or pain in an attempt to normalize life (as Figure 8.2 shows, covering up and keeping up can be regarded as two categories of the concept of normalization). What evidence does Wiener give in support of the category, how is this evidence selected from the totality of data, and how is it presented in the report? The evidence as presented is, in fact, of several different types: (a) two short direct quotations (on saying 'one feels fine' and on walking) together with Wiener's note that variations of these quotations appear throughout the interviews; (b) a section on the unfavourable social consequences of not being able to cover up, a very brief quotation (the embarrassing question about the skiing accident, though it is not clear whether this is truly a quote), and a longer quote from a woman who could walk only very slowly; and (c) a section on the painful physical consequences of covering up which includes a quote about the difficulty of walking straight and Wiener's summary of other data. On the face of it the link between the category and the presented evidence (which acts as an indicator) is convincingly argued; while it is not clear how Wiener has selected this evidence from the data as a whole, various statements are made to assure the reader that covering up is used by all rheumatoid arthritics at certain times.

The presentation of evidence in support of each of Wiener's concepts and categories follows much the same pattern: a concept or category is introduced, defined, and then illustrated by quotations and by Wiener's summaries of the patterns of data shown by the interviews. The concept-indicator links seem generally to be well argued; more will be said later about this aspect of the study, and about how the evidence is handled.

(7) *The validity of the theory.* As indicated earlier in this chapter, Wiener has constructed a discussional substantive theory of pain management. This is not propositional theory as such, though relationships between the concepts, which I have summarised in Figure 8.2, are clearly evident.

There are two stages in the assessment of the theory's validity: the first is the validity of the concepts (which has already been dealt with) and the second is the validity of the relationships. Thus we are left with the question of to what extent Wiener gives direct evidence of the relationships depicted in Figure 8.2. Certainly, many of the relationships are conceptual or logical connections which require no empirical evidence, but some can (and should) be tested – for example, what evidence is there for the four 'balancing of options' relationships?

I shall consider just one of these – the *pacing* mechanism of balancing normalization, inaction and supernormalization. The evidence is given partly in the section dealing directly with pacing and partly in the previous section, headed covering-up and keeping-up; it consists mainly of Wiener's statements (for example, the discussion of cancelled activities such as work and church) together with a few quotations from the interviews. As a whole Wiener's analysis of pacing is convincing, though this is largely due to the over-all force of the argument rather than the evidence given.

In fact, these comments apply equally well to Wiener's results *in toto,* which seem to be consistent with the evidence presented and add up to a convincing theory. Since the evidence in some sections of the report is somewhat thin, why should one be convinced? There are four points to be made. First, because the concepts are at a relatively low level of generality they are very close to participant concepts and the linkage with evidence is consequently not difficult for the reader to 'see'; this is, of course, characteristic of the grounded-theory approach. Second, most of the concepts stand in a conceptual or logical relationship to one another, and evidence in support of any one concept often supports several others; for example, much of the data presented on pacing also illustrate normalization and renormalization. Third, with this kind of theory it is sensible to ask how the participants (patients) themselves would judge it. Unfortunately, Wiener does not pursue the idea, but I have little doubt that such an exercise would substantiate the theory's validity. These three points all support Wiener's analysis, but the fourth point is somewhat less laudatory – is Wiener's theory the *only* theory that can be constructed (even from her data)? This problem will be discussed further, together with some other aspects of the theory, in the conclusions.

(8) *Sampling and generalisation.* As we have seen, this aspect of the study was reported poorly, and it is really not possible to judge what sampling methods were used. In view of the nature of the constructed theory, however, to what extent is this defect important? How, if at all, could any selectivity within the sample affect the results? In fact, the exact method of sampling is unlikely to have much effect. If Wiener had been attempting to estimate the proportion of patients who resort to folk remedies, or how long a typical patient takes to work out a pacing strategy, a representative sample would have been crucial, but these were not her concerns. Concepts like normalization and pacing are equally likely to have emerged from her analysis whatever sampling methods were used.

Generalisation raises more interesting problems. Is Wiener's theory applicable just to this one medical centre, and if not, how widely can one generalise? Wiener does not really acknowledge this problem, but generalisation is *implicit* throughout her analysis; at no stage does she give the impression that the results are to be read as if they applied just to the one centre. Assuming, then, that Wiener is generalising (perhaps to rheumatoid arthritics world-wide, though we cannot be sure), how can one justify this? Here, we must come back to the nature of the theory; there appear to be many reasons why the theory *should* be generally applicable, since all of the concepts used are common to all situations in which a person has to cope with rheumatoid arthritis. Indeed, as Wiener suggests, some of the results may be applicable to other medical conditions involving pain management.

(9) *Conclusions*. The analysis has shown that Wiener's study is comparatively well argued and that her theory is soundly based. There are, however, a number of ways in which the presentation of the report could be improved. The description of sampling was inadequate, and problems of generalisation should have been acknowledged explicitly. In the presentation of evidence direct quotes from interviews should have been distinguished from other material given in quotation marks. It would also have been helpful to identify each quotation – for example, the source could have been acknowledged as (say) 'respondent no. 12, male aged 53'; such a technique helps to reassure the reader that quotations are taken from the interviews as a whole, rather than just one or two. More information on data-collection methods should have been given, including details of note-taking and whether tape-recording was done. Despite criticisms such as these, it should be emphasised that Wiener's report compares favourably with others based on the field-work approach.

As we have seen, Wiener's purpose was to build a theory useful for the training of health-care professionals, and it appears that she has successfully achieved this objective. One can imagine this theory being taught to (say) trainee nurses, and providing a useful framework for their day-to-day handling of problems associated with pain management. 'Learning the theory' would be a process by which the nurses are sensitised about what to look for in dealing with rheumatoid arthritics, and how to respond to factors such as supernormalization or dread of dependency; the term 'discussional theory' is worth emphasising again, since Wiener is providing a framework through which these problems can be discussed.

Lastly, is Wiener's theory unique or is it only one of many discussional theories which might be developed about the same phenomena? If another researcher had carried out the study (even to the extent of collecting data in the same way and utilising the grounded-theory approach), how similar would the results have been? These are interesting questions to pose, but the answers must be somewhat speculative. In my view it is highly likely that another researcher would produce results which are different. It is doubtful, however, whether such alternative results would contradict Wiener's theory; in other words, we should have two alternative but consistent frameworks for discussing pain management.

Concluding remarks

The analysis of Wiener's study has demonstrated how research reports based on field-work may be deciphered, but before concluding this chapter some further comments on the method should be made. First, in analysing a study, one does not simply start at stage 1 of the procedure, go on to stages 2, 3, and so on, and finish at stage 9; for example, many points which emerge as part of the evaluation cause reflection on the summary. In general, the nine stages provide a framework for the presentation of the reader's analysis, rather than an inflexible step-by-step procedure. Thus another reader using the same procedure would, no doubt, decipher Wiener's study somewhat differently; even if the ingredients were the same, the format and arrangement of the material under the headings would probably differ. Over all, the approach should ensure that all methodological aspects of a study are covered, but these can be fitted together in various ways.

One limitation should, however, be mentioned. In common with the procedures given in Chapter 6, no attention is given to matters of 'external validity'; in the case of Wiener this would involve considering the implications of the study for theory and research in the relevant areas of medical sociology. As I have explained in Chapter 6, questions such as this are ultimately the most important ones, but are necessarily outside the bounds of this book.

Some final comments should be made on the field-work approach. In my view, in much of the literature on field work, qualitative data and theory-construction there is too much emphasis on a confrontation between these methods and 'conventional' quantitative theory-testing research; also, there is too little discussion of the limitations of field-work. As a result, the role of the field-work approach in sociology is often misunderstood by its critics, and sometimes by its proponents as well. For example, one might wholeheartedly agree that Glaser and Strauss's ideas on qualitative data collection and analysis are extremely valuable without granting their claim that theories constructed by their methods must necessarily be valid. More generally, many of the authors who have written on field-work (especially Strauss and Becker) do seem to capture many of the elements of data study and theorising which are central to creativity in sociology, while at the same time suggesting systematic methods which must be a considerable advance on less formal approaches.

EXERCISES

8.1 Decipher the studies of Becker, Birksted and Smith (Chapters 11, 19 and 20) using the nine-stage procedure presented above (and taking account of the summaries and other details given in Chapters 7 and 8).

8.2 Review the analysis of Wiener's study given above. Which aspects of the deciphering are explicit in the research report? Which aspects have been inferred, and are the inferences justified? Analyse the extent to which Figure 8.2 is a correct summary of Wiener's theory.

8.3 Discuss the problems which you might expect in studying any of the following groups or organisations using the field-work approach: a small factory, a large factory, trainee nurses in one hospital, a medical clinic, a leisure group, a local branch of a political party, business executives, sexual deviants, school-leavers, muggers, taxi-drivers, unemployed Ph.D.s. In each case take a *specific* example of one group or organisation with which you are familiar, and cover factors such as entry, role and field-relations, likely data-collection and sampling problems. Virtually any other groups or organisations can act as suitable examples, and may therefore be substituted for those given in the list above if preferred.

9

Conclusions and Implications

In a discussion of the existing work on research methods in sociology, Bulmer (1977: 4–5) has distinguished three separable themes: first, *general methodology,* which "denotes the systematic and logical study of the general principles guiding sociological investigation . . .[and] . . . has clear and direct links to the philosophy of science"; second, *research strategy,* which refers to the way in which particular empirical studies are designed and carried out and "what notions about the task of sociological research are embodied in the approach used"; and third, *research techniques,* which refer to "specific manipulative and fact-finding operations", for example questionnaire construction, participant-observation techniques, and methods of statistical analysis. Naturally, a textbook which attempts to be comprehensive must deal with each of these themes. In practice, however, it is extremely difficult to provide a fully integrated treatment, and even amongst the better textbooks there is a tendency to treat the three themes separately (for example, Selltiz *et al.,* 1976; Smith, 1975). Of course, many good textbooks deal only with one research strategy or technique (for example, Schatzman and Strauss, 1973; Moser and Kalton, 1971).

In this book the blend of strategy, techniques and general methodology has been somewhat different. The emphasis on the systematic evaluation, or *deciphering,* of research reports maintains a high degree of integration between different aspects of research methods. All relevant aspects of method must be considered for the systematic evaluation of a study, and they are integrated through the use of an appropriate modification of the ABCDE model (see Chapter 6), or through an equivalent procedure for studies based on qualitative data (see Chapter 8). The backbone of the approach is provided by these procedures for the evaluation of research reports.

Figure 9.1 shows the two major implications of the approach to deciphering which has been developed in this book. This approach draws on selected studies (box 1) and the literature on research methods (box 2), to provide an analysis focused on the problem of deciphering (box 3); the most obvious result is the development of the capacity to evaluate research reports (box 4). A more subtle point is that the work as a whole generates a perspective on issues of research method somewhat different from the majority of the existing literature (box 5); two examples will be given.

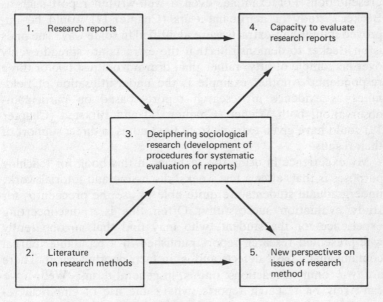

FIGURE 9.1

First, most research methods textbooks tell us that, in selecting a sample, the main problem will be to decide on an appropriate sampling procedure; conventionally, a textbook gives details of representative (probability) sampling and other kinds of samples, and discusses their relative merits. However, as Chapter 5 shows, there are several other aspects of sampling which are of equal importance: for example, the distinction between general universe and working universe, assessing the typicality of samples which are not formally representative, and the question of to what extent generalisation is possible. Questions of sampling and generalisation must be discussed within a theoretical context which admits the various informal or approximate methods of sampling often used by sociologists and enables their strengths and weaknesses to be assessed realistically.

Second, the presentation of evidence in research reports based on qualitative data is often poorly handled, and many authors seem to be unaware either of the need for evidence or the ways of presenting it. The analysis in Chapters 7 and 8 identifies this problem, and also makes some specific suggestions for data presentation. For example, even a well-written report such as Becker's study of marijuana-users (Chapter 11) would be improved if interview extracts were identified in some way. The onus is on Becker to demonstrate that the extracts are spread evenly over his sample of fifty, rather than drawn from just two or three respondents. Another example is the under-utilisation of field-notes as evidence in research reports based on participant-observation; both Wiener (Chapter 21) and Birksted (Chapter 19) could have given extracts from field-notes in direct support of their results.

My experience in using the material in this book for teaching purposes is that, after a few weeks' discussion and tutorial work, undergraduate students are quite able to use the procedures for study evaluation successfully. Often this is a disconcerting experience for the student, who may find that an apparently well-presented research report published in a reputable journal contains many basic defects and is, in fact, poorly argued. There are two common reactions: one is, in general terms, 'Well, if we can't rely on research reports, what's the use of empirical research?'; and the other is more specific, 'This article is very poor, how did it ever get published?' At the root of both reactions is the question of standards of research and research reporting.

It is interesting to consider how such questions may be answered. One fundamental point is that the undergraduate student who has a good grasp of the procedures developed in this book is in a better position to carry out a detailed *methodological* evaluation of a research report than most journal editors and referees. Referees, to whom articles are sent for approval prior to publication, are usually experts in the substantive area involved; they will be concerned mainly with what I have termed the *external validity* of the research, and will not necessarily be sensitive to the methodological issues of *internal validity* of the author's argument. These comments emphasise the professional sociologist's need to 'internalise' procedures for deciphering research studies. I would argue that this perspective on methodology is just as important as (say) technical problems of questionnaire design, statistical analysis or the problem of managing one's role in a participant-observation study. A researcher who is fully acquainted with this perspective will keep the central problems of method constantly in mind; he or she will be more likely to avoid basic pitfalls both in the conduct of research and in the writing of a research report. Additionally, a referee who uses the procedures for study evaluation is not likely to recommend that a poorly argued study be published unless it is rewritten.

These comments should not be construed negatively. I have referred to the existence of the weaker studies in sociology journals simply to emphasis the importance of the deciphering perspective. I would not argue that the general standard of research reports is low. To be sure, the standards are not uniformly high, but there is a great variety and diversity. Thus, amongst the reports included in Part Two, several emerge from the evaluation very well. It is also important to emphasise that the evaluation of a study provides an essentially *positive critique,* for the identification of weaknesses is always accompanied by specific recommendations on how they may be overcome.

THE LITERATURE ON RESEARCH METHODS

In the Preface I have mentioned that this book should be seen as complementary to the existing literature on methods, and that it takes the deciphering approach much further than any previous work. Each of these two aspects will now be explored further.

Most existing textbooks on research methods can be categorised as follows: (a) general textbooks, attempting to give a fairly comprehensive overview of the topic, either at an introductory level (e.g. Labovitz and Hagedorn, 1971) or at a more advanced level (e.g. Selltiz *et al.,* 1976; Smith, 1975); (b) textbooks which deal with one particular strategy or technique (e.g. Moser and Kalton, 1971; Schatzman and Strauss, 1973); (c) books organised as a series of practical exercises for the student (e.g. Wakeford, 1968; Wiseman and Aron, 1970); (d) general or critical analyses of existing research practice (e.g. Ford, 1975; Bulmer, 1977; Lazarsfeld and Rosenberg, 1955); (e) 'insider' accounts by researchers and personal reflections on involvement in research (e.g. Hammond, 1964; Bell and Newby, 1977; Fletcher, 1974; Golden 1976; Shipman, 1976). These five categories do not constitute a classification in the strict sense, since many individual books contain elements from more than one category, and would therefore be difficult to place unambiguously under one heading. Nevertheless, this list does illustrate, in broad terms, the content of existing work, and it also enables me to draw out some important points.

The dominant theme in methods textbooks is *instruction on the conduct of research* and the second theme, falling within heading (d), is the *critical analysis of existing practice;* in many textbooks one finds a blend of these two themes but with an emphasis on the former. Third, there is the theme of learning about methods from *reflections on personal experience by the researcher;* these writings fall under heading (e), but usually involve some critical analysis (or at least a debunking of the conventional conception of the research process) as well. If these are in fact the three main themes in textbooks on research methods, it is clear that the approach which I have termed *deciphering* is separate and distinctive – although, as I have said above, it does carry with it some critical implications. This book is therefore complementary to existing textbooks, and it can be especially valuable in providing a perspective which contrasts with both the first and third themes of 'instruction' and 'personal reflections'.

Previous work on the analysis of research reports

Some twenty-five years ago, in the foreword to Hyman's *Survey Design and Analysis,* Lazarsfeld discussed the problem of the graduate student who must review a great deal of the literature, and deplored the lack of systematic training for such an activity (Hyman, 1955: viii–ix). Much the same factors are mentioned in the introduction to Lazarsfeld and Rosenberg's *The Language of*

TABLE 9.1 *Summary of existing work on the analysis of research reports*

Source	Procedure for analysis (objectives, clarity, detail)	Limitations of procedure	Examples given?	Relationship to literature on research methods	Other comments
Knop (1967) short article	Object is evaluation – clear, quite detailed	Theory-testing, quantitative research only	None	Reader expected to be familiar with literature	Brief, but fairly thorough Intended for general use by students
MacQueen (1973: xv–xix)	"Article analysis" Not methodological – inexact. Objective is mainly a general assessment	None	None	Not stated (but methods knowledge not expected)	MacQueen's book of readings is intended for use by introductory students, and the procedures are therefore unsophisticated methodologically
Runcie (1976: ch. 2)	Object is general assessment Procedures are inexact	Unclear	One (summarises a report and raises general questions, but does not evaluate the author's argument)	Unclear	Although Runcie's is a book on research methods, the procedures do not analyse research reports systematically
Tripodi *et al.* (1969)	Object is evaluation. Procedures are clear and detailed	None	Six (some are analysed, some are left as exercises for the reader)	Reader expected to be familiar with literature Not clear exactly how such knowledge is to be used	A book intended for use by social-work students and professionals Thorough analysis of the problems of deciphering
Riley (1963)	Detailed analysis of research reports, applicable to all kinds of sociological research, but concerned with explication rather than evaluation		Many	Clearly articulated, forms backbone of the book	Very thorough analysis, but not giving procedures for deciphering research reports

Social Research, where the role of the methodologist as one who "codifies" research practices is mentioned (Lazarsfeld and Rosenberg, 1955: 4). Given the energy and enterprise of Lazarsfeld and his colleagues in the 'Columbia school' it is perhaps surprising that since then so little explicit attention has been paid to the problem of deciphering research reports. Much of the work of the Columbia school (including that of Riley (1963), which is discussed below) impinges on the problem, but it is not attacked directly. In fact, to my knowledge there are only a few existing published works which deal directly with the analysis of research reports; these are summarised in Table 9.1.[1]

Three authors – Knop, MacQueen and Runcie – have offered brief treatments of the problem; the procedures which they suggest differ in certain respects, but each has definite limitations. For example, in Knop's short article the framework, which "must necessarily be that of a model research project" (1967: 90) is in fact suitable for quantitative theory-testing research but it is not clear how it could be adapted to other kinds of research. Knop gives only an outline of his method; there is no detailed account of how it should be used, nor is an example offered of the kind of analysis which would result. It is also relevant to point out that Knop expects that the reader will have a firm grasp of the literature on theory, methods and statistics.

Riley's (1963) book is built around the analysis of the research process; a comprehensive range of reports is reprinted in the book to act as examples of the many different approaches to research. However, as Table 9.1 indicates, Riley does not deal with the problem of deciphering as such; she is concerned mainly with the explication of methodological problems from the viewpoint of conducting research. The book is of interest here mainly because it is the most thorough analysis of methodological issues which has yet been undertaken by using research reports as examples.

Tripodi *et al.* (1969) is the only source offering an analysis which is reasonably comparable with that developed in Chapters 1 to 8. The book is written for social-work students and has an orientation towards the use of research results for social-work practice. The research reports which Tripodi *et al.* consider are selected from social work, sociology and psychology journals. Tripodi *et al.* classify research reports into three main categories (1969: 54–5): "experimental", "quantitative-descriptive" and "exploratory".

Different guidelines are given for the assessment of studies in each of these categories (1969: 70–93). A distinction is made between three major aspects of any study – problem formulation, research design and data analysis, and conclusions, and a series of questions is listed under each heading. Thus Tripodi *et al.'s* procedure for evaluating any given research report consists of, first, placing the study in the appropriate category, and, second, responding to the relevant list of questions. In the second part of the book they demonstrate how these procedures work in practice by giving six examples of research reports, each of which is reprinted; three are assessed by Tripodi *et al.* and the other three are left as exercises for the reader.

In the book as a whole Tripodi *et al.* give a detailed and balanced account of their procedures, and discuss thoroughly the problems involved in assessing research reports. There are three main limitations of the work. The first, which the authors acknowledge, is the relationship to the literature on research methods (see Table 9.1). It is not really clear how the reader is expected to use this literature, and the question of how it is to be integrated with their procedures is not tackled directly. Second, the role of theory in research, both in problem formulation and in theorising generally, is given only minimal attention. Third, the evaluation procedures are based on series of questions rather than a systematic model or models; it should be evident from Chapters 1–6 that the use of a framework such as the ABCDE model gives a degree of coherence to the evaluation which is unlikely to be attained without it. A further point – which cannot really be considered as a limitation – is that, as the book is intended for social-work students, there are certain emphases which make it less valuable for the sociologist, for example the emphasis on research which is strictly experimental. Nevertheless, Tripodi *et al's.* book remains by far the most thorough previous attempt to develop procedures for deciphering sociological research reports.

Shipman's *The Limitations of Social Research* (which is intended mainly for students of education) has not been included in Table 9.1, but should be mentioned here since his intention is to provide a guide to "how to assess the reliability of research . . . reported in books and articles" (1972: ix). However, Shipman is concerned mainly with aspects of what I have termed *external validity*. For example, he deals with decision-making on how (and whether) research is to be undertaken, pressures on authors of research reports, how statistics can be used as a prop for an argument, and the use of references simply for prestige. In fact, Shipman has little to say on assessing the *internal validity* of research reports as it is defined here; nevertheless, he makes several valuable points which can in principle be regarded as complementary to the deciphering approach.

In reviewing previous work on the analysis of research reports I have, of course, implicitly made comparisons with the content of this book. There are two main points to be made. First, with the exception of Tripodi *et al.* (1969), previous writing on the problem of deciphering sociological research is rather insubstantial. Second, the principal characteristics of a satisfactory approach to deciphering have been delineated; following the headings in Table 9.1 these characteristics are: clear and detailed procedures with few limitations, examples to demonstrate that the procedures are workable, and integration with the literature on research methods so that it is shown how this literature should be used. It seems clear that the approach developed in this book satisifies these requirements better than any previous work.

THE APPLICABILITY OF TECHNIQUES FOR DECIPHERING

The twelve studies included in Part Two have been selected carefully in relation to a number of factors. They are all articles from sociology journals, they show a range of different approaches to research and are taken from a variety of different substantive areas. No studies which use complex statistical techniques are included. Some of the studies have been published quite recently, but two are from the 1950s and six are from the 1960s. The question which now arises is whether the procedures for evaluating studies, which have been demonstrated as applicable to these twelve research reports, are limited to studies of this kind. Can the procedures be applied successfully to contemporary studies, to research which uses more advanced statistical techniques, and to book-length research reports? Do the procedures have any other less obvious limitations?

I shall deal with these issues one by one. The references contain a list of research reports for which the procedures have been used successfully by undergraduate students (p. 319); many other studies could have been listed, including those summarised in Chapter 22, but a limited number have been selected as examples. Of the fourteen studies, eight have been published since 1972 (for example, Brown *et al.*, 1975; Spates, 1976). Given the nature of the procedures for case-study evaluation, there is no reason to doubt that they are readily applicable to contemporary research reports, as these examples confirm.

The question of book-length research reports deserves more comment. Four examples (Goldthorpe *et al.*, 1969; Hargreaves, 1968; Polsky, 1962; Wild, 1974) are given in the list of fourteen studies. These and many other books have been deciphered by myself and by undergraduate students. It is clear that the procedures are perfectly applicable, but more care is needed because the research itself, and hence the report too, are likely to assume a much more complex form than in a journal article. Book-length research reports commonly include much more theorising; for example, competing theories may be discussed or the data may be interpreted in the context of several different theories (Hargreaves, 1968; Goldthorpe *et al.*, 1969). A variety of data may be collected (triangulation), using several different techniques (Hargreaves, 1968) and several different samples may be involved (Wild, 1974). One advantage, however, is that rationale, field-work details and 'natural history' may be spelt out in more detail than is possible within the framework of a short journal article (Polsky, 1962; Hargreaves, 1968). Both the summary and the evaluation of a book-length research report will mirror the complexity of the book – for example, it is often advisable to evaluate the chapters separately, as each chapter may deal with a separate set of results.

The problem of studies which use relatively advanced statistical techniques (multiple regression, analysis of variance, and so on) can now be considered. Since such research is (obviously) based on quantitative data, the central question is whether the procedures given in Chapter 6 are applicable. Let us consider this problem. In the first place, a study of this kind can, in common with other research based on quantitative data, be characterised according to the various factors discussed in Chapters 1–6; thus we may pick out sampling, units, concept-indicator links, the extent to which it is theory-testing or building, and so on. The use of

advanced statistical techniques[2] does not make it any less important to analyse the basic components of the research process; of
the factors discussed in Chapters 1–6, only one is 'different' in any
sense, and that is *data analysis*. Thus, in applying the ABCDE
model to such a study, we need only recognise that stage E will be
more complex than in the reports used as examples in this book. In
short, provided the evaluator has an understanding of the relevant
statistical technique, the approach developed in Chapters 1–6 will
be applicable; the strengths and weaknesses of the author's
statistical analysis will be assessed as part of *internal empirical
validity*.

To take a well-known example, Blau and Duncan's study *The
American Occupational Structure* (1967) uses a nationally representative sample in the USA, the unit is the individual male adult
and the main variables are indicators of educational and occupational attainment. Certain problematic aspects of the operationalisation of this study can be identified quite easily; for example,
there is quite a high degree of unreliability in the placing of both
respondents and their fathers in occupational groups (1967: 15)
and surprisingly little is said elsewhere in the book about the
implications of this. Blau and Duncan's theorising is quite complex, but clearly involves elements of both theory-testing and
theory-construction. This is not the place to discuss Blau and
Duncan's research in detail, but these few points do demonstrate
that the approach can be fruitfully applied, even though so far any
consideration of the data analysis has been left aside. Naturally, to
pursue the deciphering of this study to its logical conclusion, it
would be necessary to understand the multivariate statistical
techniques which are used in the data analysis, notably path
analysis. The point to stress, however, is that the use of relatively
complex statistical techniques is not the *only* problem for the
evaluator of *The American Occupational Structure,* nor is it
necessarily the most significant or problematic aspect of the
research methods used in this study.

None of the factors considered so far constitutes a limitation on
the use of the deciphering approach. My experience is that the
methods for evaluation of research reports are generally applicable, irrespective of the level of statistical sophistication, the
length or complexity of the report, or its publication date. In
practice, the biggest obstacle is lack of information in the report;

where this occurs, it can be highlighted in the evaluation, but it may nevertheless prevent a thorough analysis of some aspects of the study. One of the criteria for the selection of the twelve studies in Part Two, the five summarised in Chapter 22 and the fourteen listed in the references was that the reports should be clearly presented and that most of the essential information should be included. In the sociological literature generally we should therefore expect to find many research reports which are less clearly expressed than those analysed in this book. There is no solution to problems such as this, but the deciphering approach can at least highlight the existence of deficiences of this kind in any given report.

One vitally important question remains to be answered. Are the procedures applicable to sociological research of all kinds, or are there some styles of research which cannot be deciphered by using the approach developed in this book? Let us reconsider the logic which underlies the procedures. In both cases (quantitative data and qualitative data) it is assumed that the research report is based on empirical evidence, and that a link is made with theory – or with other kinds of conclusions which usually have some theoretical basis. The analysis of such theory–evidence links are at the heart of the deciphering approach. I shall make two assertions: first, the procedures for deciphering a report can be applied profitably to all studies in which the theory–evidence link is construed in this way; second, that the vast majority of research reports are, in fact, consistent with this broad definition. These assertions are based mainly on my experience in applying the procedures to a wide range of research reports, but they can also be substantiated by considering some of the writing on social theory.

Mullins (1973) distinguishes eight different 'theory groups' in sociology as follows:[3] standard American sociology (more conventionally termed 'structural-functionalism'), symbolic interactionist, small-group theory, social forecasters, new causal theory, structuralist, radical-critical (including Marxist), and ethnomethodology. While this is not the place for a detailed analysis either of Mullins's work or of the research implications of each group, I am fairly confident that within each of the first seven of these groups, researchers generally construe the relationship between theory and evidence in the way I have outlined above; empirical research is therefore carried out in such a way that reports can be deciphered successfully. The last group, ethnomethodology, is a possible exception. In some cases research carried out by ethno-methodologists can be deciphered to some extent (for example, Garfinkel, 1967: ch. 2) but in others the procedures do not seem to be applicable (for example, Mackay, 1973). It is not possible to give a thorough analysis of ethnomethodological research within the confines of this book but the crux of the matter appears to be that the ethnomethodologist's conception of theory is at variance with the account given in Chapter 3. More precisely, the eth-nomethodologist eschews the deductive concept of explanation (Wilson, 1970); the nature of the theory–evidence link is therefore different, and different procedures would be needed to decipher most ethnomethodological research.

Let us return now to the main theme, which is the relationship between 'schools of social theory' or 'theory groups' and styles of empirical research. There are several further points to be made. It is quite clear that the different theory groups have different research traditions; thus 'symbolic interactionists' favour field-work and qualitative data, 'small-group theorists' often use experi-ments, and 'new causal theorists' rely heavily on large-scale social survey data. However, each of these approaches will lead to research reports which are amenable to deciphering. And, although many Marxists might dispute the claim, empirical re-search carried out by sociologists in the 'radical-critical' group can also be deciphered satisfactorily (for example, Wright and Peron-ne, 1977; Westergaard and Resler, 1975). Perhaps, as Mann (1981) asserts, "there is only one sociological methodology . . . [which he has] chosen to call the *socio-logic chain*". Mann's socio-logic chain is in fact a model for the theory-evidence relationship as it is used by the sociologist in the research process; he argues that all researchers act "*as if* they could apprehend and describe reality through the process of operationalization and *as if* they could rely on absolute standards of scientific proof for their results to be evaluated. Indeed the only choice is not to do research". From this position, the supposed strong relationship of epistemology to research practice is something of a myth.

To pursue this topic further here would be fruitless, and I must leave this contentious issue to those who are better equipped to analyse the connections between epistemological assumptions and empirical research. However, it is relevant to restate that, with the exception of certain kinds of ethnomethodological research, I have found the deciphering approach generally applicable to research reports within all 'schools of social theory'; counter-examples would, of course, modify my current views on this point.

Finally, it must be stressed again that in the analysis above I have confined my attention to research based on empirical evidence. Are the procedures for deciphering useful for the reader of a theoretical treatise such as (say) Talcott Parsons's *The Social System* or Anthony Giddens's *The Class Structure of the Advanced Societies*? To consider this question, we must first recognise that most theoretical work in sociology tries to take account of evidence, even though this may be done in a relatively informal manner; the author has not collected and handled basic data but has instead considered secondary data in a selective fashion. Thus we should often expect to find problems with the evidence which is used – for example, quality, availability and selectivity – but one would need to be an expert in the specific area (say, class relations during the last 150 years) to tease out these **problems**. Procedures for deciphering cannot be applied in any simple sense, therefore, to theoretical work in sociology. It is, however, true to say that a sensitivity to the methodological issues covered in this book may nevertheless be helpful in evaluating many aspects of a theorist's argument.

EXERCISES

9.1 Compare the account of research methods given in this book with any other source. You may find it helpful to focus on one or more of the following topics: a comparison with the other approaches to analysing research reports listed in Table 9.1 or in Shipman (1972); an assessment of the methodological lessons to be learned from the personal reflections of researchers on their experience; a comparison of the coverage of key topics (e.g. concept-indicator links, sampling) in this book and in any 'standard' textbook.

9.2 Decipher any research report with one or more of the following characteristics: (a) of book length; (b) involving 'advanced' statistical techniques; (c) written from a particular theoretical perspective.

Part Two

Research Reports

Introduction

The research reports (or studies) reprinted in Part Two act as examples for the analysis given in Part One, and provide further exercises for the reader. The rationale for the selection of the twelve studies which comprise Chapters 10 to 21 has been explained in the introduction to Part One, but the main factors will be mentioned again here. The reports deal with topics within several major substantive areas of sociology – mainly education, stratification and deviance; they do not, however, require much previous knowledge of these areas, and exposure to an introductory sociology course should be sufficient. Since only simple quantitative methods are used, the reader requires only an elementary knowledge of descriptive statistics. As a whole, the studies illustrate a range of different research methods; in each case the empirical procedures used have been explained reasonably clearly by the author(s). Each report was originally published as an article in a major sociology journal; two were published in the 1950s, six in the 1960s and four in the 1970s. Five additional studies are summarised in Chapter 22, the purpose of which is to provide additional examples for certain aspects of research method discussed in Part One.

The selection of the studies has been more difficult than it may appear. In combination the criteria above rule out the majority of research reports; although, as I argue in Chapter 9, virtually all reports *can* be deciphered by the procedures developed in Part One, only a small proportion are suitable for use as examples in a book intended to demonstrate the approach. In addition to the factors already mentioned it was a requirement that each of the twelve reports be presented in such a way that it could be edited to a shortened version but still provide a thorough account of the research.

Editing

In order to make maximum use of the space available in this book, each article has been edited. The versions reprinted here, which have been approved in this form by the authors, are on average 60 to 65 per cent the length of the original article. The main features of the editing procedure are as follows:

Details *included* are: the origins and purpose of the research, explanations of the conduct of the study, results (except for certain sections deleted for reasons of length), conclusions, and other material necessary for an understanding of the author's arguments linking evidence to theory. The material generally *excluded* is: footnotes and other details in the text referring to other studies, material peripheral to the main argument, and selected sections from the results (usually the less important sections). Although these were the main guidelines, an editing decision occasionally depended on other criteria. All major exclusions have been noted by brief editorial comments. Each edited version is intended to be as self-contained as the original article, so that all aspects of the research methods used can be analysed.

The following conventions have been used:

(1) *Footnotes and references,* as mentioned above, have been deleted unless they contain information necessary for the under-standing of the study; essential information in footnotes has been incorporated in the text. References retained are cited in the text as (say) 'Smith, 1962: 25–30'; and the full references are given in the list at the end of this book.

(2) *Editing of text*
[ ] denotes editorial comment. Where a substantial section of text has been omitted it is replaced by a paragraph or short passage in square brackets. Further editorial comments have been in-cluded where necessary for clarity of presentation. A few minor changes have been made without enclosure in square brackets; these result mainly from the inclusion of footnotes into the main text.

. . . denotes the omission of a section of text without editorial comment.

Double quotation marks have been used throughout Part Two; within *editorial comments,* material in quotation marks is taken from the original research report.

There has been no attempt to impose uniformity of presentation (apart from the requirements of printing) since clearly it is of fundamental importance that a variety of styles of research reporting be represented here.

(3) *Tables and figures* which are relevant to the edited version are, of course, included. In common with Part One, table numbers are given in decimal notation, but otherwise tables have *not* been renumbered. For example, table 2 in Dornbusch and Hickman's study is included as Table 10.2 in Chapter 10; their first table has been omitted from the edited version and is referred to simply as table 1 in an editorial comment. Consequently, Table 10.1 is non-existent in this book, and there are several chapters in which certain table numbers are 'missing'. However, I have preferred this system to that of renumbering tables, which would have resulted in more confusion. There has been very little editing of the content and layout of tables; in a few cases explanatory notes have been edited or added.

10

Other-directedness in Consumer-goods Advertising: A Test of Riesman's Historical Theory*

SANFORD M. DORNBUSCH AND LOREN C. HICKMAN

. . . In this paper an attempt will be made to formulate and test the historical trend toward other-directedness in American life posited in the work of David Riesman (Riesman *et al.*, 1950).

Although there are empirical studies applying Riesman's conceptual scheme to contemporary American society, the authors know of no research on the historical aspects of his work. He assumes, with considerable illustrative material, a general trend in recent years away from a character structure based on internalized goals towards a social character emphasizing throughout life the guiding reactions of others. Since we cannot query the dead, it is obviously necessary to use an indirect set of data which can be assumed to bear some relationship to the hypothesized shift.

THE UNIVERSE UNDER ANALYSIS

A basic assumption of this research is the belief that a shift in the verbal themes of consumer-goods advertising is likely to reflect a

*Reprinted in part from *Social Forces*, **38** (December 1959) "Other-directedness in consumer-goods advertising: a test of Riesman's historical theory" by Sanford M. Dornbusch and Loren C. Hickman. Copyright © The University of North Carolina Press 1959.

corresponding change in the values of the audience for that advertising. Riesman himself makes more than twenty separate references to such advertising. The advertising in one magazine with a long period of uninterrupted publication was selected for analysis. All issues of the *Ladies' Home Journal* from 1890 to 1956 constituted the universe to be sampled. This magazine was chosen because it is essentially middle class in its orientation (Riesman claims that it is the middle-class character which is in transition), and is directed solely at women. More than most journals, there appears to be stability in the type of readers, but it is obviously impossible to control the influences of changes in readership upon the themes to be analyzed. In our opinion, the findings reported below are of such magnitude that it is unlikely they are in any large measure a product of this uncontrolled variable.

THE SAMPLE

There were a total of 816 issues of the *Ladies' Home Journal* during this 67-year period. The sample of issues to be analyzed was drawn in the following manner. Each issue was assigned a number. By means of a table of random number, one issue from each year was selected for possible inclusion. The order in which the issues were to be analyzed was also assigned through a table of random numbers. Limitations of time and money permitted the analysis of issues from only 41 years. In the order of coding, the sample included one issue from each of the following years: 1926, 1920, 1902, 1908, 1922, 1917, 1953, 1950, 1914, 1899, 1932, 1939, 1954, 1903, 1952, 1909, 1890, 1897, 1907, 1936, 1931, 1940, 1894, 1910, 1929, 1927, 1912, 1943, 1924, 1915, 1895, 1891, 1944, 1893, 1921, 1941, 1900, 1896, 1951, 1923, 1946. This is a 5 per cent sample of the total population.

It is important to note that the random assignment of the order in which these magazines were to be read effectively prevents changes in the perspective of the content analysts from producing shifts in the amount of other-directedness found in advertising. The trends noted below are not a function of changing standards of content-analysis procedure.

INDICES OF OTHER-DIRECTEDNESS

No indices of inner-directedness are employed in this study. Rather, the proportion of advertisements with some form of other-directed appeal is the basic measure. The hypothesis is that the proportion of other-directed advertisements will increase through time. The single advertisement is accordingly the basic unit . . .

Six indices of other-directedness were used. They fall logically into two types: endorsements by persons or groups, and claims that use of a product is related to satisfactions in interpersonal relations.

Endorsements

1. Testimonials ("Billie Burke wears Minerva Sweaters.")
2. Collective endorsements ("Housewives like the Singer Sewing Machine.")
3. Quantitative endorsements ("25 million men use Star blades".)

Interpersonal satisfaction

4. Positive interpersonal ("He'll like you better if you use Revlon.")
5. Negative interpersonal ("Her perspiration drove her friends away. She should have used Mum.")
6. Both positive and negative interpersonal ("Jim lost his girl because poor breakfast foods gave him no pep. After eating Wheaties, he's won her back.")

These indices obviously bear only an indirect relationship to other-directedness as perceived by Riesman. They do have the advantage, however, of being sufficiently explicit to permit inter-subjective reliability among coders. Indices 4, 5, and 6 are mutually exclusive, but more than one appeal per advertisement may be recorded among indices 1, 2, and 3. When combined into groups of indices, advertisements are simply viewed as containing an other-directed appeal or having no such appeal, thus eliminating any possible bias due to the coding of several appeals in a single advertisement.

[An omitted section presents evidence showing a high degree of reliability in the coding of the six indices. Table 1 (omitted) compares the results of two different coders analyzing the same test sample of advertisements. Reliability coefficients based on a second test sample are given in the text.]

SUMMARY OF FINDINGS

The null hypothesis to be tested states, for each index and combination of indices, that the proportion of other-directed advertisements is the same in issues published up to 1921 and in issues appearing after that date. The year 1921 is the midpoint of our sample, therefore representing the best arbitrary cutting point. The Chi square test, a nonparametric measure, is then used as the basic statistical tool. Eight separate analyses were undertaken: one for each of the six indices, one for the use of any endorsement device, and one for the use of any interpersonal appeal.

The results of this statistical analysis can be briefly stated. In each of the eight tests, the null hypothesis is rejected at the 0.001 level. To the extent that the indices formulated here reflect the position of Riesman, the results of these statistical tests lend empirical support to his approach. When one compares the advertising of consumer goods in the period 1890 to 1921 with the themes of more recent advertisements, there has obviously been a marked change in orientation closely related to the sphere of other-directedness.

A somewhat different statistical approach is even more indicative of the magnitude of the shift towards other-directed appeals. Each issue is scored as either above or below the median of the sample for each of two measures, the use of any endorsement technique or any mention of interpersonal satisfactions. Dividing the issues into an older group, up to 1921, and a more recent set, the identical results appear for each of the two measures. Of the 21 oldest issues, 19 are below the median in other-directedness. Of the 20 more recent issues, 18 are above the median in other-directedness. The null hypothesis of no shift in other-directedness through time can again be rejected at the 0.001 level. Even more definitive, the 19 earliest issues are the 19 lowest in the use of the endorsement technique. For the interpersonal approach, there is only one advertisement using such an appeal in the first 19 issues in the sample.

There is one aspect of the findings which was not an object of our study design. As can be observed in Table 10.2, all indices except Index 1, the use of testimonials, show a sharp decline in other-directed themes from 1940 to 1956. No tests of statistical significance are appropriate here, since the choice of cutting point arose from inspection of the data. It is possible, however, to give one additional piece of evidence that indicates a decline in other-directedness since 1940, as measured by these indices. The

TABLE 10.2 *Percentage of other-directed advertisements in the Ladies' Home Journal by six indices*

		Endorsements*			
Decade	Number of advertise-ments	Index 1 (testi-monials)	Index 2 (collec-tive)	Index 3 (quanti-tative)	Indices 1, 2, 3 (any endorsement)
1890–9	1,697	2.8	3.0	1.6	6.6
1900–9	1,296	2.6	5.0	2.6	9.7
1910–19	1,138	1.6	4.8	4.0	9.8
1920–9	1,569	6.6	11.7	9.7	23.9
1930–9	502	6.8	12.4	9.2	21.5
1940–9	1,088	7.1	5.9	6.6	17.3
1950–6	1,102	6.6	6.4	7.0	15.7

		Interpersonal satisfaction*			
Decade	Number of advertise-ments	Index 4 (positive)	Index 5 (negative)	Index 6 (positive and negative	Indices 4, 5, 6 (any inter-personal appeal)
1890–9	1,697	0	0	0	0
1900–9	1,296	0.1	0	0	0.1
1910–19	1,138	0	0	0	0
1920–9	1,569	0.6	0.4	0	1.0
1930–9	502	1.8	1.0	1.0	3.8
1940–9	1,088	0.7	0.3	0.5	1.5
1950–6	1,102	0.3	0.2	0.2	0.7

[*Figures should be read as follows: of the 1,697 advertisements analysed from the period 1890–9, 2.8 per cent contained testimonials, 3.0 per cent contained collective endorsements, and so on.]

peak of other-directed appeals is found for each of the six indices, respectively, in 1932, 1932, 1926, 1936, 1936, and 1936. This is certainly contradictory to the expectations of a continual increase in other-directedness in recent years.

DISCUSSION

We have found a dramatic shift in advertising themes in the *Ladies' Home Journal,* beginning about 1920. The direction of change is harmonious with the general orientation of Riesman and his associates, thus lending some empirical support to their position. It should be emphasized that the field of consumer-goods advertising is far removed from the central core of American values, and our findings should not be generalized beyond this consumption area. For ourselves, we must confess that our initial skepticism about the usefulness of Riesman's approach has been replaced by the view that it is testable, important, and has some predictive power.

The decline in other-directedness after 1940 which is indicated by our measures cannot be appropriately evaluated in the light of this first set of data. One view assumes the reality of the peak in the 1920s and 1930s, associating it with (a) the breakdown of fixed standards when the depression overthrew faith in the American economic system, and (b) the rise of feminism after World War I and woman's corresponding search for new values. A different interpretation relates the decline to increased subtlety of advertisers. Our measures are based on explicit statements by advertisers, partly because of our concern that reliability be high. Riesman comments:

> Even though the social-class level of readers of the *Ladies' Home Journal* may not have risen, I would suspect that the educational level has risen considerably . . . The ads and the articles, if not always the fiction, have gained in sophistication as the readership has gained in education and cosmopolitanism . . . Is there more use now of polite implication rather than direct premise or direct threat? (personal communications, 9 April and 11 April 1957)

By this interpretation, the recent decline is a function of research technique rather than changes in the level of other-directedness in advertising. Only further research using different indices can answer this question.

11

Becoming a Marijuana User*

HOWARD S. BECKER

The use of marijuana is and has been the focus of a good deal of attention on the part of both scientists and laymen. One of the major problems students of the practice have addressed themselves to has been the identification of those individual psychological traits which differentiate marijuana users from nonusers and which are assumed to account for the use of the drug. That approach, common in the study of behavior categorized as deviant, is based on the premise that the presence of a given kind of behavior in an individual can best be explained as the result of some trait which predisposes or motivates him to engage in the behavior.

This study is likewise concerned with accounting for the presence or absence of marijuana use in an individual's behavior. It starts, however, from a different premise: that the presence of a given kind of behavior is the result of a sequence of social experiences during which the person acquires a conception of the meaning and behavior, and perceptions and judgements of objects and situations, all of which make the activity possible and desirable. Thus, the motivation or disposition to engage in the activity is build up in the course of learning to engage in it and does not antedate this learning process. For such a view it is not necessary to identify those "traits" which "cause" the behavior. Instead, the problem becomes one of describing the set of changes in the

*Reprinted in part from Howard S. Becker (1953) "Becoming a marihuana user", *American Journal of Sociology,* **59**: 235–42, with the permission of the publishers and the author. © University of Chicago Press 1953.

person's conception of the activity and of the experience it provides for him (Mead, 1934: 277–80).

This paper seeks to describe the sequence of changes in attitude and experience which leads to *the use of marijuana for pleasure*. Marijuana does not produce addiction, as do alcohol and the opiate drugs; there is no withdrawal sickness and no ineradicable craving for the drug. The most frequent pattern of use might be termed "recreational". The drug is used occasionally for the pleasure the user finds in it, a relatively casual kind of behavior in comparison with that connected with the use of addicting drugs. The term "use for pleasure" is meant to emphasize the non-compulsive and casual character of the behavior. It is also meant to eliminate from consideration here those few cases in which marijuana is used for its prestige value only, as a symbol that one is a certain kind of person, with no pleasure at all being derived from its use.

The analysis presented here is conceived of as demonstrating the greater explanatory usefulness of the kind of theory outlined above as opposed to the predispositional theories now current. This may be seen in two ways: (1) predispositional theories cannot account for that group of users (whose existence is admitted) who do not exhibit the trait or traits considered to cause the behavior; and (2) such theories cannot account for the great variability over time of a given individual's behavior with reference to the drug. The same person will at one stage be unable to use the drug for pleasure, at a later stage be able and willing to do so, and still later, again be unable to use it in this way. These changes, difficult to explain from a predispositional or motivational theory, are readily understandable in terms of changes in the individual's conception of the drug as is the existence of "normal" users.

The study attempted to arrive at a general statement of the sequence of changes in individual attitude and experience which have always occurred when the individual has become willing and able to use marijuana for pleasure and which have not occurred or not been permanently maintained when this not the case. This generalization is stated in universal terms in order that negative cases may be discovered and used to revise the explanatory hypothesis. [In a revised version of this article, Becker (1963: 45) points out that this is the method of *analytic induction;* see Chapters 7 and 8, and also Lindesmith, 1947 and Turner, 1953.]

Fifty interviews with marijuana users from a variety of social backgrounds and present positions in society constitute the data from which the generalization was constructed and against which it was tested. [Becker had been a professional dance musician for several years and half his sample were musicians. The other half covered people from a range of occupations. Most of the interviews were undertaken by the author, but a few interviews done by two other researchers were also used. Becker acknowledges that the sample is in no sense random; a random sample would be impossible since "no one knows the nature of the universe from which it would have to be drawn" (Becker, 1963: 45–6).] The interviews focused on the history of the person's experience with the drug, seeking major changes in his attitude toward it and in his actual use of it and the reasons for these changes. The final generalization is a statement of that sequence of changes in attitude which occurred in every case known to me in which the person came to use marijuana for pleasure. Until a negative case is found, it may be considered as an explanation of all cases of marijuana use for pleasure. In addition, changes from use to nonuse are shown to be related to similar changes in conception, and in each case it is possible to explain variations in the individual's behavior in these terms.

This paper covers only a portion of the natural history of an individual's use of marijuana, starting with the person having arrived at the point of willingness to try marijuana. He knows that others use it to "get high", but he does not know what this means in concrete terms. He is curious about the experience, ignorant of what it may turn out to be, and afraid that it may be more than he has bargained for. The steps outlined below, if he undergoes them all and maintains the attitudes developed in them, leave him willing and able to use the drug for pleasure when the opportunity presents itself.

LEARNING THE TECHNIQUE

The novice does not ordinarily get high the first time he smokes marijuana, and several attempts are usually necessary to induce this state. One explanation of this may be that the drug is not smoked "properly", that is, in a way that insures sufficient dosage to produce real symptoms of intoxication. Most users agree that it cannot be smoked like tobacco if one is to get high:

> Take in a lot of air, you know, and . . . I don't know how to
> describe it, you don't smoke it like a cigarette, you draw in a lot
> of air and get it deep down in your system and then keep it
> there. Keep it there as long as you can.

Without the use of some such technique [Becker quotes a
pharmacologist – the technique is an efficient way to get the drug
into the blood stream] the drug will then produce no effects, and
the user will be unable to get high:

> The trouble with people like that (who are not able to get high)
> is that they're just not smoking it right, that's all there is to it.

If nothing happens, it is manifestly impossible for the user to
develop a conception of the drug as an object which can be used
for pleasure, and use will therefore not continue. The first step in
the sequence of events that must occur if the person is to become a
user is that he must learn to use the proper smoking technique in
order that his use of the drug will produce some effects in terms of
which his conception of it can change.

Such a change is, as might be expected, a result of the
individual's participation in groups in which marijuana is used. In
them the individual learns the proper way to smoke the drug. This
may occur through direct teaching:

> I was smoking like I did an ordinary cigarette. He said, "No,
> don't do it like that." He said, "Suck it, you know, draw in and
> hold it in your lungs till you . . . for a period of time." I said, "Is
> there any limit of time to hold it?" He said, "No, just till you
> feel that you want to let it out, let it out." So I did that three or
> four times.

Many new users are ashamed to admit ignorance and, pretending
to know already, must learn through the more indirect means of
observation and imitation:

> I came on like I had turned on (smoked marijuana) many times
> before, you know . . . [although] . . . I didn't know the first

thing about it . . . I watched how he held it, how he smoked it, and everything. Then when he gave it to me I just came on cool, as though I knew exactly what the score was. I held it like he did and took a poke just the way he did.

No person continued marijuana use for pleasure without learning a technique that supplied sufficient dosage for the effects of the drug to appear. Only when this was learned was it possible for a conception of the drug as an object which could be used for pleasure to emerge. Without such a conception marijuana use was considered meaningless and did not continue.

LEARNING TO PERCEIVE THE EFFECTS

Even after he learns the proper smoking technique, the new user may not get high and thus not form a conception of the drug as something which can be used for pleasure. A remark made by a user suggested the reason for this difficulty in getting high and pointed to the next necessary step on the road to being a user:

As a matter of fact, I've seen a guy who was high out of his mind and didn't know it. ("How can that be, man?") Well, it's pretty strange, I'll grant you that, but I've seen it. This guy got on with me, claiming that he'd never got high, one of those guys, and he got completely stoned. And he kept insisting that he wasn't high. So I had to prove to him that he was.

What does this mean? It suggests that being high consists of two elements: the presence of symptoms caused by marijuana use and the recognition of these symptoms and their connection by the user with his use of the drug . . . [If the user does not make this connection] . . . he considers that the drug has had no effect on him: "I figured it either had no effect on me or other people were exaggerating its effect on them, you know. I thought it was probably psychological, see." Such persons believe that the whole thing is an illusion and that the wish to be high leads the user to deceive himself into believing that something is happening when, in fact, nothing is. They do not continue marijuana use, feeling that "it does nothing" for them.

Typically, however, the novice has faith (developed from his observation of users who do get high) that the drug actually will produce some new experience and continues to experiment with it until it does. His failure to get high worries him, and he is likely to ask more experienced users or provoke comments from them about it. In such conversations he is made aware of specific details of his experience which he may not have noticed or may have noticed but failed to identify as symptoms of being high:

> I didn't get high the first time . . . I don't think I held it in long enough. I probably let it out, you know, you're a little afraid. The second time I wasn't sure, and he (smoking companion) told me, like I asked him for some of the symptoms or something, how would I know, you know . . . So he told me to sit on a stool. I sat on – I think I sat on a bar stool – and he said, "Let your feet hang", and then when I got down my feet were real cold, you know. And I started feeling it, you know. That was the first time. And then about a week after that, sometime pretty close to it, I really got on. That was the first time I got on a big laughing kick, you know. Then I really knew I was on.

[Omitted is an account of other symptoms of being high and the importance of learning the awareness of symptoms from others. Three quotations from interviews are given.]

It is only when the novice becomes able to get high in this sense that he will continue to use marijuana for pleasure. In every case in which use continued, the user had acquired the necessary concepts with which to express to himself the fact that he was experiencing new sensations caused by the drug. That is, for use to continue, it is necessary not only to use the drug so as to produce effects but also to learn to perceive these effects when they occur. In this way marijuana acquires meaning for the user as an object which can be used for pleasure.

With increasing experience the user develops a greater appreciation of the drug's effects; he continues to learn to get high. He examines succeeding experiences closely, looking for new effects, making sure the old ones are still there. Out of this there grows a stable set of categories for experiencing the drug's effects whose presence enables the user to get high with ease.

The ability to perceive the drug's effects must be maintained if use is to continue; if it is lost, marijuana use ceases . . .

LEARNING TO ENJOY THE EFFECTS

One more step is necessary if the user who has now learned to get high is to continue use. He must learn to enjoy the effects he has just learned to experience. Marijuana-produced sensations are not automatically or necessarily pleasurable. The taste for such experience is a socially acquired one, not different in kind from acquired tastes for oysters or dry martinis. The user feels dizzy, thirsty; his scalp tingles; he misjudges time and distances; and so on. Are these things pleasurable? He isn't sure. If he is to continue marijuana use, he must decide that they are. Otherwise, getting high, while a real enough experience, will be an unpleasant one he would rather avoid.

The effects of the drug, when first perceived, may be physically unpleasant or at least ambiguous:

> It started taking effect, and I didn't know what was happening, you know, what it was, and I was sick. I walked around the room, walking around the room trying to get off, you know; it just scared me at first, you know. I wasn't used to that kind of feeling.

In addition, the novice's naive interpretation of what is happening to him may further confuse and frighten him, particularly if he decides, as many do, that he is going insane:

> I felt I was insane, you know. Everything people done to me just wigged me. I couldn't hold a conversation, and my mind would be wandering, and I was always thinking, oh, I don't know, weird things, like hearing music different . . . I get the **feeling that I can't talk to anyone. I'll goof completely.**

Given these typically frightening and unpleasant first experiences, the beginner will not continue use unless he learns to redefine the sensations as pleasurable:

> It was offered to me, and I tried it. I'll tell you one thing. I never did enjoy it at all. I mean it was just nothing that I could enjoy. (Well, did you get high when you turned on?) Oh, yeah, I got definite feelings from it. But I didn't enjoy them. I mean I

got plenty of reactions, but they were mostly reactions of fear. (You were frightened?) Yes. I didn't enjoy it. I couldn't seem to relax with it, you know. If you can't relax with a thing, you can't enjoy it, I don't think.

In other cases the first experiences were also definitely unpleasant, but the person did become a marijuana user. This occurred, however, only after a later experience enabled him to redefine the sensations as pleasurable.

(This man's first experience was extremely unpleasant, involving distortion of spatial relationships and sounds, violent thirst, and panic produced by these symptoms.) After the first time I didn't turn on for about, I'd say, ten months to a year . . . It wasn't a moral thing; it was because I'd gotten so frightened, bein' so high. An' I didn't want to go through that again, I mean, my reaction was, "Well, if this is what they call bein' high, I don't dig (like) it." . . . So I didn't turn on for a year almost, accounta that . . .
  Well, my friends started, an' consequently I started again. But I didn't have any more, I didn't have that same initial reaction, after I started turning on again. (In interaction with his friends he became able to find pleasure in the effects of the drug and eventually became a regular user.)

In no case will use continue without such a redefinition of the effects as enjoyable.

This redefinition occurs, typically, in interaction with more experienced users who, in a number of ways, teach the novice to find pleasure in this experience which is at first so frightening. They may reassure him as to the temporary character of the unpleasant sensations and minimize their seriousness, at the same time calling attention to the more enjoyable aspects. . .

[Becker discusses other situations in which effects may be defined (or redefined) as enjoyable. Two interview extracts are given which illustrate how the experienced user may teach the novice to regulate the amount he smokes more carefully, and to regard ambiguous or frightening experiences as pleasurable. Becker also stresses that favourable definition is "an important condition for continued use. It is quite common for experienced users

suddenly to have an unpleasant or frightening experience . . .
because they have used a larger amount of marijuana than usual or
because it turns out to be higher quality." He then discusses the
circumstances under which a user may stop using marijuana for a
substantial period, due to such disturbing experiences, and gives
an extensive quotation from one interviewee who stopped for
three years but then resumed.]

A person, then, cannot begin to use marijuana for pleasure, or
continue its use for pleasure, unless he learns to define its effects
as enjoyable, unless it becomes and remains an object which he
conceives of as capable of producing pleasure . . .

In summary, an individual will be able to use marijuana for
pleasure only when he goes through a process of learning to
conceive of it as an object which can be used in this way. No one
becomes a user without (1) learning to smoke the drug in a way
which will produce real effects; (2) learning to recognize the
effects and connect them with drug use (learning, in other
words, to get high); and (3) learning to enjoy the sensations he
perceives. In the course of this process he develops a disposition or
movitation to use marijuana which was not and could not have
been present when he began use, for it involves and depends on
conceptions of the drug which could only grow out of the kind of
actual experience detailed above. On completion of this process he
is willing and able to use marijuana for pleasure.

He has learned, in short, to answer "Yes" to the question: "Is it
fun?" The direction his further use of the drug takes depends on
his being able to continue to answer "Yes" to this question and, in
addition, on his being able to answer "Yes" to other questions
which arise as he becomes aware of the implications of the fact that
society as a whole disapproves of the practice: "Is it expe-
dient?" "Is it moral?". . .

In comparing this theory with those which ascribe marijuana use
to motives or predispositions rooted deep in individual behavior,
the evidence makes it clear that marijuana use for pleasure can
occur only when the process described above is undergone and
cannot occur without it. This is apparently so without reference to
the nature of the individual's personal makeup or psychic
problems. . . This analysis of the genesis of marijuana use shows
that the individuals who come in contact with a given object may
respond to it at first in a great variety of ways. If a stable form of

new behavior toward the object is to emerge, a transformation of meanings must occur, in which the person develops a new conception of the nature of the object . . . This suggests that behavior of any kind might fruitfully be studied developmentally, in terms of changes in meanings and concepts, their organization and reorganization, and the way they channel behavior, making some acts possible while excluding others.

12

Social Roles and Processes of Socialization in the Prison Community*

PETER G. GARABEDIAN

Studies of socialization in prison communities have utilized two temporal frames of reference within which to describe and interpret changes that occur on the part of inmates as they move through institutions. First, the usual method of treating the time variable has been to consider length of exposure to the new situation or length of time served in prison. This framework was used by Clemmer in his early study where he observed that most inmates, upon commitment, gradually assimilated aspects of the prison culture. He called this assimilation the process of *prisonization* which refers to "the taking on in greater or less degree of the folkways, mores, customs, and general culture of the penitentiary" (Clemmer, 1958: 299). The emphasis on duration of exposure to prison and its culture led Clemmer to hypothesize a direct relationship between prisonization and length of time served.

A second and more recent temporal context considers not only length of time served, but also length of time *remaining* to be served. This approach is rooted in reference group theory and emphasizes such concepts as anticipatory socialization. This is the frame of reference employed by Wheeler (1961) in his . . . study of a state reformatory. Wheeler classified inmates according to phases of the institutional career in which they were located. That is, inmates were identified as being in the early, middle, or late

* Reprinted in part from Peter G. Garabedian (1963) "Social roles and processes of socialization in the prison community", *Social Problems,* 11:139–52, with the permission of the publishers (the Society for the Study of Social Problems) and the author.

phases of their institutional confinement, and the degree to which they conformed to staff norms was determined. Two prominent trends of socialization were found to exist. The first was similar to the prisonization trend observed by Clemmer in that there was a progressive opposition to staff norms with each career phase (it is not identical with Clemmer's prisonization, because adoption of the prison culture does not necessarily involve movement away from staff norms). Second, an *adaptive* U-shaped pattern of response was observed. Inmates located in the early and late periods of incarceration conformed to staff opinion while those in the middle career phase deviated (Wheeler, 1961: 706).

Taken together the two socialization trends observed by Clemmer and Wheeler suggest that inmate norms as well as other social and cultural elements in prison not only exert a differential impact on inmates, but the point of heaviest impact also varies. For some inmates their impact is greatest during the late phase, but for others it is during the middle period of confinement. At this point a number of questions arise. Which inmates are socialized according to the pattern of prisonization and which follow the pattern of adaptation? Where are these inmates located in the informal social structure? What social processes might be responsible for the emergence of these two patterns? Are prisonization and adaptation the only two patterns of socialization? The present study reports findings that bear on these questions. Specifically, the empirical evidence to be presented support Wheeler's recent findings regarding the adaptive trend and shows that at least four alternative patterns of socialization may be discerned when aspects of inmate social structure are taken into account.

METHODS AND RESULTS: THE ADAPTIVE PATTERN

The data to be reported were collected from a maximum custody prison in a Western state. At the time of the study there were approximately 1,700 convicted adult felons housed in the institution. To derive an index of socialization, a random sample of 380 inmates and 141 staff members were asked to evaluate a series of five contrived situations referring to life in prison. The five items are as follows:

1. Two inmates, who are planning an escape, ask one of their close friends, Brown, to distract the guard's attention so that they will have a chance to get out of his sight. Brown refuses, stating that he doesn't want anything to do with the plot.
2. Officer Green discovers that Officer Black is carrying contraband into the institution and is receiving pay from some of the inmates. Green immediately reports all of his information to his supervisor.

[Omitted: items 3–5, each in a format similar to the above.]

Both staff members and inmates were asked to state as to whether they approved, disapproved, or neither approved nor disapproved of the action taken in the five situations. Weights of two, one, and zero were assigned to the approve, neutral, and disapprove categories, respectively. The weights were summed over the five items, with possible scores ranging from zero to ten.

The distribution of scores for staff members was skewed in the direction of the upper end of the scale, indicating a high degree of normative consensus. Eighty per cent of the staff obtained scores of eight to ten, and 94 per cent received scores of six to ten. On the other hand, the inmate scores approached a rectangular distribution with a slight tendency for scores to cluster between three and five (40 per cent). Compared with the staff, inmates exhibited considerably less normative consensus with respect to the five hypothetical situations. In this study inmates are classified into two groups: those obtaining scores of six to ten (33 per cent) are defined as conformists, i.e. in normative agreement with staff, while those with lower scores are considered nonconformists. (The figure for inmates is based on an N of 345. From the original 380, there was a loss of 35 cases. The extent to which the findings to be presented were influenced by these 35 drop-outs is negligible.)

With the above information it was possible to determine the number and per cent of inmates conforming to staff norms at each of the three institutional career phases. The phases were operationalized in the following manner: inmates located in the early phase were those who had served less than six months on their sentences; those who had served more than six months but who had more than six months remaining to be served were defined as being located in the middle phase; inmates located in the late phase had less than six months remaining to be served. (The questionnaire included two items which made it possible to determine institutional career phase . . . The first, "How long have you been in the penitentiary on your present commitment", provided a measure of *time served,* while the second item, "How long do you have to serve until your good-time release date", provided a measure of *time remaining to be served.* The combining of reponses to these two items identified the career phase in which inmates were located at the time of the study.)

A tabulation of the number and per cent of inmate conformists to staff norms in each of these periods gives some suggestion of the process of socialization as conceptualized within the present temporal framework. The results of this tabulation, which are presented in Figure 12.1, suggest that the trend is a U-shaped or curvilinear one and provide additional support for the evidence reported by Wheeler in his [1961] study. Inmates located in the early phase of the institutional career are proportionately twice as likely to conform to staff norms as compared with inmates in the middle period. The trend suggests that there may be a steady absorption of the prison culture between these two phases which is similar to the process of prisonization, but that this process is reversed as the inmate comes to the end of his prison career.

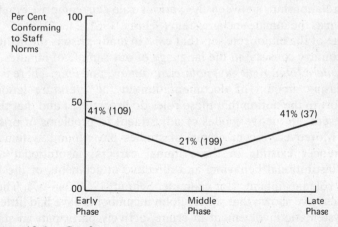

FIGURE 12.1 *Conformity to staff norms among inmates in the three career phases*

In fact, the data show that the per cent of conformists in this phase is identical to the per cent conforming at the early phase, suggesting a "recovery" or a shedding of some of the effects of the prison culture between the second and final stages of the career. This "recovery" may be due to the anticipation of relinquishing one's present status in favor of a new social position. The *adaptive* pattern of response observed in Figure 12.1 appears to be consistent with the notion that the prison culture has its greatest impact at a point where the inmate is furthest removed from the free community. However, firm empirical support of these data must await panel studies.

THE INMATE SOCIAL SYSTEM

Recent discussions of the inmate social system have stressed its problem-solving character by viewing prisoner roles as alternative patterns of adjustment to a variety of focal issues and deprivations imposed by maximum security prisons (for example, Schrag, 1961; Sykes, 1958). Many of these roles are recognized by staff and inmates alike and are frequently identified in terms of the prison argot . . . there are a variety of role sets in prison and each set is differentiated and integrated around a focal issue or issues. The interrelationships between the various role sets comprise what is known as the inmate social system (Schrag, 1961: 346–7).

One of the major role sets that exist in many prisons throughout the country consists, in the language of our sample of inmates, of the *square John, right guy, politician, outlaw,* and *ding.* There is an increasing amount of documentation in the literature lending support to the notion that these roles do in fact exist and that they represent alternative modes of adjustment to problems of prison life. Moreover, recent empirical studies have found systematic differences existing in the criminal careers, institutional and post-institutional behavior, and affective attachments of the various role incumbents (for example, Schrag, 1961: 346–57). These studies have shown that square John incumbents have had little or no systematic involvement in crime, actively participate in staff-sponsored treatment programs and have more than average contact with prison officials. Right guy incumbents, on the other hand, have been found to exhibit a rather extensive career in delinquency and crime, do not become involved in staff-sponsored treatment programs and are relatively isolated from staff contacts. Square Johns identify with conventional norms while right guys are committed to illegitimate standards. Both role types are similar, however, in that they are collectivity-oriented and thus tend to subordinate personal interests in favor of group goals.

Politicians tend to commit relatively sophisticated crimes which involve manipulating the victim by skill and wit. They become actively involved in staff-sponsored programs and have a wide range of contacts both with officials and inmates. Outlaws tend to commit crimes in which the victim is confronted with force. They are isolated from staff and inmate contacts primarily because of their preoccupation with violence and their generally disruptive behavior. Politicians and outlaws are affectively neutral with respect to group norms, but differences in cognitive knowledge of legitimate and illegitimate standards influence the manner in which the neutrality is expressed. Politicians possess a high degree of cognitive knowledge and thus shift their normative perspectives to meet the exigencies of the situation. Outlaws reject both staff and inmate norms outright with little thought or consideration of the consequences. Both types are self-oriented in that personal interests take precedence over group goals.

The term ding is used to identify inmates whose responses to focal issues and deprivations lack the consistency and reliability necessary to be assigned to one of the above roles. However, it is not unusual to find non-violent sex offenses in the backgrounds of dings, and although they tend to become involved in staff-sponsored religious programs they are nevertheless isolated from staff and inmate contacts.

In prison these roles are allocated on the basis of inmates informally observing and assessing the behaviors and verbalizations of a given inmate to a variety of real and contrived situations. The language system of inmates is used, as suggested above, to identify the role incumbent. As the process of allocation is accomplished, the role becomes a major component of the inmate's personality structure. It affects his personal orientation and in most cases attitudes toward self and others are modified or reinforced so as to be consistent with the incumbent's perception of the expectations of other inmates.

METHODS AND RESULTS: SOCIAL ROLES AND SOCIALIZATION

The method of identifying incumbents of the five roles described above consisted of the sample of inmates responding to a set of fifteen items included in the questionnaire. The items, which dealt with attitudes toward self, others and philosophy of life, are listed below.

1. You've got to have confidence in yourself if you're going to be successful.
2. I generally feel guilty whenever I do wrong.
3. "Might is right" and "every man for himself" are the main rules of living, regardless of what people say.
4. The biggest criminals are protected by society and rarely get to prison.
5. I worry a lot about unimportant matters.
6. There's a little larceny in everybody, if you're really honest about it.
7. The only criminals I really know are the ones here in the institution.
8. You have to take care of yourself because nobody else is going to take care of you.
9. Inmates can trust me to be honest and loyal with my dealings with them.
10. I am very nervous much of the time.
11. Who you know is more important than what you know, and brains are more important than brawn.
12. Most people try to be law-abiding and true.
13. It makes me sore to have people tell me what to do.
14. Police, judges, prosecutors, and politicians are just as crooked as most of the people they send to prison.
15. Most people are not very friendly toward me.

Each of the above items is assumed to reflect a component of the attitudinal organization of a given role type. Items 1, 6, and 11 are assumed to reflect some of the attitudes of politicians; items 2, 7, and 12 tap square John attitudes; items 3, 8, and 13 refer to outlaw attitudes; items 4, 9, and 14 tap right guy attitudes; and items 5, 10, and 15 are assumed to reflect ding attitudes. In short, for each of the role types there are three items designed to tap attitudes characteristic of a given type.

Inmates responded to the items by checking one of four response categories for each statement: strongly agree; agree; disagree; and strongly disagree. Weights of plus two; plus one; minus one; and minus two were assigned, respectively, to each of the above response categories. The weights for the five sets of three items were then algebraically summed for each inmate. Thus, a given inmate was represented by a set of five scores, with each score having a possible range of plus six to minus six and indicating his status on the five role types mentioned above.

Ideally, the occupant of a given role should endorse (strongly agree or agree) the three items designed to tap his attitudes, and should not endorse the remaining twelve items. That is, an inmate who has been assigned a given role in the prisoner society should exhibit a high positive score with respect to the items characterizing the role type and should exhibit low positive or negative scores on items characterizing the other role types. The highest positive score shown by an inmate on any one set of items determined his classification. (Inmates whose highest score on any of the five sets of items were three or less were not considered in the analysis; the problem of tied scores on two or more sets of items was handled by classifying the inmate in favor of the score which was furthest from the absolute mean of its distribution.) On this basis, an empirical typology was constructed classifying 251, or 73 per cent, of the inmate sample as incumbents of one of the five roles. Each of the 251 role types was then located according to career phase and the

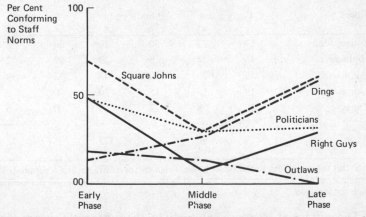

FIGURE 12.2 *Conformity to staff norms among role types in the three career phases*

number of conformists to staff norms tabulated. The results of this tabulation are presented in Table 12.1 and graphically portrayed in Figure 12.2.

Several observations can be made on the basis of the data reported above. First, not all inmates exhibit the adaptive pattern of response. However, by differentiating the sample according to role type, four distinct trends emerge. The patterns of response for square Johns and right guys appear to be *adaptive* or U-shaped; that is, both types are prisonized and "de-prisonized" as well, the trends being almost identical in form to the distribution of responses shown in Figure 12.1. For both role types the rate of absorption appears to be the same between the early and middle phases, and although the rate of "recovery" is somewhat slower for right guys, both types show definite signs of shedding some of the prisonization effects as measured by the index of conformity to staff norms. The major difference between the two types appears to be one of *degree* rather than *rate* of socialization. (This statement is made on the bais of the current data. It is quite likely, however, that had a large number of observations been made on a panel of inmates over time, square Johns and right guys might exhibit differing rates of socialization.)

TABLE 12.1   *Conformity to staff norms among role types in the three career phases*

Role type	Early phase		Middle phase		Late phase	
	%	n*	%	n	%	n
Square Johns	67	12	30	20	60	5
Right guys	46	24	8	39	29	7
Politicians	46	26	30	43	33	9
Outlaws	19	16	15	20	0	2
Dings	12	8	22	9	60	5
Total		86		131		28

(Per cent high conformity)

* In this table *n* refers to the bases upon which the percentages are computed. For example, of the 12 square Johns located in the early career phase, 67 per cent are high conformists.

The pattern of response exhibited by the subsample classified as outlaws approximates *prisonization*. That is, the net result of movement through the career phases is to reduce progressively the per cent of conformists among these role types. Although a considerable percentage of outlaws enter prison as deviants, the data suggest that processes operating within prison produce a pattern of adjustment that appears to be consistent with Clemmer's observations on inmate socialization.

The two remaining trends apparent in Table 12.1 and Figure 12.2 appear to conform to patterns of *stable conformity* and *delayed rehabilitation* hypothesized by Wheeler (1961: 709). Politicians tend to conform to staff norms throughout the institutional career, suggesting the relatively slight impact of prison culture on this role type. Although there is a slight dip in the middle phase, proportionately there are as many politicians conforming during this period as there are among the square Johns. Theoretical formulations regarding the pseudo-social orientation of the politician-type appear to be consistent with the pattern of stable conformity shown above.

Dings follow the pattern of delayed rehabilitation, showing a progressive increase in the per cent of conformists and suggesting the operation of social processes that might be therapeutic or reformative for this role type. Again, these findings should be corroborated by panel data observing shifts in attitudes on the part of the same inmates over time.

Further inspection of Table 12.1 and Figure 12.2 reveals that there is less variance in prisoners' responses to the five contrived situations in the middle than during the two extreme periods of confinement, indicating that there may be a higher degree of consensus among inmates during this period and that it tends to be in the direction of non-conformity . . .

[Garabedian discusses Table 12.2. He argues that, as the percentages falling into the first three role types are similar throughout the three career phases, it is likely that "prisoners are typed early in the institutional career and that shifts in attitude may occur without relinquishing the role." This conclusion does not necessarily apply to dings and outlaws, however, for the percentages in these two role types become "unstable in the late career phase". Garabedian therefore suggests that many outlaws assume the role of dings late in their sentence, since if they continue to be outlaws "their mobility out of the institution might be hindered". He is careful to point out that the findings of Table

12.2 as a whole are not conclusive, because they are based on cross-sectional data – thus "firm verification of the findings must await data based on panel studies".]

TABLE 12.2   *Location of role types in the three career phases*

Role type	Early phase		Middle phase		Late phase	
	%	n^*	%	n	%	n
Square Johns	14	12	15	20	18	5
Right guys	28	24	30	39	25	7
Politicians	30	26	33	43	32	9
Outlaws	19	16	15	20	7	2
Dings	9	8	7	9	18	5
Total	100	86	100	131	100	28

SOCIAL ROLES AND SOCIAL PROCESSES

At this point the question arises as to the types of social processes that might be operating to produce the various patterns of adjustment observed in Table 12.1 and Figure 12.2. For example, it is surprising to find square Johns exhibiting the U-shaped adaptive pattern of response during incarceration; the trend definitely suggests signs of prisonization as well as "de-prisonization". On the basis of recent formulations which have characterized the square John as the pro-social, isolated, non-involved inmate who openly identifies with the prison administration, a pattern of stable conformity would have been predicted for this type. But the drop in square John conformists from 67 to 30 per cent between the early and middle phase does not indicate a stable conformity pattern and suggests that they may not be as isolated as previously assumed, but rather that they become involved to some degree with other inmates.

[In the next section (omitted here) data are given on the social contact of inmates with other inmates and staff. Table 3 (omitted) shows the relationship of social contact to role type and career phase, and in the text Garabedian explains and interprets these findings. The social contact data were gathered through two items on the questionnaire, as follows: "Because of their particular jobs, activities, or interests, some inmates come into contact with other *inmates* frequently, while others do not. Comparing yourself with the average inmate, do you have more contact with other *inmates* or less contact than average? For staff contacts, the item read as above with the exception that the word *staff* was substituted for the word inmate in the appropriate places. The response categories of *much more* and *somewhat more* were considered high contact, while *somewhat less* and *much less* were considered low contact."]

CONCLUSIONS

The findings reported in this paper suggest that when aspects of inmate social structure are taken into account a variety of patterns of response to prison life emerges. Consistent with the reports of Clemmer and Wheeler, inmates are socialized in varying degrees and rates, which indicate a differential impact of the prison culture on its participants. The data also suggest that the *point of heaviest impact* varies with the different role types; the early phase being important for dings, the middle period for right guys and square Johns, and the late phase for outlaws.

[The section of the conclusions which is based on the social contact data is omitted here.]

. . . The process of anticipatory socialization, which many inmates apparently undergo prior to release, may be strong enough to "undo" or "override" many of the specific effects incurred during incarceration. On this basis, we would be led to predict a favorable post-institutional prognosis for many parolees. Yet, it is well known that a large proportion of inmates released from correctional institutions return either as parole violators or are convicted on new offences. [Garabedian concludes by discussing certain factors which may be important in understanding the issues of re-conviction and parole violation.]

13

Multiple Drug Use among Marijuana Smokers*

ERICH GOODE

Knowledge of the process through which an individual progresses from the use of a relatively mild and almost innocuous herb as a "recreational" drug, to the sometimes frequent use of drugs which have at least the potential for damaging the body and the psyche, is patchy and conflicting. An adequate explanation of this movement simply does not exist. In light of these empirical and theoretical lacunae, we wish to offer an exploratory delineation of the use of other drugs by marijuana smokers. Although our data are too incomplete and fragmentary to yield a perspective firm and coherent enough to be called a "theory" of multiple drug use, we can, nonetheless, construct some tentative generalizations and hypotheses which should clarify and shed light on some dim corners of the field.

Probably the most effective argument against the use of marijuana has inhered in the fact that it "leads to" the use of truly dangerous drugs, particularly heroin. This is the classic position of the Federal Bureau of Narcotics (later the Bureau of Narcotics and Dangerous Drugs):

> . . . it cannot be too strongly emphasized that the smoking of the marihuana cigarette is a dangerous first step on the road which usually leads to enslavement by heroin . . . Ordinarily, a person is tempted first with marihuana cigarettes. He may not

* Reprinted in part from Erich Goode (1969) "Multiple drug use among marijuana smokers", *Social Probelms*, **17**: 48–64, with the permission of the publishers (the Society for the Study of Social Problems) and the author.

even know they are dope. Then, someone already addicted makes it easy to try some heroin. *Most* teenage addicts started by smoking marihuana cigarettes. *Never let anyone persuade you to smoke even one marihuana cigarette. It is pure poison* (Federal Bureau of Narcotics, 1965).

Support for this contention is far from universal, and largely dependent on accidental factors of sampling, as well as the characteristics of the population under study: regional and rural– urban differences, race, sex, age, and social class and educational composition. Some studies have largely upheld the hypothesis of the "progression" from marijuana to the narcotics; others have found the existence or absence of the relationship almost entirely contingent on neighborhood, style of use and "type" of user, and the existence of a subculture of illicit drug use; still other studies have found that heroin use among marijuana users is virtually absent. [Goode cites a total of twelve previous studies in this paragraph.]

The search for explanations is often rewarded more readily by seemingly contradictory findings than by constant ones. What is missing in the Bureau of Narcotics position is that it contains no *variables*. We cannot discover an explanation. What we really need to know in order to understand the phenomenon of multiple drug use is the *conditions under which* it holds, and the conditions under which it does *not* hold. Only in the variation will we be able to isolate out the reasons *why* it holds. [Omitted is a passage in which the political implications of the Bureau of Narcotic's position on marijuana-heroin progression is analysed in more detail.]

A specter of more recent vintage than the fear of eventual heroin use is the alarm that marijuana will precipitate the use of the potent psychedelics, or "hallucinogens", especially LSD. [Although adequate studies of LSD-use are few in number, it] . . . should be a vexing puzzle to the student of drug use that those studies in which the marijuana–LSD connection is found generally do not find much connection between marijuana and heroin use; in turn, those studies in which the marijuana-heroin progression is strong find a low correlation between the use of marijuana and the use of LSD. It is on this seemingly paradoxical observation that we will concentrate in this paper.

THE STUDY

During the spring and summer of 1967, I interviewed about two hundred marijuana smokers, in part to unravel questions relating to their multiple drug use, particularly their use of the stronger drugs, such as heroin and LSD. The sample was drawn informally, and stemmed from two sources. I began by drawing up a list of perhaps two dozen individuals known personally to me to be marijuana users. After interviewing each one, I asked him or her to supply me with the names of a few other users. The original list "snowballed" into about one hundred interviews. Another technique, also resulting in about one hundred interviews, involved access to several places of employment at which high proportions of marijuana smokers worked. These organizations were two large New York universities, a medium-sized market research firm, and a very large publishing firm. Obviously, the individuals included in no way represented marijuana smokers in general, nor even the users within their place of employment.

[Goode discusses the drawbacks and advantages of his sampling. The key points are: (1) Co-operation of each interviewee was virtually ensured by the snowball sampling approach, as a third person had vouched for Goode's "veracity and basic harmlessness". More conventional survey methods – for example, random sampling from a list of employees in the market research firm – are not practicable since many respondents would not be willing to be interviewed by a stranger, nor would they be honest about drug use. Goode's method also avoided studying only those deviants who had come to official notice (for example, imprisoned marijuana users); samples of official deviants are known to be systematically biased. (2) It is recognized that the sample is not representative of marijuana users in general. Goode discusses the process by which respondents come into the sample – for example, their willingness to be interviewed, and that they are known by others to be marijuana users. (3) The composition of the sample is described – for example, 53 per cent are male, median age was 22, and they are mainly whites; details are also given of fathers' socio-economic background. All respondents were residing in New York or its suburbs.

The main thrust of this section of Goode's report is to argue that the snowball sample was the most appropriate for his purpose, but also that the *limitations* of the sample must be taken into account. Thus the study must be considered "exploratory, and its findings tentative", and the results "apply most directly to the New York subset of marijuana smokers . . . only by inference elsewhere in the country . . . [and] are probably without application outside the United States".]

MULTIPLE DRUG USE: AN OVERVIEW

Among the 204 respondents, the use of drugs other than marijuana was more characteristic than it was exceptional. Two-thirds of the respondents (68 per cent) had taken at least one drug other than marijuana or hashish at least once. (Some of the interviewees, I found out after it was too late, did not distinguish between marijuana and hashish – did not, that is, mention having used hashish as a drug distinct from marijuana – so that it does not appear as a separate drug.) The median number of drugs taken by the interviewees was almost exactly two, and the mean was 3.4. For the technique of deriving the number of drugs which the respondent took, see the notes to Table 13.1. More important than the sheer *number* of drugs taken is both the *kind* of drug taken, as well as the *frequency* of their use. In spite of the commonly-stated belief that marijuana use will "lead to" the use of, and eventual addiction to, heroin, this . . . was used by only a small minority of the sample. Twenty-seven respondents, or 13 per cent of the sample, had used heroin at least once. Further, extremely limited use was more common than repeated usage, whether "chippying" or actual addiction. Over half of the heroin users took it fewer than a dozen times – and of these, eleven tried it three or fewer times – and five claimed to have been addicted – although none was, or claimed to be, at the time of the interview.

The picture which LSD presents is different in the extent of its use among marijuana smokers, but similar in the characteristic infrequency of its use. Almost half (49 per cent) had taken the drug at least once. Yet 25 individuals . . . tried the drug only *once*; an additional 19 took it exactly twice. Only 14 respondents took the drug 25 times or more, and of these, four had taken it 100 or more times. No one claimed to have had more than 150 "trips". Thus, LSD characteristically is not a drug of frequent use. It is

TABLE 13.1   *Percentage taking other drugs besides marijuana** †

	%	N
LSD	49	99
Amphetamine	43	87
DMT or DET	26	54
Barbiturate or tranquillizer	24	49
Opium	20	41
Cocaine	19	38
Peyote or Mescaline	19	37
Heroin	13	27
Amyl Nitrite	8	16
Codeine	5	10
Morning Glory Seeds	5	10
Psilocybin	4	8
Romilar	3	6

* [As Goode notes in an appendix, the following rules were observed in distinguishing between separate drugs: (1) Only drugs used for pleasure (to get "high") were counted; drugs used for weight control or as pain-killers were not counted. (2) Several of the headings refer to a group of similar drugs rather than a single drug; for example, the second heading refers to all amphetamine-like drugs, including methedrine, benzedrine, etc., and the fourth heading includes all the barbiturates and tranquillizers. (3) Substances consumed in conjunction with marijuana (such as hashish "soaked in" opium) were considered as a separate drug. (4) Arbitrarily, the following substances were not considered as drugs: bananas, cleaning flud, helium, glue.]

† The table includes only the drugs which more than three respondents had taken; the less often tried drugs were: Belladonna, Dolophine, Ritalen, Morphine, Paregoric Laudanum, Renalgen, Stramonium, Resurpine, and Cava-cava.

most often taken for curiosity, for exploring unusual psychic states . . .

The amphetamines, often used for weight control or to abort drowsiness, were also used by a large percentage of the sample to obtain a "high". (It must be remembered that in order that a drug be included in the computation, it was necessary that the subject have taken it for illicit reasons, reasons which society would disapprove of. Taking an amphetamine pill to study all night for an exam would be extra-medical, but would not be included.) Forty-three per cent of the sample took at least one of the amphetamines at least once. Unfortunately, I was not aware at the beginning of the study of the importance of the amphetamines in drug subcultures, so that I did not ask a question on frequency of the use of these drugs, not did I ask whether or not the respondents had taken methedrine, a solid indicator of degree of involvement in the drug community. The conclusions on the amphetamines, then, will be more speculative than for the other drugs.

THE SOCIAL CONTEXT OF MARIJUANA USE

The most significant fact about marijuana use is that it is overwhelmingly a group activity; the drug, in other words, is highly "sociogenic". [Goode points out that much non-medical drug use takes place in relative isolation, for example housewives' use of tranquillizers, or morphine addiction amongst physicians.] What we mean when we say that marijuana (or LSD, or heroin) is sociogenic is that: (1) it is characteristically participated in a group setting; (2) the others with whom one smokes marijuana are usually intimates, intimates of intimates, or potential intimates, rather than strangers; (3) one generally has long-term continuing social relations with the others; (4) a certain degree of value consensus will obtain within the group; (5) a value convergence will occur as a result of progressive group involvement; (6) the activity maintains the circle's cohesion, reaffirms its social bonds by acting them out; (7) participants view the activity as a legitimate basis for identity – they define themselves, as well as others, partly on the basis of whether they have participated in the activity or not. In these senses, then, marijuana use is sociogenic.

What we find is that marijuana users form a kind of subcommunity. This does not mean that a powerful bond of identity holds all users together in a closely-knit social group. But it does mean that users are more likely to identify and interact with other users than with someone who does not smoke marijuana. In a sense, they are part of a subculture. Crystallizing all of the possible meanings of this term, the following three are probably of most importance: (1) *Sociologically*: the degree to which a given category of individuals form *associations* with one another, whether or not that category is a subcommunity, the degree of concentration of one's most intimate and frequently interacted-with friends and acquaintances within that social category; (2) *Anthropologically* and *ethnographically*: the degree to which members of a given social category share a distinct way of life, whose patterns of social life and basic social outlook set them off to some degree from members of other social categories; (3) *Social psychologically*: the degree to which *identities* revolve about the category, the degree to which both members and non-members define group membership as significant, binding, and strongly indicative of the "kind of person" who belongs to it. "Subcultureness" must be seen as a continuum, not a dichotomy. Subcultures vary as to *degree of institutionalization*: the higher the "score" on one or all of these three dimensions, the more that a given group may be called a subculture.

[In a passage omitted here, Goode discusses the importance of group processes for first introduction to marijuana. Ninety-three per cent of the sample were "turned on" for the first time in the company of at least one individual who had already smoked marijuana. In this way the neophyte smoker is "subject to group definitions of the desirability of the experience, as well as . . . its reality". At its inception, marijuana use is thus "*simultaneously, participation in a specific social group*". This is equally true for continued use. Marijuana is "characteristically smoked in groups, not in isolation . . . only five per cent claimed to smoke at least half of the time alone, and . . . 45 per cent said they never smoked alone". Further details are then given of the sociogenic nature of marijuana use – for example, smoking is normally in intimate groups, and the emphasis is on sharing a "joint". Goode goes on to suggest that marijuana use can be seen in *Durkheimian* terms, for example there are elements of *tribal ritual*, and a vigorous *mythology* connected with use.]

What holds for marijuana use *per se* holds *a fortiori* for frequent and long-range use. Heavy marijuana use is not only an indicator of but also a *catalyst* in generating and reaffirming commitment to a drug-using subculture. Moreover, higher levels of use tend to involve the smoker in related sets of activities which, likewise, implicate him in the marijuana subcommunity. Involvement can be thought of as a stepwise movement toward the "core" of the group, each step representing a kind of progressive commitment to a subculture. None of these steps is dramatic; the smoker does not think of himself as suddenly becoming a new social animal as a result of taking these steps. Yet it is possible for the sociologist to discern a number of broad concomitants and changes associated with them.

The most obvious indicator of this progressive involvement is, of course, the *amount* that the individual smokes. The "experimenter", the individual who has tried marijuana once or twice or a dozen times and has discontinued using, is clearly a member of this subculture in only the most superficial way. The more that an individual smokes marijuana, the greater the probability of his being involved in the subculture. The more that he smokes, the more extensive and intense are his social bonds and activities among smokers – and the weaker are his social bonds and activities among non-smokers.

Clearly, a dynamic and *dialectical* relationship obtains between friendships and the amount one smokes. One does not generally acquire a great many marijuana-smoking friends until one already smokes. Yet the fact that one has friends who smoke further increases the likelihood that one will smoke more, and the fact that one smokes implicates one in relationships with those who also smoke [see Table 13.2]. Rather than one or another being causal here, the two mutually influence and feed into each other.

TABLE 13.2 *Percent of closest friends who are regular marijuana smokers**

Marijuana use†	0 to 29%	30 to 59%	60 to 100%	N
Every day	4	35	62	26
3 to 6 times per week	14	36	50	42
1 to 2 times per week	35	24	41	54
1 to 4 times per month	42	31	28	36
Less than monthly	72	19	9	43

* Designated as at least once per week.
† An average of over the past six months.

Moreover, the more that an individual smokes marijuana, the greater is the likelihood that he will also be involved in drug-related activities which *further* strengthen his social ties with the drug-using group. For instance, the more that he smokes, the greater the chances of his having bought and/or sold marijuana [see Table 13.3]. Again, we are hesitant about imputing causal direction here, since use feeds into these activities, and these activities feed back into use. The more that he smokes, the greater the need to purchase marijuana; the more that he smokes, the greater is the chance of being able to take advantage of the economy in large purchases, and thus the greater is the likelihood of having a surplus to sell; the more that he smokes, the more that he associates with others who smoke, especially heavily, and thus the more centrally located he is in the marijuana distribution system, and the more knowledge he has about buying and selling.

TABLE 13.3   *Buying and selling by marijuana use*

	Percent "Yes"		
Marijuana use	Ever bought	Ever sold	N
Every day	96	92	26
3 to 6 times per week	93	80	42
1 to 2 times per week	84	40	55
1 to 4 times per month	67	14	36
Less than monthly	29	11	45

With extended and frequent use, and its invariable concomitant, subcultural association, attitudinal shifts generally take place relative to drug use and drug-associated identities. The more that one smokes, the greater the likelihood that one will see oneself as a marijuana smoker, the higher that drug-connected identities will rank on one's "who am I?" responses. And the more that one will look for drug cues in others, the more that one will think of others in drug-associated terms. And the more that one will think that it is necessary that others with whom one associates also smoke. The more that one smokes, the greater the *salience* that marijuana has in one's life, and the greater the likelihood that it is involved in one's evaluation of others [see Table 13.4].

Heavy marijuana use, then, (1) implicates the individual in intense and extensive social interaction with other marijuana users, (2) involves him with numerous marijuana users, (3) involves him in numerous marijuana-related activities, (4) alters the role of marijuana as a relevant criterion in his conceptions of others, (5) changes his conception of himself as a drug user. Moreover, it increases the likelihood of taking drugs in addition to

TABLE 13.4 *Salience of marijuana by marijuana use**

Marijuana use	First half-dozen things	Preferable that friends smoke	Turn on sibling
Every day	81	56	88
3 to 6 times per week	69	53	73
1 to 2 times per week	45	37	65
1 to 4 times per month	39	33	57
Less than monthly	16	31	41

* Percent saying "yes" to the following questions: 'When you meet a person for the first time, is the fact that he smokes marijuana one of the first half-dozen things you think about?' 'Is it preferable that your friends smoke marijuana, or not?' "Do you think that you would turn on your younger brother or sister, if you had one?"

marijuana *which the subculture approves of*. (Even daily use of marijuana will not involve the individual in heroin use if it is absent from the group in which he interacts and finds his significant others.) This will come about as a result of a favorable definition of the drug experience, and opportunities for taking drugs other than marijuana. The more that the individual smokes marijuana, the greater is the likelihood that he will have taken drugs other than marijuana [see Table 13.5]. The more that he smokes, the more *extensive* his drug experience is likely to be.

TABLE 13.5 *Non-marijuana drug use by marijuana use*

Marijuana use	Percent having ever tried at least three drugs aside from marijuana	N
Every day	92	26
3 to 6 times per week	69	42
1 to 2 times per week	29	55
1 to 4 times per month	19	36
Less than monthly	9	45

Moreover, the greater the proportion of one's friends who are also regular marijuana smokers, the greater is the likelihood that one has taken drugs other than marijuana, and the more extensive one's experience with other drugs is likely to be [see Table 13.6].

Likewise, buying and selling impel the individual into social relations which shift the individual's conception of himself as regards drug use, and provide opportunities for non-marijuana drug use. The fact that the individual has bought and sold marijuana means that he has had contact with other individuals who are likely to be heavily involved in drug use, and who define drug use in favorable terms [see Table 13.7]. Moreover, it clearly means that other drugs are more *available* to him.

TABLE 13.6 *Percentage non-marijuana drug use by marijuana-smoking friends*

Percent of friends who are regular marijuana smokers	Taken marijuana only	Taken 1 or 2 other drugs	Taken 3 or more other drugs	N
60–100%	16	25	59	73
30–59%	23	30	46	56
0–29%	53	32	15	72

TABLE 13.7 *Percentage non-marijuana drug use by buying and selling marijuana*

		Taken marijuana only	Taken 1 or 2 other drugs	Taken 3 or more other drugs	N
Bought marijuana	Yes	27	27	49	147
	No	49	37	14	57
Sold marijuana	Yes	13	22	64	89
	No	45	35	20	115

Marijuana can be looked upon as a kind of *lingua franca* in the drug-using world. It is used in extremely diverse settings, in groups whose members have little or nothing to do with one another. Heavy marijuana use, and involvement in significant marijuana-related activities, generally implicates the user in *some* kind of stronger drug-using group, but which drugs this group uses, aside from marijuana, is determined less by the chemistry of any of the drugs used than by the social conditions which marijuana use implies. In social and ecological areas wherein heroin addiction is more frequent, in the slums and the ghettos, marijuana use often involves the user in heroin-associated activities and peers. Often marijuana use "leads to" experimenting with the narcotics in a working class urban area not because of the search for an even-bigger and better "kick", but because the associations one makes as one's use level moves upward are increasingly also likely to experiment with the narcotics. Obviously, the process is anything but inevitable . . .

In contexts other than the slum, marijuana use does not imply experimentation with narcotics; on the college campus, for instance, heroin use involves a very tiny segment of even the drug-using contingent, and its use is distinctly frowned upon . . . The psychedelic drugs are still the category most likely to be used among college marijuana smokers, by far (Blum *et al.*, 1969:101–9) . . . [Omitted here is a discussion, based on the results of other studies, of the relationship between frequency of marijuana use and experimentation with LSD-type drugs, for middle-class and college-campus users.]

In our sample, for every drug which we computed, the daily marijuana smoker was far more likely to have tried it than was the less than monthly marijuana smoker. For instance, only 4 per cent of the least involved smokers had tried heroin at least once, while over 35 per cent of the daily smokers had. Only 24 per cent of the less than monthly smokers had taken one of the amphetamines to get "high", while 81 per cent of the daily smokers did. Thus, the greater the amount of marijuana use, the greater the chance of having tried *nearly any* drug. Intense and continuing involvement with marijuana use implies involvement in a drug-using subculture. But it must be recognised that this is a highly *conditional* statement; it refers specifically to heavy use and intense involvement. At the lowest levels of use, the use of drugs which are considered dangerous is highly unlikely; moreover, if it does occur, it is likely to be discontinued very quickly. Thus, it is crucial to understand the *differential* impact of crucial variables on multiple, or "progressive", drug use. Our data do not support a simple and ineluctable conception of the use of stronger drugs by marijuana smokers.

Our model of progressive drug involvement is probably most unambiguously illustrated by the later use of LSD by differentially using marijuana smokers. The more that one used marijuana, the higher were his chances of having taken LSD at least once. The higher the proportion of friends who were also regular marijuana smokers, the greater were the individual's chances of taking LSD

[see Table 13.8]. The fact that he bought or sold marijuana also
increased his chances of having taken LSD.

TABLE 13.8   *Taking LSD by marijuana use*

	Percent taking LSD	N
Every day	82	26
3 to 6 times per week	71	42
1 to 2 times per week	49	55
1 to 4 times per month	25	36
Less than monthly	22	45

It can be seen in the last set of tables [see Tables 13.9 and 13.10]
that since marijuana *selling* is a more intense commitment than
mere *buying* is – it takes one further into the "core" of the
drug-using subculture, particularly the psychedelic drug community – it serves as a more effective predictor in differentiating
whether a person will have taken LSD: 13 per cent more of the
sellers of marijuana have taken LSD than is true of the buyers, and
7 per cent fewer of the nonbuyers have taken it than the
non-sellers. To never have bought marijuana is a better indicator
of one's noninvolvement.

TABLE 13.9   *Taking LSD by marijuana-smoking friends*

	Percent	N
60–100%	64	73
30–59%	57	56
0–30%	26	72

TABLE 13.10   *Taking LSD by buying and selling marijuana*

		LSD			
		Yes	No	Total	N
Bought	Yes	59	41	100%	147
marijuana	No	23	77	100%	57
Sold	Yes	72	28	100%	89
marijuana	No	30	70	100%	115

QUALIFICATIONS

However unambiguously that our data point to the fact that the use of other, stronger drugs, particularly the psychedelics, increased with increased marijuana use, several strong qualifications seem to be in order.

(1) Increasing involvement with marijuana is not only not inevitable, it is not even typical. Although everyone who now smokes marijuana daily once smoked it less frequently, and thus became "progressively" involved, the sporadic user very rarely becomes a daily user. Our sample is weighted more heavily in the direction of the frequent user; therefore *incidences* of marijuana use are far less valid than *relationships between variables*. In studies where some representativeness obtains, the majority of all those who have tried marijuana at least once smoke it only occasionally. [Goode cites two previous studies of drug use amongst college students, and discusses their findings.]

(2) Any study has to stop at some point in time. The *eventual* drug use of our respondents *after* we stopped interviewing is impossible to determine. Although certainly some of the indices of the eventual use of some of the stronger drugs will be higher than we reported – probably not a great deal higher, however – it seems unlikely that the *patterns of use* which we described will be significantly different.

(3) There has been some recent evidence that the use of some of the specific drugs reported during the period of our study are used at a different frequency today. [Goode cites two recent sources.]

(4) It must be remembered that our marijuana use index is an average of the past six months. Although most of the nonmarijuana drug use occurred within that period a not negligible minority of it did not. The time factor, therefore, should be kept in mind in understanding the drug use dynamics here.

(5) The marijuana use figure refers to the average and continued use of the drug, while for the other drugs, such as heroin and LSD, we always relied on the figure which referred to whether the respondent *ever* took the drug.

(6) The role of social class background as a variable in our study influencing drug use is ambiguous and even contradictory. [Omitted is a passage in which Goode explains that, because of the nature of the sample, his data are not suitable for a study of the

relationship of social class to drug use. Some data on the social
class background of the respondents is nonetheless given, but no
clear relationships emerge.]

(7) This study does not discount the role of personality factors in
the generation of multiple drug use; it is not an attack on what
Albert Cohen calls "kinds of people" theories of drug use (Cohen,
1966). I have limited myself to social and cultural factors for
reasons of space (and expertise). I readily admit the possibility –
indeed, the certainty – that psychological variables must be
included as one of the various factors worth exploring. I leave that
study to those who are inclined and trained to do so.

14

Occupational Prestige and Social Mobility of Suicides in New Zealand*

AUSTIN L. PORTERFIELD and JACK P. GIBBS

This analysis of the social circulation of suicides in New Zealand includes ranking of the victims by the prestige accorded to their occupations and a description of the route followed by victims from their position at birth to their position at death, with a consideration of its implication for suicidal behavior. Our foremost concern is with the dynamics of suicide, not static conditions surrounding the suicide at the time of his death, and we shall concentrate on his social situation from birth to death. A great deal of information has been secured on the social history of the 955 persons who committed suicide in New Zealand between 1946 and 1951.

. . . Data on each case were gathered in several steps: (1) Suicides were identified by inspecting all coroner's reports on deaths in the dominion in the six-year period. (2) There was an attempt in each case to record all relevant testimony included in the coroner's report. (3) All demographic and social characteristics reported on death certificates were recorded. (4) The same step was repeated with birth certificates of victims born in New Zealand. (5) Finally, the data were assembled and prepared for analysis. The data are such that the victims' pasts can be considered from several points of view. We have selected the mobility of suicides as particularly worthy of consideration, since it is

* Reprinted in part from Austin L. Porterfield and Jack P. Gibbs (1960) "Occupational prestige and social mobility of suicides in New Zealand", *American Journal of Sociology*, **66**:146–52, with the permission of the publishers and the authors. © University of Chicago Press 1960.

closely related to basic structural characteristics of societies and is a determinant of the fulfilment or frustration of social expectations.

The major problem of procedure is the establishment of a measure of prestige of occupational positions. This was needed in determining the distribution of suicides as reckoned by the difference between the prestige position of their families of orientation and their position as to occupational prestige at the time of death. We began with the traditional designation of classes as "lower", "middle", and "upper". These terms were applied first to the total male working population of New Zealand and then to males who had attained or passed the age of thirty-five years. In both cases our goal was to estimate the number of persons who belonged to upper, middle, or lower classes.

We used the findings of Congalton (1953) on occupational prestige in New Zealand. The scores on the Congalton scale are based on the rank order assigned by four samples of 974 interviewees to thirty occupations, selected to represent all occupations, from the medical doctor to the road-sweeper. Congalton's scale is similar to the North–Hatt scale for the USA (1947) [and] the Hall–Jones scale for Britain (1950) . . .

In the eyes of Congalton's interviewees the occupations in order of their prestige were: doctor, lawyer, company director, business manager, minister, public accountant, civil service head, works manager, farmer, primary-school teacher, jobbing master-builder, news reporter, commissioned policeman, commercial traveler, news agent or bookseller, fitter, routine clerk, insurance agent, carpenter, bricklayer, shop assistant, carrier, chef, tractor-driver, agricultural laborer, coal miner, railway porter, barman, wharf laborer, and road-sweeper.

By applying the Congalton scale to the occupations listed in the census reports, we estimated the total number of male workers and the number of males thirty-five or more years old on each of the three levels of prestige represented by Class I (ranks 1–9 in Congalton's scale), Class II (ranks 10–19), and Class III (ranks 20–29). These class designations are our own, not Congalton's. Estimating the number of workers in each class on the basis of the Congalton scale was a tedious process, the results of which can be no more than tentative. For one thing, the scale does not cover all occupations listed in the census. Also, only twenty-five of Congalton's thirty occupations were listed as occupational groups in the 1945 New Zealand census. Therefore, the application to the twenty-five occupations was made on a comparative basis, depending upon the judgment of the observer as to what occupations are comparable to those on the scale. Hence, while the process is not fully replicable, other persons employing the same procedure would probably arrive at estimates very similar to those made in Table 14.1.

OCCUPATIONAL PRESTIGE OF THE VICTIMS OF SUICIDE

The occupations of the 689 male suicides of all ages were located along the Congalton scale, except that 14 without occupations or whose occupations are unknown were classed in rank 31 and a few pensioners were placed in rank 30. Those who were retired were accorded the prestige scores of the vocations they had pursued, and it was assumed that they should be included in our aggregate estimates but excluded in tests which concerned only active workers.

If we inquire whether suicides are distributed according to occupational prestige in much the same way as are all male workers, we discover that they are not (Table 14.1). The differences between the number of suicides observed and the number expected, from the total working population in each class, are great (Chi square = 43.41, 2 degrees of freedom, p <0.001). Class I had more than its share, while Class II and III had less.

TABLE 14.1 *Distribution by prestige groups of classes of the male working population and of male suicides in New Zealand*

Class	No. of workers	Percentage of all workers	No. of suicides	No. expected*
I	90,000	19.2	200	132
II	130,000	27.7	171	191
III	250,000	53.1	318†	366
Total	470,000	100.0	689	689

* Based on the percentage of the population of each class as shown in the table.

† Fourteen persons with no occupation are included in this number.

VICTIMS THIRTY-FIVE OR MORE YEARS OLD

The application of the Congalton scale to the occupations listed in the census for males thirty-five years of age or older leads to the results presented in Table 14.2 in terms of the number of active workers in each class in the designated age group. Table 14.2 also indicates the number of suicides which occurred in each class as compared with the number that would correspond with its proportion of the 270,000 active workers in all classes.

TABLE 14.2   *Class distribution of active male workers thirty-five or more years old and of 348 male suicides of corresponding age who were active workers at death*

Class	No. of workers	Percentage of all workers	No. of suicides	No. expected*
I	73,000	27.0	124	94
II	74,000	27.4	94	95
III	123,000	45.6	130	159
Total	270,000	100.0	348	348

*Based on the percentage of the population in each class as shown in the table.

The 348 victims who belonged to this age-group of active workers were not distributed by classes in the statistically expected proportions. The differences in the number of suicides observed and expected in Classes I and III remain significant at a high level of confidence (Chi square = 14.88, 2 degrees of freedom, $p < 0.01$).

It is difficult to estimate the class distribution of the male population over thirty-five years old which is retired, sick, of "independent means", or unemployed; but the relation of the distribution of income to various levels of prestige makes it possible to move tentatively from estimates of the former to estimates of the latter. Data on the former are available; these were estimated on the basis of data in the New Zealand *Population Census, 1945: Incomes*: table 2, 6–7. By assuming that the per capita income of males in these categories was probably not more than two-fifths of their per capita income during employment, we placed all non-workers in the designated categories with incomes of more than £225 a year in Class I, those with incomes of £100–225 in Class II, and all with incomes of less than £100 in Class III. It is not likely that this procedure leaves the upper class underrepresented or overestimates the population of the lower class. The comparison of the distribution by classes, thus determined, of 175 suicides among non-workers in these groups is given in Table 14.3. As shown, the upper class of older non-workers contained a larger proportion of suicides than was found in the classes below. It it unlikely that these class differences are the result of chance (Chi square = 14.27, 2 degrees of freedom, p <0.01).

TABLE 14.3   *Class distribution of suicides among the non-working male population above thirty-five years of age*

Classes	No. of non-workers	Percentage of all non-workers	No. of suicides	No. expected*
I	12,500	18.9	52	33
II	16,500	25.0	43	44
III	37,000	56.1	80	98
Total	66,000	100.0	175	175

* Based on the percentage of the population in the class as shown in the table.

VERTICAL MOBILITY

The vertical mobility of suicides in New Zealand tends to be downward – sometimes sharply so – yet suicides occur in great numbers among men who are on the way up. In the whole of New Zealand there appears a small aggregate deficit in the ranks of prestige gained and lost among the 523 male suicides thirty-five or more years old, as compared with the highest rank attained by their fathers. The 523 men fell 477 ranks below their fathers – an average loss of less than one rank per suicide. In the four major New Zealand cities – Auckland, Wellington, Christchurch, and Dunedin – the aggregate deficit in prestige positions was 614 – an average of less than 3.3 ranks per suicide.

We have no adequate data on the aggregate prestige gains and losses in the succession of generations in New Zealand, but we did obtain a 2 per cent sample, chosen at random, among registrations of death attributed to natural causes in 1948. The year 1948 was chosen as being near the middle of the whole period of study, 1946–51. The sample of 321 is almost exactly 2 per cent of the 15,812 deaths occurring in 1948. Within the sample of 321, there were 149 males above 35 years of age. Of these 149, only 56 passed upward or downward from one class to another – 32 (21.5 per cent) were upwardly mobile and 24 (16.1 per cent) were downwardly mobile. Ninety-three (62.4 per cent) remained in the class of their fathers, among whom 50 registered no change . . .

The interclass patterns of mobility of persons who become suicides may be observed more specifically in Table 14.4. Of the 523 male victims thirty-five or more years old, 233 originated in upper-class families. Of these, 119 had moved downward, with the result that upper-class fathers provided their own class with two-thirds of its suicidal sons and fathered nearly two-fifths of those who became suicides in the middle class and nearly three out of ten who died by their own hands in the lower class. Middle-class families bred only one out of six of all suicides, and only a little more than one-fourth of those who died in this manner in the middle class. Lower-class families bred 87 sons who went up to die, 40 of them in the upper class. In all, 104 suicides moved up from their fathers' to a higher class; 149 moved down.

TABLE 14.4   *Class at death and class of origin of 532 male victims of suicide thirty-five or more years of age*

| | | | Class of origin | | | | | |
| | | | I | | II | | III | |
Class at death	No.	Per cent	No.	Per cent*	No.	Per cent*	No.	Per cent*
I	176	33.7	119	67.6	17	9.7	40	22.7
II	137	26.2	54	39.4	36	26.3	47	34.3
III	210	40.1	60	28.6	35	16.7	115	54.7
Total	523†	100.0†	233	46.6	88	16.8	202	38.6

* Based on the number in the corresponding row of column 1.
† Totals refer both to columns 1 and 2 and to the corresponding subtotals in row 4.

Many suicides are mobile to a very high degree. In the group above thirty-five years of age, 156 died after attaining an occupational prestige score 10 or more ranks above or below the highest attainment of their fathers. Of these, 90 moved downward and 66 upward. Here it should be observed that 60 moved down from the upper to the lower class, as compared with 18 who slipped to the middle class, and that 40 moved up from the lower to the upper class, as compared with 18 whose climb terminated in the middle class.

One may well ask whether tension in those who moved upward is not a factor in suicide, just as frustration in those who think of themselves as failures may be. If it is an influence among climbers, what are its sources? There may be two sources of tension. The first relates to the lack of satisfying expectations and the threat of losing status; the second, to social mobility as tending to weaken social relationships.

Assuming that most fathers want their sons to exceed the parental attainments, that the sons would like to do so, and that society applauds them for doing it, those who fall far behind may suffer from a keen sense of failure. The frustration may be difficult to tolerate, particularly when a depressed status is accentuated by events which are perceived as catastrophes. On the other hand, the sons who have surpassed their fathers may feel greatly depressed by threats to their new status. As a consequence, the climbers may furnish a relatively high rate of suicides. Finally, it is suspected that both climbing and descending weaken social relationships and that weak social relationships are not conducive to a normal reaction to crisis.

MOBILITY AND CRISIS

In an effort to establish the frequency of crises preceding suicide among the climbers and the "sliders", as compared with those who maintained the status of their fathers, we matched, by age, each of 50 males who "stayed put" with (1) a man who fell 10 or more positions below his father on the Congalton scale and (2) a man who climbed at least 10 ranks above his father's highest attainment. We then examined the available data on each case to determine whether some special crisis preceded the suicidal act.

Distinguishing the crisis cases is not easy, but every case included in that category involves suicide following shifts in social or medical situations which might be regarded as an added burden. If no new difficulty confronted the victim before the suicidal act, he was not included. If he had been isolated over a long period, as was often the case, but fell a victim to suicide without any apparent change in his situation, he was not included. If he had been long depressed and not subject to any new event which would be likely to increase his depression, he was not included. Said a physician:

> This particular type of mental disease, "melancholia", is always accompanied by the urge to self-destruction, and the urge is independent of outside happenings or circumstances. The subsequent suicide is the result of the mental affliction, and not of an upset in their affairs.

Such cases we have not included. We regret that necessity precludes a description of individual cases here, and we recognize that the incompleteness of the case materials makes such an evaluation tentative at its best; but, for what it is worth, we concluded that 35 of the 50 climbers, 15 of those who "stayed put" on their father's level, and 26 of the sliders committed suicide after some precipitating event. For them the situation was a crisis. These differences are clearly significant only if our judgments are valid, but they lead us to make the comparisons which follow.

COMPARATIVE BEHAVIOR OF CLIMBERS AND SLIDERS

The climbers and sliders, as we have indicated, were confronted with a crisis in more instances than were the non-mobile males. The differences observed in Table 14.5 are statistically significant (Chi square = 16.08, 2 degrees of freedom, $p < 0.01$). The climbers were confronted with loss of economic status more often than were the sliders or the non-mobile group. Both climbers and sliders were confronted with a disruption of close personal ties in more instances than were the non-mobile, with the sliders slightly exceeding the climbers in this respect. It is difficult to determine from the cases what relationship climbing or sliding bears to the

TABLE 14.5   *Crisis among suicides in three age-matched groups of males above thirty-five years of age*

Group[†]	Total no. of cases	No crisis	Crisis	Nature of Crisis[*]		
				Career crisis	Disrupted social relationships	Health poor
Climbers	50	15	35	17	11	7
Sliders	50	26	24	8	13	5
Non-mobile	50	35	15	6	3	6
Total	150	76	74	31	27	18

* Example of crises: *career crisis* – business failure, fear of business failure, loss of job; *disrupted social relationships* – death of spouse or close relative, divorce; *health poor* – impending surgery, diagnosis of cancer.
† Climbers and sliders are persons who moved at least 10 ranks above or below the prestige positions of their fathers.

strength of social relationships. Yet differences of status between father and son may be an index of decline in their relationships in ways in which the data we have presented do not show.

It is possible that the suicide has low tolerance for frustration, whatever else enters into his behavior. He may have no major problems, as viewed by others, but may suffer attrition from small adversities. "Why did you shoot yourself?" the doctor asked one dying victim. He replied, "There is no grass; the cows are starving. The cow kicked over a bucket of milk this morning, and that was the end of everything!" But this man's annual income was probably more than £750, and the current outlook was not as bad as he pictured it. Other victims suffer from headaches or worry about a slight scab in the nose, but we have not considered a scab in the nostril as a crisis. Low tolerance of frustration, as a possible factor in suicide, is not proposed as an individual trait, unrelated to the past of the person. More data are needed on the sociogenic factors involved in personality development in order to understand human differentials in the tolerance of disappointments such as suicides suffer.

Nothing short of longitudinal case studies, which take account of the processes of the family conditioning of children who later, as adults, develop suicidal tendencies, will give us an understanding of some of the conditions to be considered in an adequate analysis of suicidal acts. Such longitudinal studies would make it possible to observe class differences in psychogenic conditioning which could play a part in producing variations in the ability to tolerate frustration. Do upper-class children have a lower tolerance of frustration than those in the lower class? In the United States? In New Zealand? We do not know. Our data give us no answer to this question.

15

Some Sociological Concomitants of Academic Streaming in a Grammar School*

COLIN LACEY

A great deal is now known about the macro-sociology of secondary education in Britain. Recent studies (for example, Floud *et al.*, 1957; Douglas, 1964) focusing on selection for entry and on the performance in secondary schools of pupils with various social and psychological characteristics, have sketched in the major dimensions of the problem. This paper, on the other hand . . . is an attempt to lay bare some of the micro-sociological mechanisms within one school and dwells primarily on processes of differentiation and sub-culture formation. It must therefore be seen against the background of well-established findings in the field.

The paper contains three sections: (1) A description of some of the sociological characteristics of boys entering the school; (2) A descriptive analysis of some aspects of the developing informal structure of one class in the school, with particular reference to two case studies, and an attempt to establish a model which describes the passage of pupils through the school; (3) An attempt to verify the model through the use of quantitative indices – in particular, the concepts of differentiation and polarization which are developed in section 2. The overall aim is to provide a picture of the stratification and subsequent sub-culture development associated with academic streaming.

* Reprinted in part from Colin Lacey (1966) "Some sociological concomitants of academic streaming in a grammar school", *British Journal of Sociology*, **17**: 245–62, with the permission of the publishers and the author.

THE INTAKE

The grammar school is a highly selective institution. To start with, therefore, it is important for us to investigate the ways in which this selection affects the composition of the newly recruited first-year classes. It is only possible to talk about subsequent sub-cultural development if the initial characteristics of the group are clear. The particular factors that will concern us here are: (1) The way selection restricts the intake to a particular type of student; (2) The way selection isolates the successful candidate from his fellow pupils and friends at his junior school.

Though not completely conclusive, the evidence gathered supports my contention that the new intake to a grammar school will consist largely of 11-year-olds who have been accustomed to playing what I have called 'best pupil' role in their junior schools, and are, in their new environment, often separated from their former school friends. It is useful to look at Hightown Grammar School as an illustration of the way the selection process works. Hightown is a pseudonym for the town in which the school is located. I conducted eight months full-time and ten months part-time fieldwork in the school. In all I have been associated with this school and others in the area for three and a half years.

[Lacey describes the school system in Hightown, as it relates to the transition from junior to secondary school. While the situation is quite complex, there are four main factors: (a) entry to a grammar school is restricted to the 15 per cent of junior-school pupils who pass the 11-plus examination; (b) there are several grammar schools, with some degree of specialised selection of intake (for example, on the basis of religion, and occupational aspirations); (c) the annual intake of Hightown Grammar is about 120 boys, representing 4 per cent of their age-group in the community. The 1962 intake was 118, and these boys are from thirty-five different junior schools; (d) the school splits the intake, at random, into four classes – thus half the boys have no friend from the same junior school in their class. Lacey's table 1, showing the size of junior-school contingents in the 1962 intake, is omitted here.]

The homogeneity of the intake and the relative isolation of individual new boys from their junior-school friends are both important factors affecting patterns of behaviour in the first-year classes. The first-year pupils show a high degree of commitment to the school. School uniform is rigidly adhered to; caps and blazers are proudly displayed; school functions and clubs are attended disproportionately by first-year boys. Their behaviour in the classroom is characterized by eagerness, co-operation with the teacher and a high degree of competition among themselves. [Lacey stresses the desire to participate in class; data on a typical incident are given, based on his observation of the first-year classes.]

The type of enthusiasm characteristic of a first-year class was occasionally found in second- or third-year forms but there were a number of observable differences. The second and third forms were more likely to 'play dead' and to allow five or six people to 'do all the work' . . . [Lacey mentions a residue of boys in the second and third years who hardly participated in classes; an incident is described in which a class is intentionally disrupted.]

THE INFORMAL STRUCTURE – TWO CASE STUDIES

As soon as this highly selected first-year population meets at Hightown Grammar School and is allocated to the four first-year classes, a complex process of interaction begins. This process takes place through a variety of encounters. Boys talk and listen to each other, talk and listen to teachers, listen to conversations, notice details of accent, gesture, clothing, watch others at work and at play in various situations and in innumerable different permutations.

During the first few days much of this interaction appears to take place in a fairly random way influenced mainly by the physical and organizational arrangements. Soon, patterns of selection begin to emerge. Various initial interactions yield information and experience, which are retained by the individual and provide some basis for the interpretation and partial control of other interactions. This partial control is extremely important because it soon gives rise to a recognizable, although unstable and changing structure.

When I started observing the first-year classes in March 1963, the members of each class had only been together for about six months, but each class already had a definite structure of which the pupils clearly had detailed knowledge. When a master called a boy to read or answer a question, others could be seen giving each other significant looks which clearly indicated that they knew what to expect.

[Omitted here is a discussion of two boys – Priestley and Cready – from the same first-year class, IA. Lacey describes several incidents observed in IA which show how the structural position in the class and the expectations of the class and the teacher towards the pupil differ between the two boys. Priestley has "fallen foul of the system". He is the "butt of the class" and is often in trouble with the teachers. He does poorly in first-year examinations, is placed in a low stream (2C) in the second year and is generally failing academically. In the first term of the first year Cready's academic performance was similar to that of Priestley. However, by the end of the first year Cready is doing well in examinations; he is placed in the highest stream (2E) in the second year, and continues to do well. Lacey comments that, in contrast to Priestley, Cready associated with a "different group of boys. He behaved differently in class, and had a markedly different reputation." Observational data based on pupil-teacher interaction in one class show that differential treatment is sometimes given to the two boys for what is essentially the same behaviour; table 2 (omitted here) illustrates this point. The main thrust of Lacey's argument is that the micro-sociological processes operating, both within the peer group and through interaction with teachers, are important factors affecting academic success or failure. Priestley is from a middle-class family and Cready is working - class in origin, so these two cases do "not conform with the established correlation between academic achievement and social class". This point reinforces the importance of the micro-processes emphasised by Lacey.]

. . . I reiterate that this is not an attempt to disprove the general established trend [that middle-class boys do better academically than working-class boys] but to highlight the fact that there are detailed social mechanisms and processes responsible for bringing it about which are not completely determined by external factors. By studying these mechanisms it will be possible to add a dimension to our understanding of the general processes of education in our schools.

DIFFERENTIATION AND POLARIZATION

It is important to discuss these processes in a more general way and set up a model which describes the passage of pupils through the grammar school. To do this, I will need to introduce two terms – "differentiation" and "polarization". By differentiation is meant the process of separation and ranking of students according to a multiple set of criteria which makes up the normative, academically orientated, value system of the grammar school. This process is regarded here as being largely carried out by teachers in the course of their normal duties.

Polarization on the other hand is regarded as a process taking place within the student body, partly as a result of differentiation but influenced by external factors and with an autonomy of its own. It is a process of sub-culture formation in which the school-dominated normative culture is opposed by an alternative culture which I will refer to as the anti-group culture. The content of the anti-group culture will, of course, be very much influenced by the school and its social setting. It may range from a folk music, CND group in a minor public school to a delinquent sub-culture in a secondary modern school in an old urban area. In Hightown Grammar School it fell between these extremes and was influenced by the large working-class and Jewish communities of Hightown.

There are a number of scales on which a master habitually rates a boy. For the purposes of the analysis I will consider two.

(a) Academic Scale.
(b) Behaviour Scale. This would include considerations as varied as general classroom behaviour and attitudes, politeness, attention, helpfulness, time spent in school societies and sports.

The two are not independent. Behaviour affects academic standards not only because good behaviour involves listening and attending but because a master becomes favourably disposed towards a boy who is well-behaved and trying hard . . . There is another reason why good behaviour is correlated with academic achievement. A boy who does well and wishes to do well academically is predisposed to accepting the system of values of the grammar school, that is, he behaves well. This is because the system gives him high prestige and it is therefore in his interest to support it . . . He is thereby supporting his position of prestige. On the other hand a boy who does badly academically is predisposed to criticize, reject or even sabotage the system, where he can, since it places him in an inferior position.

A boy showing the extreme development of this [phenomenon] may subscribe to values which are actually the inverted values of the school. For example, he obtains prestige from cheeking a teacher, playing truant, not doing homework, smoking, drinking and even stealing. As it develops, the anti-group produces its own impetus. A boy who takes refuge in such a group because his work is poor finds that the group commits him to a behaviour pattern which means that his work will stay poor and in fact often gets progressively worse. [Lacey gives a short extract from an essay written by a boy, Badman, illustrating "development of anti-group values of an extreme nature for a first year pupil". The extract ends "I would much rather be a hooligan and get some fun out of life than . . . being a dear nice little boy doing what he is told."]

Earlier we saw that at the beginning of the first year, the pupils constitute a relatively homogeneous and undifferentiated group. They are uniformly enthusiastic and eager to please, both through their performance of work and in their behaviour. The pupils who are noticed first are the good pupils and the bad pupils. Even by the Spring term some masters are still unsure of the names of quiet pupils in the undifferentiated middle of the classes they teach. It is fairly rare for an anti-group to develop in the first year. Although one or two individuals may develop marked anti-group values, they are likely to remain isolates. In the 1962 first year, I was able to recognize only one, Badman . . . He wished to be transferred to a secondary modern.

The more usual course of events associated with a marked degree of (relative) failure in the first year is for the child to display symptoms of emotional upheaval and nervous disorder and for a conflict of standards to take place. Symptoms that occurred in the first-year intake of 1962 included the following: Bursting into tears when reprimanded by a teacher . . . Sleeplessness, Bedwetting [seven other symptoms are listed] . . . The 15 cases recorded probably represent all the cases of major disturbance but a large number of cases of minor disturbance probably never became known to the school.

The individual significance of these cases cannot be discussed here but their general significance is important to the model under discussion. We have seen that the "eleven-plus" exam selects the "best pupils" from the top forms of the junior schools . . . The pupils . . . have internalized many of the expectations inherent in the position of "best pupils". Their transfer to the grammar school not only means a new environment, with all that such a change entails – for example, new class-mates, new teachers and new sets of rules – but also for many of them a violation of their expectations as best pupils. It is when this violation of expectations coincides with "unsatisfactory" home backgrounds that the worst cases of emotional disturbance occur.

In the second year the process of differentiation continues. If streaming takes place between the first and second years as it did in the year group I am studying it helps speed the process and a new crop of cases of emotional disturbance occurs. In the 1963 second year most of these cases were associated with boys who were failing to make the grade in the top stream and boys who were in the bottom half of the bottom stream. After six months in the second year this bottom stream was already regarded as a difficult form to teach because, to quote two teachers: (i) "They are unacademic, they can't copy with the work"; (ii) "Give them half a chance and they will give you the run around."

The true anti-group starts to emerge in the second year, and it develops markedly in the third and fourth years. It is in the third and fourth years that strenuous efforts are made to get rid of anti-group pupils. [Lacey describes the processes through which anti-group pupils may leave the school, officially or unofficially. It was not possible to give exact figures – the estimate was that between 10 and 15 "officially" left each year.]

INDICES OF DIFFERENTIATION AND POLARIZATION

The indices developed in this part of the paper are prepared from two questionnaires completed by all members of the 1962 intake. One questionnaire was given at the end of the first year and one at the end of the second. The indices are designed to illustrate the processes of differentiation and polarization. On both occasions the boys were asked who had been their close friends over the last year. They were asked to restrict themselves to boys in the school and to six choices, unless they felt they definitely could not do so.

There was virtually no difference in the average number of choices *received* per boy in the four *unstreamed* first-year classes [see Table 15.3]. The boys were streamed on academic criteria at the end of first year; approximately the top one-quarter of each first-year form went into 2E, the second quarter into 2A, and so on. These same (first year) friendship choices were related to the new forms 2E, 2A, 2B and 2C as shown in Table 15.4(a). Not only do the figure reveal striking differences but these differences are related to academic achievement. At the end of the first year, the higher up the academic scale a boy was placed, the more likely he was to attract a large number of friendship choices.

TABLE 15.3

1A	4.1 choices per boy
1B	4.1 choices per boy
1C	4.2 choices per boy
1D	4.5 choices per boy

TABLE 15.4   *Average number of friendship choices received per boy after streaming: first year and second year*

	Average number of choices per boy in each class	
	(a) 1st year	(b) 2nd year
2E	4.8	5.0
2A	4.5	4.5
2B	3.9	3.9
2C	3.3	4.3

At the end of the second year the boys were asked the same question. The response was equally striking. Column (b) of Table 15.4 shows that the year spent among a new class of boys has hardly changed the overall positions of 2E, 2A and 2B, although the actual friendship choices for any one boy will have undergone considerable change. However, 2C has undergone a substantial change. The increase from 3.3 to 4.3 for 2C represents an increase of something like 30 choices, in a class of 30 boys. That the new

TABLE 15.5 *Distribution of friendship choices according to class: second year 1963 (1962 intake at end of second year)* *

Number in each class in brackets	2E	2A	2B	2C	Others	Total of choices made	% of choices in own class
2E (31)	**96**	24	13	7	11	151	63.2
2A (31)	28	**94**	16	6	14	158	59.5
2B (28)	20	17	**63**	23	20	143	45.6
2C (30)	9	4	18	**92**	13	136	67.2
Totals (of choices received)	153	139	110	128	58	588	

* Read across for choices made, down for choices received by each class.

popularity of the boys in 2C is brought about by the growth of a new set of norms and values or the beginnings of the anti-group sub-culture is demonstrated by Table 15.5. The boys of 2C have become popular for the very reasons that they were unpopular in their first year.

The boys of 2E and 2A who according to our hypothesis *should* be positively influenced by the academic grading, since they are successful in relation to it, show that it does in fact have a marked positive influence on their choice of friends (e.g. 2E make 24 choices into 2A, 13 choices into 2B and only 7 into 2C). There is no element in the organization of the school that could bring this about. In 2B a change takes place. Their choices into 2E and 2A have the expected form but there is an unexpectedly large number of choices into 2C, i.e. 23, more than into either 2E or 2A. Similarly, the boys of 2C show a marked tendency to choose their friends, outside 2C, from 2B rather than 2E and 2A. There must be a basis, other than the school-imposed academic values, on which these friends are chosen. This alternative set of norms and values I have already referred to as the anti-group sub-culture.

Table 15.6 shows that in the second year academic achievement is related to social class. To some degree this is a problem of working-class and middle-class culture (see, for example, Holly, 1965). That this is not the whole answer is demonstrated by reminding ourselves of Table 15.4(a) and (b) where it is clearly demonstrated that this anti-group development took place between the ends of the first and second year. If it were solely a social class phenomena it would have been apparent at the end of the first year.

TABLE 15.6   *Distribution of the sons of non-manual workers between the four second-year streams*

	Non-manual/manual ratio	Ratio
2E	18/14	1.3
2A	18/13	1.4
2B	13/14	0.9
2C	8/23	0.3

This analysis is confirmed by another set of data which is in many ways complementary to the first. In the second year questionnaire I asked "What boys do you find it difficult to get on

TABLE 15.7 *Distribution of choices of unpopular boys: second year, 1963*

	2E	2A	2B	2C	Others	Prefects	Total of choices made	Average number of choices received
2E	38	4	4	26	3	0	75	1.71
2A	5	33	1	9	22	1	51	1.45
2B	7	4	24	20	1	0	56	1.14
2C	3	4	3	42	3	6	61	3.23
Totals (of choices received)	53	45	32	97	29	7	243	

with?" Once again I allowed them to put up to six names unless they felt they could not possibly confine themselves to six. This time, however, many boys refrained from putting any names down and only a few put six. Enough names were mentioned to establish a pattern of unpopularity. Once again the largest number of choices were made into the informants' own class (see Table 15.7). The number of choices made into other forms was always less than 7 with one notable exception – 2C received 26 from 2E, 9 from 2A and 20 from 2B and so received the highest number of unpopularity choices, 97 compared with 53 for 2E which is the next highest. The preponderance of choices into 2C is explained by the anti-group development in 2C. These boys are now regarded as bullies and "tough eggs" who in Badman's terminology would rather be hooligans and having a good time than be nice little boys. They are aggressive, loud-mouthed and feared by many who are successful in terms of the dominant school norms.

An expectation that is considerably altered by academic streaming is the school-leaving age. Boys who are successful will expect to continue after "O" level at 15 or 16 into the sixth form. At the end of the first year the boys were asked "At what age would you like to leave school?" The results demonstrate the overall optimism of the first year. Only 25 per cent wanted to leave at the end of the fifth year, 75 per cent desiring a sixth-form career. In practice only something like 50 per cent ever achieved this. When the figures were broken down into the second-year classes they reveal, even so, considerable foresight. [Lacey discusses the first column of figures in Table 15.8; he points out that these are rational estimates made by the boys based on their own knowledge at the time.]

TABLE 15.8   *Average age at which the boys in each class would like to leave school*

	Before streaming at end of first year	After streaming at end of second year
2E	17.4	17.4
2A	17.7	17.3
2B	17.3	17.4
2C	17.0	16.7

By the end of the second year, the averages of the desired leaving age revealed a number of puzzling features (see Table 15.8). 2E remained the same while the average age for 2A fell below 2B. 2B's average in fact increased to the same level as 2E, 2C's average value decreased, but not as much as one might expect. The situation has been complicated by an additional factor which I have called "streaming reaction".

When the top seven or eight boys from each of the first year house-groups are put into 2E it is fairly obvious that most of them are not going to be able to maintain a high position in the form. In fact Table 15.9 shows that only two were able to maintain their position, the rest were all placed lower in 2E than in their first-year class. This was less marked in 2A with only 16 boys doing less well. It was reversed in 2B and 2C.

TABLE 15.9 *Examination performance before streaming compared with examination performance after streaming*

	Number of boys who were placed higher in second year than in first year	Same	Number of boys who were placed lower in second year than in first year
2E	0	2	28
2A	7	4	16
2B	17	2	6
2C	15	0	2

[In a section omitted here, Lacey argues that streaming reaction has a special effect on the E stream and a minimal effect on the C stream. By contrast, in classes 2A and 2B "streaming reaction was a major factor affecting the length of time that the boys wanted to stay at school". Additional discussion, and two further tables, show some other effects of streaming reaction. Table 10 (omitted) gives data on the boys' personal estimate of success in the second year. 2E shows the lowest proportion of boys regarding the year as successful and 2C shows the highest – results which probably represent personal reactions to the examination performance differences shown in Table 15.9. In table 11 (omitted) the estimated average time per night spent on homework in the first year is contrasted with the corresponding estimates for the second year. There is little change for those in 2C, but the figure for 2E almost doubled (approximately from one hour to two hours). Lacey comments that "streaming has given rise to distinctively different climates of expectation in relation to homework"; this is taken as another illustration of the process of differentiation.]

CONCLUSION

In this article I have attempted to develop a model which describes the internal processes of a grammar school in terms of sub-culture formation, differentiation and polarization. The indices presented in the last section are an early attempt to verify quantitatively some of the impressionistic data presented earlier. The research is, however, still continuing and a great deal of the material already collected is still at an early stage of analysis.

It is expected that material yet to be collected, as well as that already in the pipeline, will clarify and modify this early formulation. [See Lacey (1970) for a full report on the project, and also Lacey (1976) for a review of the methodology of the research.] Nevertheless the evidence presented here seems to indicate that the relationship between the internal organization (Jackson, 1964) and development of pupil sub-cultures (see Coleman, 1961) is an important factor in the process of education that warrants careful examination in further research.

16

Girls, Boys and Politics*

ROBERT E. DOWSE AND JOHN A. HUGHES

Some of the most solidly researched and validated findings in the
social sciences relate to the differential participation of men and
women in political activities . . . Women have been found to vote
less than men, to participate in political parties less than men, to
know less about politics than men, to have less interest in politics
than men and to be more conservative than men. [A number of
sources are cited documenting these differences, and the proposed
explanations reviewed below.]

A number of explanations of these findings have been suggested. One type of explanation stresses the structural restraints
militating against women's participation; the restraints, including
the tasks of child-rearing and maintaining a home, are held to
account for the lower political participation and knowledge since
women, contrasted with men, are prevented from linking up with
the wider network of social contacts which helps to maintain male
political involvement. This explanation is obviously a powerful
one and does account for the well-documented finding that
women's rate of participation increases when such burdens cease
. . .

The structural explanation stresses that most adult females
experience more or less structural impediments to political involvement and interest. If very strictly interpreted this explanation

* Reprinted in part from Robert E. Dowse and John A. Hughes (1971) "Girls,
boys and politics", *British Journal of Sociology*, **22**: 53–67, with the permission of
the publishers and the authors.

must insist that differences between the sexes acting or thinking politically emerge only when the female role set changes with marriage and during the period of child-rearing and other household duties. That is, that significant sex differences with regard to politics will not be present in childhood.

Another proposed and alternative explanation is based on the idea of differential role modelling in which the dominant cultural norm stresses that politics is eminently a male preserve. An implication of this explanation is that one would expect at least some elements of adult role behaviour and attitudes to politics to be learnt during childhood, and that such sex difference noted amongst adults should to some extent be detectable amongst young children. Drawing on a very large number of published reports on child socialization Hyman suggested that "already at early ages, boys are directed towards politics and here lie the seeds of adult differentiations everywhere found in studies of political participation" (Hyman, 1959: 31). An implication of the differential socialization explanation is that sex differences in political attitudes have their foundations in childhood, and it is reasonable to suppose that such differences are reinforced in the child as it grows older. If this implication is correct then it should be possible to observe the development of these differences between boys and girls. Hence, we hypothesize that any political sex differences apparent in childhood will increase with age as the roles become more clearly defined. This relationship we call hypothesis I.

It is the pre-adult roots of these differences that we wish to discuss in the paper. The expectation we started out with was that the sex differences observed in adults in terms of political interest, knowledge and sense of potential efficacy would be present in the young, but the differences would not be strongly marked for girls because of the absence of family responsibilities. We also expected that childhood differences would, however, consistently anticipate adult political differences; that is, that girls would regularly have lower levels of political interests, etc., than boys. But it is known that the gross differences amongst adults are reduced by intervening variables such as education. In the light of the relatively widely confirmed findings that middle-class women of higher educational levels differ only very marginally from similar middle-class men (for example, Milbrath, 1965: 136–7) we expected that if the socialization theory is correct, the roots of this resemblance would be detectable in childhood. On the grounds that higher education on the part of women seems to offset the cultural pressure toward socializing women into less salient political roles we would expect that middle-class girls will resemble middle-class boys. On the other hand since working-class girls receive neither the benefits of more education nor cultural direction we would expect that they will not resemble working-class boys. Thus, we expect that since middle-class girls are better educated than working-class girls they will consistently be more like middle-class boys than working-class girls resemble working-class boys. This hypothesis we will call hypothesis II.

In this paper we will empirically test our two hypotheses using English data in an attempt to discover whether or not the socialization explanation of adult sex–political differences is plausible. We cannot use a stronger word than plausible since in a strict sense there are no formal political socialization theories and, therefore, our hypotheses are inferences from previous empirical studies. But if our hypotheses are supported by the current evidence then at least we will have shown a strong possibility that adult sex differences are rooted in pre-adult experience.

THE DATA

The data presented here are based upon a survey whose major focus was an examination of the extent to which transmission of political attitudes within the family took place. The data are drawn from a study of a sample of school children from Exeter between the ages of 11 and 17 plus years. This sample consists of a girls' grammar school ($n = 148$), a boys' grammar school ($n = 146$), two girls' secondary modern schools ($n = 193$) and a boys' secondary modern school ($n = 140$). The number of children in each school sampled represents a randomly selected 20 per cent of children in each school. The sample constitutes a good cross-section of the state secondary education sector of the town. Each child in the sample was asked to complete a paper-and-pencil questionnaire under the supervision of the investigators. In this way we obtained questionnaires from 627 children.

FINDINGS

Our most clear-cut sex difference emerged from a series of 24 questions designed to measure the children's knowledge of political facts. The kind of question we asked the children was to name the local MP, name a local councillor, who was Sir Winston Churchill? Which party forms the government? Name four members of the government, the names of the two Houses of Parliament, etc. The political knowledge categories were constructed by dividing the distribution of scores for the total sample into three groups on the basis of the nearest tertile scores. This gave us three almost equal categories – high, medium, and low.

We found that controlling for education, girls were consistently less well informed than boys [see Figure 16.1]. But grammar school girls by the age of 13 years scored higher on political knowledge than secondary modern boys of 15 years and above: by 15 years 78 per cent of grammar school girls were high scorers but

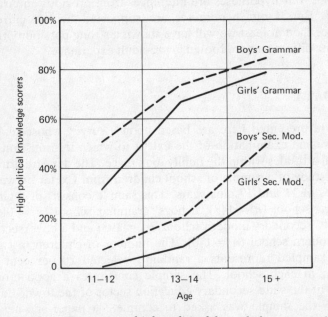

FIGURE 16.1   *Percentage high political knowledge scorers by age, school and sex*

at the same age 48 per cent of secondary modern boys were high scorers (83 per cent of grammar boys above 15 years were high scorers). By 15 years only 29 per cent of secondary modern girls were high scorers (Unless otherwise stated all relationships cited are acceptable at least at the 5 per cent level of significance employing the Chi-square test.) In all cases the percentage of children scoring high increased with age, but starting from a lower base girls increased more rapidly than boys and in the case of 15-year-old boys and girls in grammar schools the differences were relatively trivial.

The problem here is why the improvement in political knowledge amongst girls in secondary modern schools (from 0 to 29 per cent) is so much less than amongst secondary modern boys (from 5 to 48 per cent). Controlling for social class (all manual occupations of parents were defined as working-class and all non-manual as middle-class) working-class children in all the schools fell consistently below middle-class children so that class has an effect (but chi-square not acceptable). Further, working-class girls in both grammar and secondary modern schools fall below their middle-class age peers. Hence, we can assume that class makes a contribution in determining political knowledge of girls, but whether this is simply a consequence of an anti- or of an a-political home environment for working-class girls or of a more generalized cultural impoverishment we cannot say.

Hypothesis I, drawn from socialization theory, that with increasing age there will be increasing differences between the sexes, was not confirmed for political knowledge amongst the two sexes in grammar schools, but was weakly confirmed in secondary modern schools. Hypothesis II . . . is partly confirmed by the following evidence: middle-class girls in grammar schools were more like middle-class boys in grammar schools (65 per cent girls and 67 per cent boys scored high) than they were like working-class girls in grammar schools (60 per cent scored high). Taking the spread of political knowledge across the whole sample the hypothesis is confirmed. It is apparent from Table 16.1 that middle-class girls as a group are politically more like middle-class boys than working-class girls are like working-class boys, and hence we have an element of confirmation for the socialization theory explaining mature sexual differences in politics.

TABLE 16.1   *Percentage differences on political knowledge by sex and class*

| | Political knowledge | | | |
	High	Medium	Low	Total
Working class*				
Boys	43% (73)	31% (52)	26% (45)	100% (170)
Girls	22% (39)	36% (63)	42% (72)	100% (174)
Middle class†				
Boys	48% (42)	36% (31)	16% (14)	100% (87)
Girls	47% (52)	27% (35)	27% (35)	101% (128)

* Gamma = 0.34, $X^2 p < 0.01$.
† Gamma = 0.12, $X^2 p > 0.10$.

[Dowse and Hughes discuss table 2 (omitted), in which data are given on the attribution of party preferences to selected occupations (doctor, lorry-driver and nine others). These data, which stem from items on the questionnaire, asking whether doctors, lorry-drivers, etc., are likely to prefer Labour, Conservative or Liberal, or to vary, were designed to test political cognition. Table 2 shows little sex difference, except that "girls were more likely than boys to be undecided . . . in all cases". Dowse and Hughes suggest that "the girls political world is less sharply defined than is that of the boys".]

Thus our evidence is relatively clear that at a cognitive level there are important differences between girls and boys . . . Further it seems clear that parents' class has an effect on the child's level of political knowledge; in grammar school although working-class girls increase their knowledge score slightly more rapidly than middle-class girls they do not catch up since by 15 years and above 75 per cent of working-class girls score high whilst 81 per cent of middle-class girls score high. Again, in secondary modern schools, middle-class girls starting from the same base as working-class girls with 0 per cent scoring high have by the age of 15 years and above increased to 33 per cent scoring high whilst for working-class girls the comparable figure was 22 per cent. Also working-class girls in grammar schools by 15 plus fall well below working-class boys in grammar schools and start well below them (boys = 40 per cent at 11 years and 83 per cent at 15 plus; girls = 29 per cent at 11 years and 73 per cent at 15 plus). Finally, in the boys' grammar school by the age of 15 years and above the percentage of high scorers by class was exactly the same (83 per cent). Thus it would appear that in all cases working-class girls fall below working-class boys and below middle-class girls and we suggest that this relationship may be explained by assuming that for the working-class the role definition of a female (in home and school) tends to de-emphasize political knowledge. In the middle-class the female role is not quite so a-politically defined. Thus our analysis up to this point confirms the explanation of differential sexual interest, etc., which stresses early role modelling.

However, all our other findings which relate to the affective or normative level are far more ambiguous suggesting that affective differences, such as they are, are reinforced and developed within the working and marital situations.

The most persistent differences between boys and girls that emerged in response to our questions designed to tap affective orientations to politics and politicians was that the girls tended to be more unsure than the boys, and over the whole range of questions were more likely to answer "Don't know" or not to answer at all [the example is the political cognition data presented in table 2 (omitted); see the editorial note above]. This may represent another element of sex role modelling and is slightly clearer in the case of girls in secondary modern schools.

Sex was unrelated to declared levels of political interest with school being a much stronger predictor of interest than sex or age (see Table 16.3) . . . 40.5 per cent of children in grammar schools fell into the "strongly interested" or "interested" categories compared with only 21 per cent in secondary modern. The comparable figures for all boys and girls were 35 per cent and 30 per cent respectively (Chi-square not significant, gamma = 0.06). There were no significant or consistent differences in the data on political interest that would in any way confirm hypothesis I since the differences between the children in expressed political interest did not increase with age.

TABLE 16.3 *Children either "strongly interested" or "interested" in politics by sex and school*

School	Male	Female
Secondary modern	26.3%	26.6%
Grammar	44%	42.6%

TABLE 16.4 *Social class, sex and political interest in secondary modern schools*

	Political interest		
	High	Low	Totals
Working class*			
Boys	24%	76%	100% (91)
Girls	26%	74%	100%(117)
Middle class†			
Boys	26%	74%	100% (35)
Girls	27%	73%	100% (58)

* $Q = -0.15; X^2 p > 0.10; N = 208.$
† $Q = -0.04; X^2 p > 0.10; N = 93.$

TABLE 16.5 *Social class, sex and political interest in grammar schools*

	Political interest		
	High	Low	Totals
Working class*			
Boys	35%	65%	100% (48)
Girls	28%	72%	100% (57)
Middle class†			
Boys	51%	49%	100% (87)
Girls	43%	57%	100% (70)

* $Q = -0.17; X^2 p > 0.10; N = 105.$
† $Q = -0.05; X^2 p > 0.10; N = 157.$

Looking at the combined effect of school type, social class and sex on adolescents' declared level of political interest we find that within secondary modern schools neither sex nor social class made any significant difference [see Table 16.4]. In grammar schools on the other hand it is the non-manual boys who show the highest level of declared political interest followed by non-manual girls followed by manual boys and then manual girls [See Table 16.5]. Apart from manual girls, all groups within grammar schools show significantly higher reported levels of political interest than any of the same groups in secondary modern schools but none of these relationships are significant. It is clear that these findings do not confirm hypothesis II since the overall differences postulated are not apparent, and it is evident that during adolescence the strongest factor is education (Dowse and Hughes, 1971). In Figure 16.2 this factor is demonstrated by age and we discover that although secondary modern boys start below all grammar school children their trend of interest is upward. This suggests the *possibility* that if in their work situations working-class boys find support for political interest and involvement this upward trend may be maintained. In other words structural factors are probably more important in maintaining working-class political interest and involvement than is early political socialization. A very interesting trend among both boys and girls in the grammar schools is the precipitous decline of interest between the ages of 15 and 16 years and their rapid increase to a similiar high level of political interest by 17 years and above. Hence hypothesis I which predicted that with age sex differences would become greater is not confirmed for either school type. However, when we break down by class in the grammar schools we find that middle-class children are always more interested in politics than are working-class children. Another point is that taking age cohorts in grammar schools *both* boys and girls decline in interest at the same age and this decline is *common to both* class groups. Hypothesis II was not confirmed for grammar schools since no consistent sex differences on political interest by class emerged, i.e. middle-class girls did no more resemble middle-class boys than working-class girls resembled working-class boys. [There] are class differences, but education is far more important.

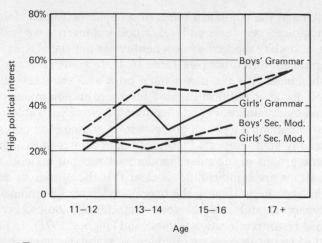

FIGURE 16.2   *Political interest by age and school*

[Omitted is a brief discussion of the results for questionnaire items on attitudes to women in politics; no tables are given.]

We found a moderately strong association between sex and choosing a party to support with boys much more likely than girls to choose a party (gamma = 0.24, Chi-square p <0.01). [See Table 16.6]. Hypothesis I was not confirmed by our data on choosing a party since by age girls were *increasingly* likely to choose one of the three major parties offered whilst boys were *less* likely! With our data we are able to offer no explanation of this finding except to note it. A possibility is that since boys have a greater knowledge of politics by age than girls, they might find that a clear cut choice is more difficult to make and this possibility is enhanced by our finding (see Table 16.7) that boys are more exposed to political media, with its contrasting and varied messages, than are girls. Hypothesis II also was not confirmed since sex differences by class on choosing a party were negligible. [Omitted is a further discussion of data on (a) party preference, and (b) attitude to political efficacy. In each case, comparisons are made between the results for the sample and those of their parents.]

TABLE 16.6   *Choosing a party by sex and age*

Age	Boys	Girls
11–12 years	63% (60)	39% (40)
13–14 years	52% (50)	42% (68)
15+ years	50% (43)	46% (36)

TABLE 16.7   *Sex and exposure to media with political content*

Sex	Percentage who select political TV programmes	Percentage who "always" watch the news on TV	Percentage who "regularly" hear news on radio
Boys	37	89	81
Girls	29	25	25

It has been found in various studies of women's political interest that they are comparatively less exposed to political media than are men, and in order to discover whether this was rooted in childhood we asked three questions about children's selections of political material on radio and TV. The differences here were quite startling and are summarized in Table 16.7. Controlling for social class did not significantly increase the association between media exposure and sex but this was hardly likely since the one to one relationship is a very strong one; nor were there any significant relationships between social class and media exposure or age. Thus, neither hypothesis I nor hypothesis II was confirmed. However, the lower media exposure may well help to explain why girls have less political knowledge at their disposal than boys . . .

[The Findings section concludes with a brief discussion of other data from the survey. Several questionnaire items are listed as showing no perceptible difference between boys and girls; these items include conservatism in party preference, and discussion of politics with parents and friends. No further tables are given.]

CONCLUSIONS

It would be possible, but tedious, to go through the questionnaire item by item detailing the lack of significant differences between boys' and girls' political attitudes since the fact is that our survey revealed very few and although differences were usually in a predictable direction (pointing to adult differences) this was not always the case. Boys and girls, in the Exeter state school sector at least, are not obviously and grossly differentially socialized in terms of political attitudes. Certainly girls have significantly lower levels of cognitive awareness than boys and this is strongly the case with working-class girls. Certainly they appear to inhabit a less sharply focused political world than boys and in most of our questions working-class girls were marginally (but not statistically significantly) more likely to be 'blurred' than any other group. Further, we found that many differences between boys and girls did not significantly increase with age so that hypothesis I, drawn from socialization theory predicting an increasing disparity (controlling other factors), was not confirmed. In most cases hypothesis II also was not confirmed. Given that there are quite discernible differences in the political involvement of men and women and that our data point to these differences only to a rather limited extent, a number of problems of interpretation emerge.

Quite possibly a finer-tuned study employing more sophisticated techniques to probe hypothesised underlying differences might have given other results, but we do not really think that this is the case and in this belief we are strengthened by American findings that "The sex differences that we find are small and . . . they do not present a simple pattern" (Easton and Dennis, 1969 : 343). It is also possible that our hypotheses drawn from childhood socialization as an explanation of adult differences are either wrongly inferred or the assumption that the next generation more or less replicates previous generations is incorrect. We do not believe our inferences from the theory, such as it is, are implausible and are therefore driven to conclude one of two things: (a) that generations are not politically replicated on the basis of childhood political socialization or (b) that structural factors are more important than socialization theory suggests. Obviously generations do change, but we suggest that adult life situation is more important than child socialization patterns, at least as far as political participation, etc., [are] concerned.

We suggest that socialization theory overstresses the importance of children's attitudinal predispositions to become involved as adults since there may well be a whole range of "accidental" structural features such as differential possibilities of trade union membership, the accidents of casual friendships, sudden issues which galvanize the previously politically inactive into action, the accident of living in a homogeneous political environment, etc., etc., which may cause people to become involved when otherwise they might have remained passive (Dowse and Brier, 1968).

At the cognitive level, tested by the political knowledge scale, girls certainly scored below boys and in the cognition of likely voting patterns girls were less sensitively aware than boys. Further, in most of the affective or attitudinal items girls were very much more likely to answer "Don't know" than boys. Boys know more than girls and are more likely to have an opinion, but when girls do have an opinion it is not siginficantly different from that of boys. When the children move into the adult world the structural factors affecting the male and female role may reinforce the marginal differences observed in school children.

There is no compelling reason to believe that the structural and socialization theories are really alternatives since they may be seen as being more or less operative in conjunction throughout the life history of the person with structural impediments to political interest and involvement operating with maximum effect upon women during the first ten to fifteen years of married life. That is to say, married life for a woman constitutes a structural restraint reinforcing those cultural patterns inimical to women's involvement in politics learned during girlhood . . . Adult males are much more likely than adult females to join a trade union, to meet political activists on the shop floor and office, and to link up with a more political milieu, and are less likely than women to be confined to home and children. Thus the likelihood is that men's political socialization is a continuing process whilst most women for a crucial period of their lives, roughly between 18 and 35 years of age, operate in a more a-political environment.

17

Father-to-Son Mobility: Australia in Comparative Perspective*

LEONARD BROOM AND F. LANCASTER JONES

This report of findings from the first national survey of social stratification and social mobility conducted in Australia attempts to fill a gap noticed by students interested in the comparative analysis of mobility . . . The findings of our Australian survey serve as the point of departure for comparisons with recent data for Italy and the United States . . .

METHOD

The data reported in Tables 17.1 and 17.3 were obtained in a sample survey of Australia's adult male work force conducted between February and May 1965. We designed the survey and interviews were carried out by the Roy Morgan Research Centre (the Australian Gallup Poll), with some supplementary interviews conducted by the Department of Sociology at the Australian National University. Electoral rolls were used as a sampling frame in twenty-three of 122 federal electorates in Australia, and ten names (starting addresses) were randomly selected from the rolls for each sampled electorate. Interviewers were instructed to call at the starting address and adjoining residences until ten interviews had been completed with an adult male worker twenty-one years

* Reprinted in part from Leonard Broom and F. Lancaster Jones (1969) "Father-to-son mobility: Australia in comparative perspective", *American Journal of Sociology*, **74**: 333–42, with the permission of the publishers and the authors.

of age or older (or with his wife). Only one interview per dwelling was attempted in 2,319 "eligible" dwellings, yielding 1,925 completed interviews, an over-all response rate of 83 per cent.

The geographical representativeness of the sample was good, with 56 per cent of respondents resident in capital cities, 27 per cent in "other urban" centres, and 17 per cent in rural areas. The comparable figures for the 1966 Census of Australia (total male population) were 57, 25, and 18 per cent. There was some underrepresentation among younger workers, the foreign-born, and the lower occupational strata, where the young and the foreign-born tend to be concentrated. A more detailed statement on the representativeness of our sample must await the publication of the relevant 1966 census tabulations. No adjustments of our data have yet been attempted. [In certain later publications based on the same data, these adjustments were made; see, for example, Broom and Jones (1969).]

Occupational data for three points were secured: (1) the occupation of the respondent at interview; (2) his occupation when he began regular employment; and (3) his father's occupation at the time of interview or, if the father was deceased or retired, his last regular job. The survey also explored the major elements of the Australian stratification system and called for information on other measures of social rank, and on attitudinal and life-style correlates of social rank (Broom *et al.*, 1968). This paper is limited to an analysis of what is customarily called intergenerational occupational mobility, that is, the relationship between the present occupation of respondents and that of their fathers.

In Table 17.1, our findings are presented in terms of the conventional non-manual, manual, and farm division of occupations. The detailed list of sixteen occupational categories shown in Table 17.3 was derived from the Australian Census classification of occupations. Census code books were used in allocating responses to specific occupational groups (Broom *et al.*, 1965). Although the sixteen categories form a scale of occupational prestige, we have preserved meaningful industrial divisions where possible. It should be noted that shop assistants (in American commerce, low-skilled retail store employees) are ranked below craftsmen, a position that reflects more accurately the standing of these occupations in Australia, the United States, and the United Kingdom. [The authors cite several previous studies in which this finding was demonstrated.] Our non-manual category consists of groups 1, 3, 4, 5, 7, and 8 as shown in Table 17.3; manual, of groups 9, 10, 11, 12, 13, 14, and 16; and farm, of groups 2, 6, and 15. The location of farm occupations at three points in the hierarchy recognizes different levels of prestige in rural work.

INTERNATIONAL COMPARISONS

The main value of statistics presented in the broad categories of Table 17.1 is for comparative analysis. Comparisons should, however, be confined to surveys whose data derive from similar sampling frames and whose occupation variables are reported in comparable categories. Prior Australian data are unsuitable for comparisons . . . We therefore limit ourselves to comparisons with two . . . published national surveys on Italy and the United States which appear to satisfy the criteria mentioned (Lopreato, 1965; Blau and Duncan, 1967).

Table 17.1 shows the outflow mobility from fathers' occupational strata to the strata currently occupied by their sons, as recorded in surveys in Australia in 1965, Italy in 1963–4, and the United States in 1962. An immediate observation is the large proportion immobile in non-manual and manual occupations in all three countries. In Italy and America seven out of ten sons from non-manual backgrounds were themselves in non-manual jobs at the time of interview. The Australian figure, while less (six out of ten), is nevertheless high in absolute terms. In all three countries, between one-quarter and one-third of sons of non-manual fathers were downwardly mobile into manual occupations and a much smaller proportion were mobile into farm occupations.

The pattern of mobility among sons of manual fathers, while similar in general outline in all three countries, exhibits greater variety. The figures for upward mobility into non-manual jobs are particularly interesting. More than one in three sons from manual origins in the American sample were upwardly mobile, compared with only one in five in the Italian sample. The Australian figure is intermediate, but is closer to the American than to the Italian experience. If this movement can be taken as indicative of the degree of openness in the stratification system, then the United States has the most open, and Italy the least open, stratification system of the three countries.

TABLE 17.1   *Father-to-son mobility in Australia, Italy and the United States*

Occupational division	Father's occupation (columns)		Son's occupation* (row percentages)			
	Number	Percentage	Non-manual	Manual	Farm	Total
Australia						
Non-manual	486	26	60	35	6	101
Manual	935	51	31	65	4	100
Farm	427	23	19	40	41	100
Total	1,848	100	35	52	13	100
Italy						
Non-manual	209	16	70	26	4	100
Manual	526	39	20	76	5	101
Farm	603	45	8	39	53	100
Total	1,338	100	22	51	26	99
United States†						
Non-manual	7,517	22	69	29	1	99
Manual	15,985	47	36	62	2	100
Farm	10,470	31	22	56	22	100
Total	33,972	100	39	53	8	100

* Cells are to be read as follows: of Australian workers whose fathers were non-manual workers, 60 per cent were themselves non-manual workers, 35 per cent were manual workers, and 6 per cent were farm workers.

† The American numbers (in thousands) represent population estimates derived from an initial sample of about 20,700 respondents.

The pattern of mobility from farm origins varies markedly and throws light on the processes of occupational mobility in societies at different stages and with different rates (perhaps different types) of industrial change. The United States shows by far the highest rate of mobility out of farm occupations; only one of five sons from farm origins remained in farm work, three moved to manual, and one into non-manual occupations. In Australia twice as many, proportionately, remained immobile in farm jobs. While farm to non-manual mobility was comparable with the high US rate, mobility from farm to manual jobs in Australia was only two-thirds that of the American figure. The Italian pattern is similar to the Australian, except that its larger degree of immobility is associated with quite low mobility into non-manual jobs.

Observed differences and similarities in mobility rates illuminate, and are illuminated by, differences in the opportunity structures within which they occur. For example, the similarity between the percentage immobile in non-manual occupations in Italy and the United States masks the different implications of these statistics, which must be seen in the context of a more rapid expansion of non-manual job opportunities in the United States. As Table 17.1 shows, in the American sample there were almost twice as many non-manual sons as fathers (39 and 22 per cent, respectively), whereas in the Italian sample this relative difference was much less pronounced (22 per cent, compared with 16 per cent). This means that while the percentage of immobile non-manual sons was the same in the two countries, the opportunities for upward mobility among sons of manual or farm origins were much greater in the United States than in Italy. In the Australian sample, the comparable difference in the relative number of non-manual jobs was less marked than in the United States but greater than in Italy. However, because of lower immobility in the non-manual stratum, the rate of movement from manual to non-manual jobs more nearly approached the United States figure than the outflow percentages suggest. Viewed from an inflow perspective, the proportions of non-manual sons from manual origins were similar in Australia and the United States (44 and 43 per cent, respectively), but rather lower in Italy (35 per cent). These percentages are not shown in the table.

[Omitted here is a substantial section in which Broom and Jones analyse in more detail the comparative rates of occupational mobility in Australia, the United States and Italy. The observed rate of mobility is partitioned into structural (or "forced") mobility and circulation (or "free") mobility. Summary statistics for the three countries are derived from Table 17.1 and presented in table 2 (omitted). The United States is shown to have the highest rate of observed mobility, but also the highest figure for structural mobility. Australia has a somewhat lower rate of observed mobility, but, as structural mobility is also less evident, the Australian figure for circulation mobility (31.5 per cent) proves to be higher than the comparable figure for the United States (25.7 per cent). Thus Australia could be regarded as more egalitarian. Italy has the lowest rates of observed mobility and circulation mobility. While this section contains Broom and Jones's most important substantive findings, it has been omitted here as the focus is on the research methods used in the Australian survey, and on the Australian data, rather than the comparative analysis.]

AUSTRALIAN TRENDS

In Table 17.3 we present our findings for Australia in more extended form. The first point that merits comment is the over-all low degree of immobility. Only one in four sons (24 per cent) is found in the same occupational niche as his father, and in most categories the figure is much smaller. To some extent the high level of mobility reflects the number of measurement categories, but even so it is noteworthy that in no case does the diagonal element (the percentage immobile) exceed 50 per cent. Occupational inheritance is most marked among graziers (large scale pastoralists), craftsmen, farmers, and to a lesser degree upper professionals, but in the remaining twelve categories an average of only one in seven sons filled the same occupation as his father. The impression of high mobility is further strengthened by the fact that the father's occupation was the commonest destination of his son in only five of the sixteen categories.

In most groups, mobility was more heavily concentrated within the broad divisions of non-manual, manual, and farm jobs. Thus, while only 27 per cent of the sons of upper professional fathers were themselves in that stratum at time of interview, the majority of the mobile sons were in other non-manual rather than in manual

TABLE 17.3 *Father-to-son mobility in Australia (percentages)*

Father's occupation	Son's occupation

Father's occupation	1	2	3	4	5	6	7	8	9	10	11	12	13	14	15	16	Total %	No. of fathers
1. Upper professional	**27**	4	11	19	2	2	18	4	12	2	2		2			4	101	56
2. Graziers	4	**45**	1	7		7	4	1	8	2	4	7	1		4	4	99	91
3. Lower professional	20		**8**	24			24		4	4		4	4		4	4	100	25
4. Managerial	10	4	7	**21**	1	3	19	1	13	2	8	3	4		2	3	101	173
5. Shop proprietors	6		2	10	**12**	6	14	2	15	4	14	8	2	2	2	2	101	51
6. Farmers	1	4	1	10	1	**35**	4		12	2	10	9	3	1	3	4	100	276
7. Clerical workers	13	1	6	15	2	1	**21**	1	17	2	10	3	3	1	2	2	100	146
8. Armed services, police	14		3	11		3	14	**6**	17	3	3	6	9			11	100	35
9. Craftsmen	4		4	10	1	1	12	1	**39**	2	9	5	4	1	2	7	100	341
10. Shop assistants	13			9			13	4	39	**17**	4						99	23
11. Operatives	3	1	4	9	1	7	11	1	26	1	**17**	9	5		1	5	101	148
12. Drivers	2	2	2	12	1	3	11	1	26	1	11	**17**	7	2		5	101	119
13. Service workers	6		4	17		2	14	1	29	4	8	4	**7**	1		3	100	91
14. Miners				5	2	2	7		32	3	11	3	7	**14**		14	100	57
15. Farm workers	2	2	2	10	3	5	5	2	20	5	8	8	7		**8**	13	100	60
16. Laborers	3	4	4	7	1	3	14		28	3	13	6	5		4	**10**	101	156
17. Not stated	4	1		8	3	1	9	1	17	4	12	18	4	3	5	10	100	77
Total %	6	3	4	12	1	7	12	1	23	3	9	7	4	1	2	6	101	
No. of sons	109	64	70	225	26	145	228	19	434	48	182	132	79	19	37	108		1,925

jobs; and of those in manual jobs, two out of three were skilled workers. A similar pattern can be observed in the lower professional category and to a lesser degree among sons of managerial and clerical fathers. Only among shop proprietors and members of the armed services and police (a small but inevitably heterogeneous category) was mobility into manual jobs as high as the percentage remaining within the non-manual category.

For the sons of manual fathers, it can be similarly observed that a minority left manual for non-manual strata. The rate of upward mobility was lowest among miners (16 per cent), somewhat higher among unskilled, semiskilled, and skilled manual workers (29–32 per cent), and highest of all among shop assistants and service workers: about two in five sons from these strata of origin were mobile into non-manual jobs.

The pattern among farm occupations is less uniform. Only among graziers did a majority of sons remain in farm occupations (56 per cent). Slightly less than half this number moved into manual jobs; one in six moved to a non-manual job. In all three farm categories, most mobile sons entered manual rather than non-manual jobs, a pattern evident in the Italian and American figures cited above. It is also interesting that the rate of mobility from farm occupations was inversely related to prestige. It was highest among farm workers (85 per cent), lower among farmers (68 per cent), and lowest among graziers (44 per cent).

The differential nature of farm mobility directs attention to the changing composition of the rural labor force and to the selective social characteristics of rural-urban migrants. In advanced industrial societies, the character of rural work itself is changing. As the scale of agricultural enterprise increases, urban-industrial technology and formal education supplant traditional farming methods and the managerial revolution extends to farm as well as non-farm occupations. It is tempting to interpret the higher movement from non-manual to farm jobs in Australia (Table 17.1) as evidence that the translation of urban skills into the rural environment has proceeded further than in the United States or Italy and to suggest that the superficial similarity between the Italian and Australian figures for non-manual farm mobility reflects in fact opposite processes.

The Australian scene is peculiar and prophetic. Australia has never experienced the smallholder settlement of the New World or the peasant agriculture of the Old. Large-scale primary industries geared to export markets have long dominated the Australian economy. Under such circumstances, there is little transitional strain to the further rationalization of capital-intensive, highly skilled, large-scale agricultural enterprises, which we perceive as the emergent and characteristic mode of rural activity in advanced societies. As this transition is completed, and if, consequently, the relative distribution of primary, secondary, and tertiary jobs approaches stability in industrial nations, structural determinants of occupational mobility between the generations will diminish. Observed differences in mobility between industrial nations would then no longer be related to changing opportunity structures, but would reflect the degree of openness of their stratification systems.

18

Class Conflict and Images of Society*

JOSEPH LOPREATO

[The article commences by referring to a resurgence of interest by social theorists in conflict and coercion in society. Among recent works, Dahrendorf's (1959) theory of social conflict "stands out for its clarity of expression and its generality". The purpose of Lopreato's study is, then, to "examine the empirical validity of some aspects of this . . . approach".]

In examining those changes in industrial society since Marx's time that have interfered with a proper validation of Marx's classical theory, Dahrendorf is particularly impressed by what has come to be known as "the separation of ownership and control", whereby contemporary industrial organizations are increasingly comprised of "capitalists without function" (the stockholders) and "functionaries without capital" (the managers). For Dahrendorf, once control is separated from ownership, the concept of property, so critical a variable in Marx's scheme, is no longer relevant to the analysis of class formation and conflict. Moreover, what is property if not the *right* to exclude others from the use of a given item, in other words, a form of authority? It is, however, only one form of authority. Wherever there is property, Dahrendorf rightly suggests, there is authority, but not every form of authority implies property. Authority is, therefore, the more general social relation (Dahrendorf, 1959: 137). Accordingly, class conflict is best seen

*"Class conflict and images of society" by Joseph Lopreato is reprinted in part from the *Journal of Conflict Resolution*, volume XI, number 3 (Sept. 1967). © 1967, pp. 281–93, by permission of the publisher, Sage Publications Inc. (Beverly Hills/ London).

as arising out of a dispute over the distribution of authority in a given authority structure. The basic units of analysis, therefore, are "imperatively coordinated associations", that is, those associations within which "some positions are entrusted with a right to exercise control over other positions in order to ensure effective coercion" (Dahrendorf, 1959: 165).

[Lopreato outlines further aspects of Dahrendorf's theory of conflict within such associations. The central point is that, under certain conditions, *two* interest groups will emerge, based on authority relations (domination/subjection). Thus far, Dahrendorf's model is "a tool for the analysis of conflict in specific associations within an industrial society". However, because of a tendency for the many different "conflict fronts" in a society to be "superimposed"] . . . Dahrendorf's model transcends its narrow value and lends itself to the study of more comprehensive social phenomena. One of these concerns the "images" of the social structure that may exist in a society. In this connection, the logic of Dahrendorf's argument would seem to suggest that, given the tendency toward the superimposition of class interests in society, in the absence of severe hindrances to class consciousness, there would be a general tendency in an industrial society toward a dichotomous image of the class structure as an expression of a basic class cleavage in that society. Dahrendorf appears to be under the influence of this particular implication of his argument when he discusses the problem of "how people see society" (1959: 280–9).

[Lopreato then points out that "when confronted with certain bodies of findings, Dahrendorf is forced to depart greatly from the logical implications of his theory". A quotation is given in which Dahrendorf (1959: 284) suggests that dominant groups tend to see class relations as hierarchical and consensual, whereas subjected groups visualize society as dichotomous with conflict as the basis of class relations.]

Taking all the above arguments into consideration, it seems altogether reasonable to generate the following three predictions, whose joint validity will be considered evidence of at least the partial validity of Dahrendorf's theory:

1. There is an "appreciable" tendency within a population at large to view the class structure of its society in dichotomous terms.

2. This tendency is more pronounced among those occupying positions deprived of legitimate power (the Obey Class) than among those partaking of the exercise of such power (the Command Class).

3. Assuming a dichotomous image of society to be reflective of a conflict-ridden perception of class relations, such conflict can be traced to relations of authority in the society.

METHODS

The data are part of a national survey on various aspects of social stratification carried out in Italy between December 1963 and January 1964. The original sample consists of 1,569 male family heads interviewed through the research facilities of DOXA, the major private public opinion research institute in that country. In accordance with certain restrictions specified by Dahrendorf's theory, the working sample, however, is necessarily smaller. Specifically, it includes only individuals who at the time of the interview were employed in imperatively coordinated associations and whose position in the authority structure was clearly definable. This means that the sample excludes the unemployed, agricultural and independent workers, petty proprietors, and certain other occupational categories that, according to Dahrendorf, "stubbornly resist allocation to one or the other quasi-group", e.g., "staff" members, routine clerks, foremen and the like (Dahrendorf, 1959: 255, 287).

The effect of all these exclusions has been the construction of a sample of 780 cases which is preponderantly urban, occupationally active and industrial in character, and which more than meets the general characteristics of the postcapitalist industrial society as described by Dahrendorf. Dahrendorf (1964: 227) also has some doubts as to whether the southern regions of Italy may be considered under the rubric of "the industrial society". A preliminary comparison between north and south in terms of the variables examined in this study showed, however, that there are no differences at all between the two parts of the country. The southern regions are, therefore, included in the sample.

The sample is divided into a Command Class and Obey Class in Table 18.1.

TABLE 18.1   *Number and percent of sample in the two classes*

Class	N	%
I. Command class		
1. High functionaries, proprietors and managers of larger establishments	8	4
2. Professionals	32	15
3. Proprietors and managers of medium-sized establishments	39	18
4. Middle grades of officials	132	63
Total	211	100
II. Obey class		
1. Skilled workers	238	42
2. Semiskilled workers	236	41
3. Unskilled workers	95	17
Total	569	100

CLASS IMAGES

Table 18.2 summarizes the information elicited by the following question: "Nowadays there is frequent talk of social classes. In your opinion, what are the social classes to be found in Italy?" The first and most striking finding refers to the large number of respondents in the Obey Class who have no class image of their society at all. No doubt, this very pronounced lack of class awareness is at least in part a function of poor education . . . The finding is nevertheless surprising in terms of any theory of class conflict. For it does indicate that at any given time a very large number of those on whose behavior the validity of the theory fundamentally rests do not possess even that minimum degree of class sensitivity that is the first step toward a class consciousness and the theoretically predicted class struggle. For the sample as a whole, the lack of class awareness comprises 32 per cent of the total. While large, this proportion is not entirely unusual when an open-ended question on class awareness is used. [Lopreato cites three previous studies each reporting between 10 and 25 per cent of respondents lacking class awareness.]

TABLE 18.2 *Detail of class awareness, by authority class (percentages)*

Detail of class awareness	Authority classes	
	Command class	Obey class
Two classes	15	9
Three classes	45	30
Four classes	12	10
Five classes	11	5
Six classes or more	5	3
Lack of awareness	9	41
Unclassifiable	4	2
Total*	101	100
(N)	(211)	(569)

* Totals do not always add to 100 because of rounding.

. . . The reader will recall the prediction stated above that the respondents will evince an appreciable dichotomous image of their society. I was led to state this prediction not only by Dahrendorf's particular conceptualization of the class structure but also by his conclusion, on the basis of an examination of analogous studies, that – as a way of seeing society – the dichotomous class view is "a solid and, probably, powerful social fact" (Dahrendorf, 1959: 289).

In fact there can be some disagreement about this conclusion when those studies are carefully examined. In any case, the data from Italy provide little support for a statement of that sort. Here too the dichotomous view of society is a fact, but, contrary to expectation, it is not terribly imposing in its frequency. Thus, less than 11 per cent of the entire sample hold a dichotomous image of their society. But what is even more surprising is that such a view is almost twice as frequent in the dominant class, where it is held by 15 per cent of the respondents, than in the Obey Class with a total of only 9 per cent. Even if the sample is reduced in order to focus only on those who had a specific image of their society, the proportion of dichotomous views in the Obey Class increases to a percentage of 16, while in the Command Class it continues to be more frequent for a total pecentage of 17.

The most frequent view of the class structure, in *both* classes, is a trichotomous one. Widespread evidence exists that this is the most common view among samples representative of national or at least urban populations (see, for example, Kahl and Davis, 1955). Moreover, if we again focus on that part of the sample that holds a specific image of society, the trichotomous view is slightly more prominent in the Obey Class, with a total of 53 per cent, than in the Command Class, where the total is 51 per cent. Contrary to expectation, therefore, the dichotomous image of society is some-what more prevalent in the dominant group than in the subject group, while the opposite is true with respect to what might be called a continuous or hierarchical view of the class structure.

[In a section omitted here, Lopreato asks whether these patterns of findings are peculiar to Italy – and suggests (tentatively) that they may be "indicative of a more general phenomenon". It is then argued that the findings are consistent with reference group theory (Merton, 1957), and this connection is discussed in some detail.]

. . . It remains now to be seen whether, given a dichotomous perception, it in fact represents a conflict-laden view of society . . . that a dichotomous class image represents a conflict-laden view is an assumption, however, which to my knowledge has never been contested in the literature. The same may be said of the assumption (ironically general, particularly among students of class conflict) that a hierarchical image of society represents a view of harmonious social relations. Underlying both these assumptions there is a third, more fundamental one, to the effect that a fight always involves two, and only two, parties. This, of course, is a patently false assumption, as countless historical instances reveal . . .

Table 18.3, in which I have taken only the respondents holding dichotomous perspectives and examined the factors of division they employ, presents some very interesting findings. Two among them are of chief interest to us. They concern two major questions central to the argument of this paper: (1) whether the twofold division of the class structure is, as is usually assumed, expressive of feelings of conflict; (2) whether this division follows problems of authority distribution – in view of Dahrendorf's intention to offer an alternative to Marx's theory of classes, does Dahrendorf's theory receive more support than Marx's own?

TABLE 18.3 *Distinguishing criteria used in class dichotomies, by authority class (percentages)*

Distinguishing criteria	Authority classes	
	Command class	Obey class
Economic	35	45
Occupational	10	8
Political-ideological	29	8
Political and work dependency	10	25
Other	16	15
Total	100	101
(*N*)	(31)	(53)

The class criteria used by the respondents have been grouped into five general categories. The first, the *economic* dimension, represents such expressions as "the rich and the poor" and "the rich and those who have to work". This group of class images is most closely representative of Marx's conception of the classes in terms of holders and nonholders of property. Next, the *occupational* category is suggested by such expressions as "white collar workers and manual workers" and "those who work in an office and those who work with their hands". This class of perceptions is more difficult to attribute either to Marx's or to Dahrendorf's theory, for obviously it can be claimed by both. Accordingly, we shall avoid considering it as evidence in support of either. Likewise, what I have termed the *political-ideological* dimension presents evidence in support of both theories. It comprises images of society expressed in such terms as "the bourgeoisie and the workers" and "the powerful and the poor". The fourth category, *political and work dependency,* is the clearest expression of the Dahrendorfian conceptualization, and on it, therefore, must fall any burden of proof in favor of that formulation. It is represented by such class images as "the rulers and the populace" or "the *dirigenti* (managers) and the workers". Finally, the fifth category is a residual one, encompassing various class images that follow neither Marx's line of thought nor Dahrendorf's. It is also the category that is irrelevant to any theory of class conflict. It includes prestige-like expressions such as "those who command respect and the rest of us"; moralistic notions such as "the smart ones and the *cretini*"; and "intellectual" expressions such as "the educated class and the masses" or "the intelligent and the common people".

It is worth noting, however, that the number of choices falling within this fifth group of class criteria is quite appreciable, comparable to all others except the economic or Marxian dimension, which out-distances the others by far. This finding constitutes direct evidence that not all dichotomous images of society are expressive of class conflict. Whether the other types of dichotomies in Table 18.3 represent in fact conflict-ridden images of society is a question that cannot be answered with the present findings. However, Table 18.4, as we shall presently see, provides some basis for a direct answer to this query.

Concerning the question whether the findings at this point provide any basis of support for Dahrendorf's theory . . . it may be seen that only relatively small numbers in both classes have an image of society bearing authority connotations, as reflected by the category of responses that has been termed "political and work dependency". On the other hand, omitting from consideration those class criteria which, as I have suggested, do not lend themselves to unequivocal allocation, support is more substantial for Marx's theory of classes, as represented specifically by the "economic" category, wherein more than one-third in the Command Class and nearly half of the workers are represented.

PERCEPTIONS OF CLASS RELATIONS

In discussing the findings so far, concern has been with the basic problem, *inter alia*, of determining whether relations of conflict obtain in the Italian class structure. We have not been in a position, however, to observe conflict directly . . . it is now advisable to take a more direct approach to this question. The findings organized in Table 18.4 represent a step in this direction. They have been obtained on the basis of the following questions: "Judging by your own experience, what kinds of relations exist among the various social classes? Would you say that on the whole they are relations of amity, hostility, or something else? What?"

TABLE 18.4   *Perception of types of relations existing among social classes, by authority class (percentages)*

Types of relations perceived	Authority classes	
	Command class	Obey class
Amity	22	22
Hostility	29	45
Work relations, collaboration, mutual convenience	15	8
Tolerance, suspicion, distance	9	4
Indifference	14	8
Lack of perception	3	7
Unclassifiable	8	6
Total	100	100
(N)	(211)	(569)

We should begin by making two necessary observations. First, it must be noted that, strictly speaking, what we are about to measure is not relations of hostility, but only *perceptions* of it. It is reasonable to assume, however, that in this case perceptions of hostility are very probably representative of actual relations of hostility; after all, the question posed to the interviewees required them to answer it on the basis of personal experience. Second, conflict and hostility are not one and the same phenomenon, so that what we are about to assess is not conflict as a distinctive form of actual interaction, but only a predisposition to it. Theoretically, the two phenomena are independent of each other . . . it may be said, however, that, in view of the particular wording of the interview question, we are essentially on the right track.

Glancing now at Table 18.4, we note that, even without taking account of kindred expressions suggesting "tolerance, suspicion, distance", a perception of hostile class relations occurs with greater frequency than any other type of perception in both classes. To this extent, the predisposition to conflict mentioned above is real enough, and support in favor of theories of conflict – though not necessarily Dahrendorf's – is quite substantial. Moreover, such support comes, as predictable, more heavily from those in the Obey Class . . . The next most frequent response after hostility is that of amity, with 22 per cent in each class perceiving this type of class relations, thus providing some support also for scholars of consensus or integration theory, and at the same time making it all too obvious that an ideology-free and mature sociology . . . must develop a sensitivity to problems of consensus and of conflict as equally real properties of social relations.

In point of fact, the data point to still a third major form of social relations . . . a considerable number of respondents, particularly within the Command Class, perceive a form of class relations which is based essentially on conditions of potential conflict, but which is resolved, it would seem, deliberately and consciously, because the parties in basic contention find it mutually convenient . . . Truly, it is an expression of the "social contract" come true in industrial society. It is a demonstration of the great degree of interdependence existing in society today which to some extent checks tendencies toward basic cleavages. The fact that this particular perception of social relations is considerably more marked among the dominant groups than in the working class is also direct confirmation of the numerous accounts of the particular efforts made by contemporary entrepreneurial classes to interpret the exercise of authority in a favorable light . . .

Finally, the reader will note that the number of respondents who perceive relations of hostility among the social classes far exceeds the number of those who, as reported in Tables 18.2 and 18.3, hold a dichotomous image of society. This finding is direct proof of my earlier suggestion that, contrary to a general assumption, a hierarchical image of society is not *prima facie* evidence that class relations are perceived as harmonious. More detailed calculations show, for instance, that 94 individuals in positions of superordination and 171 in the Obey Class had perceived three classes. Of these, 25 and 51 per cent, respectively, now perceive hostile relations among the classes.

But how about the relationship between a dichotomous image of the social structure and perceptions of the nature of interclass relations? On an earlier occasion some doubt was raised concerning the widespread assumption that dichotomous class perceptions reflect conflict-ridden class images. We are now in a position to question that assumption directly. As Table 18.3 showed, 31 respondents in the Command Class and 53 in the Obey Class held a dichotomous image of their society. Of these, it can now be ascertained that 35 and 53 per cent, respectively, perceive hostility in interclass relations. In short, the difference in perceptions of class hostility between those who hold a dichotomous image of society and those who have a hierarchical view is hardly noticeable. The critical, distinguishing factor is class position. Working-class people are much more likely than their middle-class fellow citizens to define class relations as being fraught with animosity. Whether their perception reflects defensive behavior of the kind of class consciousness that theories of class conflict demand of them is hard to tell. Whatever the answer, there is little or no evidence in support of a theory that would account for class conflict in terms of relations to an authority structure.

DISCUSSION AND CONCLUSIONS

In conclusion, data from Italian society seem to indicate that Dahrendorf's theory has little if any validity. The reality of the case reveals that to the extent that they exist, conflicts follow the articulation of heterogeneous interests. Dahrendorf's particular etiology fails to receive any but the slightest degree of substantiation. Even when dichotomous class images, central to the logical implications of his theory, are scrutinized with a view to ascertaining the interest basis of such images, concern with authority distribution in society appears to be minimal, while sensitivity to the economic basis of society, so central to Marx's theory of class conflict, comes more heavily into view. It follows that whatever evidence exists to substantiate a theory of conflict based on a dichotomous class division is more favorable to Marx's theory of classes than to Dahrendorf's . . .

[Omitted here are ten paragraphs which begin with a discussion of certain central aspects of Dahrendorf's theory; some comparisons are also made with the theories of Marx. Lopreato also takes into account certain structural conditions that, according to Dahrendorf, must be fulfilled before his theory can be properly tested. On the bases of this analysis, Lopreato reaffirms that Italy provides an appropriate test for Dahrendorf's theory. Lopreato goes on to discuss some features of recent Italian history and their impact on class relationships.]

In a sense, therefore, Italy may very well represent a special case, but one which should be especially favorable to a proper validation of Dahrendorf's theory. The failure of that formulation to be supported by the data presented in this paper may, therefore, be particularly damaging to its assumed validity. Fortunately, *non tutti i mali vengono per nuocere* – there is a saving grace. Whatever the merits of Dahrendorf's theory, one thing stands out about it as a tool for the analysis of social conflict. In Italy, at least, it has led us to observe that social conflict, whatever its source or its basis, is a real and bold property of social relations. To that extent, Dahrendorf's underlying intent to revive interest in the analysis of "the ugly face of society" is a most justifiable and fruitful one. As such, his endeavor represents a most important contribution to sociological analysis and vindicates the still largely unheeded advice – his own and that of a few other keen intellects in the discipline – not to neglect, as we have for a long time done, the analysis of phenomena of social conflict.

19

School Performance viewed from the Boys*

IAN K. BIRKSTED

School, in the literature of the sociology of education, is a place where some children succeed and others fail. The focus has been on the selection processes operating on the children. These selection processes have been located in three principal areas: the family background, the school itself, and the peer group (Banks, 1971).

[Birksted contrasts the two main bodies of previous work on academic performance – first, "comparative study between the culture of the school with its educational values and the culture of the pupils with their social-class values", and second, the "interactionist view of classroom processes which stresses the importance of teachers in the success and failure processes". He then argues that both approaches define success in the school's own terms; this is legitimate and important but accounts become biased unless children's own views of their behaviour are also studied.]

It was to avoid the biases of these approaches that I tried another, similar in orientation to that literature which sees behaviour as stemming from choices and strategies appropriately adapted to the actors' views of themselves in their social environment. In considering children, this literature attributes to them a coherent system of reasons for their performance. Lacey (1970) describes how pupils use schools in accordance with their occupational plans and their perceptions of the resources at their disposal
. . .

* Reprinted in part from Ian K. Birksted (1976) "School performance viewed from the boys", *Sociological Review*, **24**:63–77, with the permission of the publishers and the author.

THE RESEARCH PROBLEM AND THE AREA

The research problem was exploratory: to clarify what "school" meant to a selected number of adolescents. I was interested less in seeing how they fitted into the structure of the school than in how the school fitted into the structure of their lives. I was thus interested in school from the adolescents' own point of view, rather than from the school's point of view. Consequently I planned to carry out participant observation both inside school and outside school. The area I selected was the catchment area of a comprehensive school. This catchment area consists of a Victorian terraced and economically depressed area, a post-war council and owner-occupier development, and a 1960s owner-occupied bungalow estate giving directly onto the surrounding countryside . . .

THE RESEARCH METHODS

The methods to be used had to be suited to eliciting how people construe their environment. I was not interested in testing hypotheses but in finding out about other people's point of view. Participant observation was clearly the sort of research which would be suitable to the problem under study. I first entered the field-work situation by regular attendance at a youth and community centre . . . Staff were young and on friendly terms with adolescent members. It was thus relatively easy for me to mix in with adolescents and staff. After about two months I began approaching the local school which these adolescents attended. When I gained entrance to the school, I thus knew many adolescents who introduced me to friends, but I knew no school staff. I suddenly found myself in a situation where my position as full-time sociology research-student on friendly terms with the pupils stuck out as anomalous and made me feel very uncomforatble. Since I persisted in spending most of my time with pupils I was only accepted by a few members of staff. I avoided teaching, and the one class I was pushed into taking ended by complaints about noise from the teacher next-door. It was in this general situation that I met the boys whom this article is about. My friendship with these boys was the breakthrough which gave me a legitimate position at the school in the eyes of the school staff: I became the person who could get on with these boys, taking them out on visits and keeping them busy. I thus got to know them well before the summer holiday, during which I saw them frequently. All through the research, staff and adolescents knew that I was a research-student interested in adolescents about whom I was writing a book.

At the outset of the participant observation, I knew that I was not interested in attitudes and opinions such as have been documented before, as I wanted a much more in-depth picture. The methods of cognitive anthropology seemed to be the best adapted to this task. [Birksted explains that cognitive anthropology places major emphasis on how "natives" see their world, particularly categories of description used in natives' language.]

I was interested in the concepts and categories of the adolescents. I could not assume from the start that "school" would be a significant category to them, nor, if it were, what it would mean. Thus I would have to elicit the adolescents' own concepts and the relational patterns between these concepts. One of the central features of the method is to map the cognitive world of the informants into "contrast sets" . . .

The advantages of the approach are many . . . The method has in common with ethnomethodology the stress on process and on the continual construction of social reality. At the same time as the method allows the researcher to describe native categories, it also allows him to bring in his own research problem and interests; ethnography and problem-oriented research can be combined. [See the original article for notes on selected aspects of cognitive anthropology. A range of previous works is cited, including Tyler (1969).]

THE BOYS

As part of this research project I studied a group of eight adolescents. Six belonged to a group of boys who spent much time together both inside and outside school. This article is mainly about these six boys. Two other boys were peripheral to the group, spending time with the group inside school but seldom outside. All these boys were fifteen at the time of the research and were ending their fourth year at school. The six boys were Rob, Steve, Garry,

Peter, Frank and Ken . . . The two boys . . . peripheral to the group were Russ . . . and Jerry . . . [Omitted is a passage introducing each of the group of six, and also the other two boys; in contrast to the other seven, Ken is a high achiever academically.] The six boys saw themselves as a group. Group lore consisted of certain items of clothing which they had bought together on an expedition to Brighton: boots and sweaters. They had a "high rate of social interaction", a "system of mutual obligations" with a lot of cigarette borrowing and some status differentials, as described in Whyte (1955).

The teachers also saw the six boys as a group. They saw this group both as a menace and a cause of despair. Ken was in a different position: he was frowned upon because of his association with the group and because of his refusal to wear school-uniform, but Ken was highly praised for his school-work. Ken was seldom with the group in lessons, and had, in this way, more leeway for manoeuvre as he was less observable during lessons by the other members of the group: he could work hard and perform well without his every school success being observed by the other members of the group. The others often found themselves in twos or threes during lessons.

A DIFFERENT VIEW OF SCHOOL

[Birksted describes how he observed the group spending their time. In school time they would usually spend breaks between classes in an unused room, smoking and listening to music, etc. Over the summer holidays the pattern varied a little from day to day, but was nevertheless very predictable.] It struck me how similar were their days during term-time and holiday-time. The impression of the run of the day was that of a relaxed and informal gathering, playing cards, listening to music, having a smoke, chatting, laughing and talking. Occasionally this atmosphere was broken by having to attend classes. School breaks did not seem to be gaps between classes, but classes seemed to be interruptions in the gathering. After these blanks, normal life had to be picked up again and continued. Such was my first experience of participant observation inside and outside school with this group of boys. No great distinction seemed to be made between term-time and holiday-time since classes slotted into the normal run of life relatively easily. So if the distinctions which adults make and assume to be significant to school-pupils did not appear as significant to the boys, which distinctions did they make? How was life organized?

WORK, LEISURE AND SCHOOL

The boys distinguish between "work" and "leisure". In one interview I arranged for Steve to do the interviewing. I handed him my question-cards and sat back, letting him put the questions to the others. My question-card read "please tell me where you spend your time?" Steve read the card, and changed the question:

Steve: Where do you spend your leisure time?
Rob: Over the park.
Peter: Up somebody's house.
Rob: Sometimes in Brighton.
Garry: Play cards . . . Listen to records.
Steve: Do you work anywhere?
Frank: Yeah, I work at the Alliance.

(The dialogues are transcripts from tape-recorded interviews. I have reduced the amount of repetition, and cut out parts where we talked about something else.)

Work, for the boys, is not exemplified by or identified with school. Work is the daily cleaning job which they do at the offices of the Alliance Building Society between 5.00 p.m. and 7.00 p.m. on weekdays. These office-cleaning jobs are handed down from one year to the other as the children leave school to take on full-time employment. The boys were told of the jobs by friends, and all went along and applied. Other children from the same comprehensive work there too. All six boys work there, and so does one of the two peripheral boys, Russ. Some of the boys have other jobs as well. Frank works in a restaurant twice a week, and Garry works in a pub every morning before going to school. These individual activities, though, tended not to be mentioned in group discussions. The boys earn £4 a week each at the Alliance. How do they see these different activities in terms of time during a normal day?

Rob: A day sort of goes in three: in the mornings and afternoons, you sit about. In the evenings, five to seven, you go to work, and after than, to half past ten, you sit up the park usually.

We can represent this diagrammatically [see Figure 19.1]. In this scheme, school has its place:

"Morning"	"Afternoon"	"Evening"	
"Sit about"	"Sit about"	"Work"	"Up the park"

FIGURE 19.1

Steve: At least school takes up your time, gives you something to do. Same as the Alliance, takes a couple of hours.
Garry: Normally from school we just come home, sit down and watch telly.

It can be seen that school is something which takes up time, which occupies time. During the course of my participant observation, I was so struck by the unexceptional place school played that I tried to introduce the subject in an interview.

Ian K.: Does school make a difference?
Rob: . . . (silence) . . . Pardon?
All: . . . (silence) . . .
Ian K.: Uh, I was saying . . .
Steve: Ah, school? . . . (silence) . . . School divides up a lot really, if you think about it. Nine to what, four. There's a school club.
Ian K.: Do you go there?
Rob: Not really, I get bored.
Garry: It's the same every week.

Not only is school a time-filler, but it is also something which 'divides up' time. School is something which the boys describe not as an activity in itself, but as something which helps to pass the time.

We have seen how school fits into the day. How does school fit into the week? The week consists of three parts:

Rob: I don't see Frank every day. I don't see Ken and Steve every day.

Steve: We see each other Monday to Saturday, but not normally on Sunday. We don't come out on Sundays. On Sunday, I get up late, and watch telly in the afternoons.

Garry: Saturday is rest day from work.

Rob: Saturday is lounge-around day.

Monday to Friday	Saturday	Sunday

FIGURE 19.2

We can represent this [in Figure 19.2]. These divisions are made according to three sets of criteria: (1) whether the group are together or not, (2) whether it is a work day or not, and (3) particular events that take place in the evening:

Frank: Thursday and Friday I baby-sit. Mondays is bingo. Last night we won a pair of tights!

These events were mentioned less frequently in the group as they took place individually with family or girl-friends. Once again, school is not an organizing principle.

Though I had not specifically asked about the day and the week, the above descriptions came out of the discussion. I did ask about the year, as I felt this would complete the picture which had begun to emerge. The year, however, proved not to be a very relevant time-period, as can be seen from the initial hesitation.

Ian K.: How do you divide up the year?

Ken: The whole year?

All: . . . (silence) . . .

Ken: It's so big, really, that you just got to take it as it comes. We stay in more in winter. It's colder.

Frank: It's more boring, in summer. In winter, it's colder, you dress up, feel like mucking about, doing something.

Rob: You're walking down the street. Somebody says "Feel like a run!" You ring somebody's door-bell and run! Keeps you warm!

Steve: I prefer it to the summer. Playing football in the rain, it's good fun.
Rob: I like summer on the beach. I don't like when it's cloudy.
Ken: I don't like a summer school-day.

The boys see the year [as in Figure 19.3]. Here again, the organizing principle is not school, but something else. In this case, the weather and the effect it has on you.

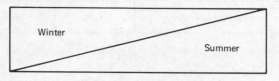

FIGURE 19.3

HOLIDAYS

Over the summer, we often talked about holidays. The boys told me about a holiday they once had in Wales. This was organized by the school and they all went. A teacher supervised the group, which included other children. They said they enjoyed the trip, and told me many stories about what they had seen and done. We also discussed people away on holiday. Peter went away for a week's training course with the Cadets, and Ken went away with his family for a week. They said such things as "He's away on holiday." In one interview they described the summer as follows:

Frank: School only changes the holiday-time. It gets boring because we're normally at school.

The distinction between "holiday" and "holiday-time" is an important one. To be on "holiday" is to go away – away from where the boys live and spend their lives. A holiday is not to be away from school, thus a holiday can be a school-trip. But "holiday-time" is merely to be away from school without going anywhere. Holiday-time is merely when the powers-that-be have decided to close the school temporarily. The concepts relate to each other in the . . . way [shown in Figure 19.4].

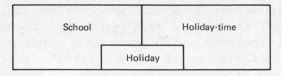

FIGURE 19.4

The distinction between "holiday" and "holiday-time" throws light on the meaning of school to the boys. I would like to emphasize that this is a conceptual difference, not a difference of attitude or preference. I am not saying the boys prefer "holiday" to "holiday-time", and "holiday-time" to "school". Whether they prefer to go on holiday or to stay at home depends on what kind of holiday it is. And school, as we have seen, "gives you something to do" and "divides up" the day . . .

All along we have seen how school for the boys is not a place to which life is oriented and which constitutes an organizational principle of life. School conveniently provides certain advantages: it fills time, it is somewhere to be at. School is like a waiting-room. Of all the boys, it is least like this for Ken, the good pupil. Ken, who wants to be a surveyor, sees classes as significant. This brings me to the next point: the boys' evaluation of the usefulness of school to them.

EXAMINATIONS

Steve: If I could choose, I'd go to metalcraft and woodwork. And you have to have a maths exam to be a carpenter.
Russ: It doesn't help me. To get into printing, all I have to do is to take a general exam.

The boys see the purpose of school to be to get exams for jobs. If you need exams, school is useful, if you don't school is useless. In metalcraft and woodwork, the boys are conscientious and make difficult things: furniture in particular. They are on good terms with the teachers. They spend more time in these classes than the school requirements demand . . . Russ, who plans to go into printing, has already put himself down for the entry-examination, and applied for a job at a local printer's office. What more can he do? In so far as Russ does not need school, why should he compete to do well? The boys see good performance at school as an exercise in conformity and obedience not in usefulness . . . [All the boys but Ken] see good marks and doing well as belonging to a closed system. It is a system in and for itself . . . They can, though, see the usefulness of school to other pupils. Ken is mildly teased because of "the pin-striped suit and bowler hat you'll be wearing one day". But in the life of the group, these differences in school-performance and occupational plans do not govern how the boys treat each other. They do not evaluate each other according to school-grades, but as whole people.

The boys therefore evaluate the usefulness of school to them in terms of their occupational plans for the future, and they aim at passing the appropriate exams accordingly. They see school not as the embodiment of Good which must be sought for its own sake, but as a dispenser of exams – which some people need and others do not. The idea of school success and school failure is an idea which they understand . . . They know they are "the school dunces". They joke about it. But they see themselves as failing in the sense of not conforming to the standards of the school . . . [however] being school failures is irrelevant to them. For other boys whom I studied, school was also evaluated in terms of occupational plans for the future, but found relevant and important.

DISCUSSION

Adolescents with whom I did participant observation inside and outside of school during their fourth and fifth year at a comprehensive did not see school as an organizational principle of their lives. They evaluated the usefulness to them of exams in terms of their occupational plans for the future. This evaluation governed their perception of the usefulness of school and their performance at school. Thus school achievement and performance can be seen as strategies decided upon by pupils in terms of their perceptions of ends and means. A group of boys who were seen as hostile by the teachers and who would be, with the exception of one of them, classified by sociologists as a typical under-achieving clique "that the school most needs to teach" (Nash, 1973), can only be thus labelled by ignoring the logic and meaning of their decisions, strategies and choices . . .

. . . What commonsense and sociology both see as failure in a non-differentiated way, these boys see as failure *at school*, not particularly important in the broader view that they have of life. They see failure at school as specific to that setting, and not as applicable to life in general. Whereas teachers and sociologists fail to consider school-pupils' purposes, and construe success and failure in terms of institutional standards, pupils have a much more operational and differentiated view.

[Birksted argues that the findings raise "interesting questions for the general debate about schools and schooling". The school was "de-pressured", i.e. there was no great pressure to perform well academically. The boys "did not react against school in a very hostile way. They could be described as a-school rather than anti-school" (compare with Lacey's findings – see Chapter 15). Thus school "was a kind of waiting-room for them". Birksted suggests that this may be a tolerable situation, but it can hardly be seen as exciting and valuable educationally. The answers may lie "in the directions indicated by Freire (1972)" and others who stress the importance of the students' own life-experiences and preoc-cupations, and the experiences of the process of learning itself. Applying Freire's framework to his boys, Birksted notes that the two situations in which "the boys seemed most involved were craft classes and our tape-recorded discussions".] The craft classes gave them the freedom to make things they wanted, to ask the teacher for his advice when they felt they needed it, and to be together as a group. They liked our tape-recorded discussions and were very proud of them, telling other people about them. They had very interesting ideas about things we could do together and did eventually do, like taking photographs of important places in their lives, such as the park-shelter where they spent a lot of time.

Rob: You've done some change, coming and talking to us like that . . . You've made us like a friend. You're doing a job at the same time . . . We act more adult. We discover we're more adult than we think.

Steve: Do you find we act different now from in a classroom? Now it's nothing like Mr X's class. It's more grown up now.

20

Kids, Cops and Conflict*

GREG SMITH

This article is based on a participant-observation study of an
adolescent delinquent group at a Brisbane Housing Commission
Estate. The members of the group are mostly male, although there
are a few girls who are core members and who appear to have
equality with the males. Ages of members ranged from thirteen to
twenty, but the majority were in the fifteen to seventeen age
range. Of one hundred and fifty relatively regular attenders,
approximately thirty could be considered core members. The
group was also mixed racially, with about twenty-five Aboriginals,
mainly male, belonging. (The area itself has a relatively high
proportion of Aboriginals.) There is no formal or institutionalised
structure or rules for membership. Whoever turns up at the locale
in which the group members spend most time is accepted virtually
without question if he or she is from the same suburb. The period
of observation was four months during the latter half of 1973, and
most of the comments which I have reproduced here are taken
verbatim from tape recorded conversations and interviews.
Names, where used, are pseudonyms.

While this article contains a report of interactions with, and
attitudes towards, the police, this is only part of a wider study of
the leisure activities and interest of delinquents. Relationships
between group members and the police, while not initially a major
topic for investigation, became such a recurring theme that I felt it

* Reprinted in part from Greg Smith (1975) "Kids, cops and conflict: a participant-
observation study", *Australian and New Zealand Journal of Sociology*, 2: 21–7,
with the permission of the publishers and the author.

needed further analysis. In many cases it seemed apparent that positive steps could be taken as a result of this analysis to reduce conflict between the two groups. I have loosely defined these juveniles as a "delinquent group" because of the frequency with which members come into conflict with the police. Nearly all of the core members of the group have police records, some dating back several years. In addition, even many of those who do not have official records have still had a number of encounters with the police and freely admit to activities which the law defines as illegal.

I met many of the group members through a local coffee shop. After a few Saturday evenings there I felt sufficiently confident to approach the group on its own territory (a park in the centre of the estate). Here, anywhere from five to seventy-five group members would gather every evening of the week around dusk. They would sit in the dark to listen to the music drifting across from a skating rink across the street, engage in the continuous talk and bantering which Yablonsky (1967) called "sounding", make plans for the weekend, catch up on news about friends, pool money for a trip to the pub, watch cars go by, or drink beer. The darkness and a gully in the centre of the park made it possible to drink out of sight of the police. Despite the fact that I was older than group members (25) I could blend in when police arrived and they (police) were unaware of the study.

ATTITUDES TOWARDS POLICE

As might be expected, delinquent gangs have been found by many researchers to be suspicious and cop-fearing, and the police are an enemy in perpetual war with the delinquent gangs. [Smith quotes Reiss (1971: 137) and Chappell and Wilson (1969) on police attitudes to juveniles. The latter survey also showed that "a majority of young people in Australia had little respect for the police".]

The group which I observed was no different, although occasionally attitudes to police were somewhat more ambivalent. The following remarks are typical:

> Lately the coppers have been real good. They know there's nothing in (this suburb) for us to do and they're pretty good . . .

> They just do what they have to. (Female, 17, core member)

> You get your good coppers and your bad ones here. (Male, 14, marginal member)

The statement of the last boy sheds some light on why this ambivalent attitude exists. Generally, a policeman is good *despite* being a policeman. When a group member expresses tolerance for a policeman it is because that constable has distinguished himself from what the boys perceive to be the normal role and personality of a "copper" . . .

The tougher a cop is, the greater the hostility towards him. Despite the occasional concessions that "you get some good coppers", most kids feel that the good ones don't last long, before being transferred out of the area. Incidentally this viewpoint was supported by one of the leading citizens in the community – a local businessman.

However, despite a certain ambivalence towards individual policemen who may *sometimes* prove to be not so bad, distrust and hostility were most commonly expressed. Because the park was in a highly central and therefore visible position in the community, and because it was well known as a hangout for some of the most delinquent teenagers, it was visited often by police. They would shine their spotlights on the kids as they sat in the dark, or drive right into the park, to question people. This happened so frequently it became commonplace. But police intervention also arose from incidents other than routine patrols. Drinking or fighting at dances, vandalism, complaints about disorderly conduct from residents or recreation leaders, boys yelling obscenities or other taunts, and reports of crime for which a boy fell under suspicion – all caused police–youth interaction.

Since many of the boys have had convictions for several offences, and the police were the agents who caught such offenders, they therefore became the enemy. In the view of group members – many of whom had no official records – there was justification for their suspicion and hostility. They felt, for one thing, that they were being maligned by the police, who had more opportunities to present their side of the story. The roots of this hostility towards the police are often based upon personal experience or the experience of friends.

ALLEGATIONS OF POLICE VIOLENCE

An allegation I heard frequently was that the police beat up kids
they detained . . .

> You know the time I was in that home for a day? You know they
> punched me up first in the lockup. I tried to get away you know,
> and a copper grabbed me and I hit him a couple of times and he
> started going down and all these coppers grabbed me and took
> me inside and they punched - - - out of me, you know. On the
> way to the home they were real good to me. They said do you
> want a smoke – so I wouldn't tell anyone what they had done to
> me. (Male, 16, core member)

This belief is a widely-held view of what happens to anyone
unfortunate to be arrested by the police. Surprisingly enough,
though, the boys do not mind admitting that they may have
provoked the police. Such was the case with the sixteen-year-old
quoted above who punched back. Generally, though, they claim
that they only fight back as a form of self-defence. While I have
never witnesed any of the incidents described above, I have on one
occasion seen a policeman use physical force against a group
member. The boy, 16, was ejected from a dance for drinking and
rushed across the street to cool off away from a potentially
explosive crowd of his peers. He was leaning against a car when I
saw the policeman punch him in the stomach. Although I drifted
over to the scene as an observer, I and another boy were warned
away on penalty of being charged ourselves. Later I found out
from the boy involved what he felt had happened: "The copper
said put your hands on your head, eh? So I did and wham he
punched me right in the gut". A girl who was a core member
played a role which I saw two or three times. Although she was
only a friend, she went over and pretended to be his girlfriend to
help win sympathy for him with the police. This time it apparently
worked, for he was let off with a warning. Another factor was
probably, in the boy's own words, that "When he hit me I told him
I'd dob him in [report him] for hitting me, so he let me off with just
a warning."

ALLEGATIONS OF DRINKING ON DUTY

If police violence against kids is, in their view, a common habit, they allege that drinking on duty, and even drunkenness, is another. One constable in particular appears to be best known among the group. Their opinion of McDonald varies from "pretty good" to "he's all right to a certain extent, but you get him when he's drunk he's a - - -"

When I first started spending time with the group, I began to hear stories of policemen drinking on duty:

> The coppers came back here. They took two dozen cans off him and gave him a dozen back again.
> –Yeah, you know what the coppers do? They pinch your beer off you. They do. They save it up and take it round to the cop shop.
> **G.S.:** Have you seen them drink it?
> **Several:** Yeah.
> – That's an old trick that, everywhere, the coppers been doing that ever since they began. They've always done that, police.
> – That's all they - - -ing do, get your grog, save it all up and have a big party.
> – Yeah, most people know that. I know that. (Exchange among several boys)

This discussion group included several of those who claimed to have seen policemen drinking, or drunk, on duty. However, in this case resentment of the police appeared to be more because they confiscate the beer, than because they (the police) drink themselves. On the contrary, the fact that some policemen appeared at parties and drank themselves seemed to humanise them to some extent among the boys:

> Sometimes they go to the parties (in the area), even the trainees they go to the parties sometimes you know. Oh, some of 'em are good blokes you know. (Male, 16, core member)

"NEVER TRUST A COPPER"

Another common criticism of the police by the boys is that they are deceitful. As one boy said, "I reckon you can never trust a copper." When I asked him why, he told of the time he had been picked up drunk with another fellow he had met at a party in the city. The other fellow had tried to steal his watch and the ensuing argument brought the police, who took them both to "the lockup". The police then asked him to write out a statement accusing the other fellow, who was well known to them:

> I said "no". They said "look, if you just tell us that he done it we'll let you off from being drunk in a public place . . . Go ahead just do it and we'll forget about everything about you."
> So I said "all right" and I wrote it out that he pinched it. Then they grabbed me, took me to the thing and started punching into me (the boy admitted that they had already scuffled previously), and says "righto, you have to go to court on Monday for resisting arrest and drunk in a public place". (Male, 16, core member)

The same boy alleged that he had also been deceived another time. The most prevalent perception of the police then is that while there may be one or two "good coppers", they are the exception rather than the rule.

STATE OF RIVALRY

This belief, which the boys consider to be well-founded as a result of their experience, encourages them to operate in a continous state of rivalry with the police. This rivalry, coupled with peer group pressure to appear tougher and smarter than the police, leads to abrasive encounters. These usually take the form of open defiance when confronted or more subtle attempts to outsmart the police verbally . . .

I have witnessed a few examples of the former, usually at dances, where the large number of people appears to encourage face-saving belligerence. Typically, a boy is ejected from a dance for drinking and rowdy behaviour. As he is rushed outside by one or two policemen, he resists – but usually only to a point slightly below that which would provoke severe reaction against him. Usually, however, although a boy would try to push the constable as far as he could, he would eventually back down just short of being booked. It was making the gesture which was apparently the face-saver. Attempts to outsmart the police appeared to be about as successful as the attempts to defy them. Usually outsmarting a policeman consisted of pretending to be old enough when caught drinking. More often, though, it was the boys themselves who were outsmarted by the police . . .

[In a passage omitted here, Smith gives three quotations which illustrate verbal exchanges in encounters with the police. He makes three main points: (1) usually, the policeman has the upper hand, but "occasionally, a boy would get the best of the police in one of these verbal duels"; (2) whatever the outcome of the verbal duel, it does not enhance the policeman's image with the group; (3) in the eyes of the group, being caught by the police (for drinking, etc.) is "not a mark of failure . . . it was only another example of how devious policemen can be".]

POLICE ARE ILL-INFORMED

One sure way for a policeman to lose respect among the group was to be hopelesly ill-informed about something which was obvious to the group. Thus, when a very drunken boy yelled loud insults to two policemen across the street from the park, they came over and accused the wrong boy of the offence. This was seen as a mark against them, because the boy who had yelled the obscenities was in plain sight at the time, and in fact had walked over very close to the police. Incidentally, it is an indication of the solidarity of the boys that the one who was mistakenly charged never made the slightest reference to his friend being the actual offender. After the police had left, however, the real offender was severely criticised by the others for getting his mate into trouble.

Another incident which earned the policeman involved the disdain of the group occurred one evening while we were sitting in the park quietly chatting. A cruiser came into the park and two policemen got out. Most of the boys there at the time were Aboriginals. A constable said: "What are all you darkies doing here, waiting to punch up all the white boys?" Relating the story later, one of the boys described it this way:

We says "no, we don't want to hurt them too much". Then he rabbles on about how they got called down here because there's supposed to be brawl starting. Then as he's walking off he turns around and says "Aw well, don't hurt 'em too much."

The boy laughed scornfully and said: 'Weren't even going to be no - - -ing brawl."

In this case the policeman was misinformed not only about the potential "brawl", but also about the internal relationships of the group. In four months I detected no sign of any friction between Aboriginal and white members. There were about twenty-five Aboriginal and one hundred and twenty whites who made up the larger group of core and marginal members. In every respect they were equals, although I noticed a slight tendency for Aboriginals to spend more time with members of their own race. Even this, however, was not strongly marked, and interaction by and large seemed to ignore race. This applied for relationships between males and females as well. In the eyes of the group, then, this confirmed their opinion of the police as somewhat distant, ill-formed adversaries.

CONCLUSION

It would be wrong to say that individual policemen have not earned the respect of the group members. On many occasions I have heard people refer to a particular policeman as "not a bad bloke" or "a good copper". However, this tolerance is extended only intermittently to particular individuals – and virtually never to police as a group. Overall, the attitude of group members to the police is one of suspicion, disrespect, distrust, dislike, contempt and occasionally even fear. Group members allege repeatedly that police are violent, hypocritical in their attitudes towards drinking and the law; deceitful in their dealings with arrested offenders; remote from the daily lives and activities of the group; and in some cases plain foolish.

This derogatory opinion of the police appears not only to emanate from but to help perpetuate a continual state of conflict between the members of the group and the police. Occasionally this strained situation leads to physical violence between the two groups. A large scale fight in the park two years previously resulted in several arrests for assault. More recently, as this article was being written, several dozen members of the group were again involved in a half hour brawl with police which resulted in several injuries.

The hostility of group members does not seem to be so much directed against the *role* of the police as enforcer of the law. It appears rather to be directed against the *ways* in which the local police fulfil this role. The policeman operating from the remoteness of a cruiser has little opportunity to defuse this hostility, since he normally only interacts with people when an offence has been committed. The policeman then becomes a sort of "bogeyman" who lacks any dimension as a real human being, and who appears to lack knowledge of, or interest in, the constructive side of group activity . . .

. . . It is worth sounding a cautionary note regarding the accuracy of the stories which group members tell. While they appear to be largely consistent, at least one researcher has found such stories to be exaggerated. Voelcker found that:

> . . . the youths who relate and believe these stories have absolutely no wish to doubt their authenticity. To them the police are a bad lot and the stories go towards confirming this conviction. And to complete the circulatory, these stories are likely to be true *because* the police are a bad lot! (1962: 82))

However, whether the hostility of these boys, and others like them is justified or not, the fact remains that it exists as a force which militates against the effectiveness of the police – not only to detect offenders but to prevent offences from occurring initially.

IMPLICATIONS FOR POLICY

It has been suggested by interactionists that the police are actually amplifiers of deviancy in some cases (Young, 1970: 27–61). Becker (1963: 31) considered "the experience of being caught and publicly labelled as a deviant" to be "one of the most crucial steps in the process of building a stable pattern of deviant behavior".

Young argues that the police are susceptible to stereotypes held about certain groups. They therefore select evidence to support these views which leads to apprehension and the stereotypes becoming reality. Cain, in a study of police on the beat, has noted the importance of their seeing individuals "in the round as total people" so that they "respond to them as such and not just to the action they perform" (1970: 80). Such arguments appear to be applicable to the group in this study. The present state of friction and lack of mutual understanding between police and delinquents is undoubtedly impossible to eliminate completely. However, there are measures which could improve the situation, make the work of the police more effective, and reduce the extent of inaccurate stereotypes (such as widescale racial conflict within the group) common to both parties.

[Omitted is a section describing "juvenile liaison schemes", through which informal contacts are made between police and juveniles. The implementation of such a scheme is advocated. It is also suggested that the procedures for pressing civilian complaints about police behaviour are in need of change.] It seems clear from the experiences of police forces throughout the world that there are ways of reducing juvenile hostility towards the police. When a concentrated effort is made, it also appears methods such as those suggested here may meet with some success.

21

The Burden of Rheumatoid Arthritis: Tolerating the Uncertainty*

CAROLYN L. WIENER

All living requires tolerating a considerable amount of uncertainty – to state this is to state the obvious. But a study of the victims of rheumatoid arthritis provides an insight into the demands placed upon living when uncertainty is exaggerated beyond the usual level of toleration. This paper examines the disease conditions which produce variable uncertainty. It then analyzes the strategies arthritics develop in order to tolerate this uncertainty . . . The ultimate social-psychological tyranny of tolerating the uncertainty lies in balancing [the use of these strategies] one against the other. Compounding this is the additional problem of balancing drug side effects against relief. This burden of balancing limited options is examined at the conclusion of the paper.

RESEARCH METHODOLOGY

All patients referred to in this paper were participants in a research project on *Nursing Care and the Management of Pain in Patients*. Field work was conducted on hospital wards by means of observation and interviews, focussed upon interaction between patients and the attending staff, between staff members and the patient's family, and among the staff members themselves . . . The objective of the project was the collection and analysis of data

* Reprinted in part from Carolyn L. Wiener (1975) "The burden of rheumatoid arthritis: tolerating the uncertainty", *Social Science and Medicine*, **9**: 97–104, with the permission of the publishers and the author.

pertaining to the sociological aspects of pain management, to be used in teaching health professionals how to give better care to patients who are in pain.

This paper deals only with that aspect of the project concerning the management of rheumatoid arthritis. Twenty-one arthritics were interviewed either as out-patients in the Arthritis Clinic of a major medical center, as in-patients in the center's orthopedic unit, or in their homes. Analysis of field data was conducted in the following manner: indicators in the data (descriptions by the arthritic, or observations by the researcher, of an action, episode or event) were coded into categories and their properties. For example, all descriptions of behavioral attempts to continue a normal life were initially coded as *normalization* and then broken down into categories of normalization, such as *covering-up*, *keeping-up* and *pacing*. Concepts which have been dictated by the data, and thus coded, can then be interrelated. Moreover, they have imagery for the reader, and can be carried forward in the writing (one can carry forward a concept such as *covering-up* to demonstrate its relationship to another concept such as *justifying inaction*, but one cannot constantly carry forward a description such as "When I walk, I walk as normally as possible" and demonstrate its relationship to another description such as "My husband doesn't really understand"). It is intended that conceptually specifying behavior will strengthen its applicability as a guideline for health professionals . . .

Under the framework employed for this study, data collecting and analysis proceeded simultaneously. Emerging concepts were constantly compared to new indicators as they arose in the field, as well as to indicators in data collected on other illnesses under study in the pain research project. Through this systematic coding, and constant comparison of indicators, *uncertainty* emerged as the core category, i.e. uncertainty accounted for most of the variation in the social/psychological problem of living with rheumatoid arthritis. It should be understood that the objective of this mode of analysis is not to test already existing theory but to suggest hypotheses – to generate substantive, "middle-range" theory. [Following Glaser and Strauss (1967), Wiener defines substantive theory as that developed for a substantive, or empirical area of inquiry, such as patient care and the management of pain. Wiener also acknowledges the guidance of Strauss and Glaser, who were joint directors of the project.] Such theory-making (in this paper that of *tolerating the uncertainty*) develops a dense integration of the relationships among conceptual categories and their conceptual properties, each of which has earned its way into the theory by being "grounded in the data", i.e. derived from the meanings and the interpretations made by the subjects of the study.

RESOURCE REDUCTION AS A SOURCE OF VARIABLE UNCERTAINTY

The term "arthritis" dates back to the days of Hippocrates, and literally means joint inflammation, i.e. joints which are hot, red and swollen. As popularly used to describe a disease, "arthritis" is a misnomer, less than the full picture. There are many diseases that manifest arthritis as part of their symptoms, but rheumatoid arthritis, the disease under examination here, is now understood to be a systemic disease that affects the connective or supporting tissues which are ubiquitous throughout the body. The etiology of rheumatoid arthritis is unknown, but the result is that the involved tissue becomes inflamed. When the disease attacks joint tissue, pain becomes the signal for patient and physician. In most cases, the onset is insidious, with ill-defined aching and stiffness . . .

[Wiener gives a description of the basic symptoms of rheumatoid arthritis, together with many examples. The main points are these. First, the patient is "faced with an intermittent *reduction in personal resources*", namely *mobility, skill* and *energy*. These resources are affected because of factors such as pain, inflammation of joints, loss of dexterity and strength, and the metabolic effects of the disease. Second, patients learn that "the disease is not only incurable, but its specific manifestations are unpredictable . . . in only a minority of cases does the disease follow a downhill course of severe disability. Most cases are marked rather by peaks and valleys of flare-up and remission." The timing of flare-ups and remissions is quite unpredictable; Wiener calls this condition *variable uncertainty*.

Third, in these circumstances "two imperatives press their claims upon the arthritic". The *physiological imperative* is the impairment due to pain and disability. In competition with this is the *activity imperative*, which has to be acknowledged if the arthritic is to maintain what is seen as a normal life. All of Wiener's inter-viewees "were still coping with the demands these two imperatives were making upon them". Finally, Wiener states that "the very uncertainty which makes the disease so intolerable also mitigates against acceptance of . . . invalid status, for there is always hope of another remission. It is this dimension of tolerating which we shall examine next."]

SOCIAL-PSYCHOLOGICAL TOLERATING STRATEGIES

The psychological strategy of hope

Faced with the whipsaw of a physiological imperative which reduces activity and an activity imperative pushing one forward, arthritics tolerate the uncertainty by *juggling the hope of relief and/or remission against the dread of progression.* Although they know the disease does not follow a decided downhill course, there is always the fantasy of the disease progression: dreading the next place and the next time it is going to hit. As one person expressed it, "I think of my body like a used car, waiting for the next part to go." In a clinic such as the one under examination here, they see others who are worse off and when they say "I'm lucky it's not in my . . .", the implication is clear. This leaves one constantly on the alert. Pain, when it hits in a new place, makes the uncertainty intolerable. Knowing the possibilities is one thing; having them occur is another. The arthritic must wait to see if the pain persists and while waiting the uncertainty is heightened. One begins to worry that the new pain is not really arthritis, but something even more serious, requiring professional diagnosis. Arthritics are inhibited by a selectivity in reporting symptoms: "If I tell the doctor about all my aches and pains, he won't be listening when it's really important."

The dread of a progressively worsened state brings with it a *dread of dependency,* expressed frequently as "I don't want to be a burden". Some patients fear the dependent role to such an extent that they will live alone at tremendous sacrifice in order to avoid the dependent status they would have in the family home. To illustrate, one woman, now 44, recalled the onset of her disease at 22, her move to an apartment, and her struggle to continue working:

It was harrowing. When I got up in the morning my feet were so painful I couldn't stand on them. I would slide out of bed and with my elbow and rump get into the bathroom. I learned to turn the faucets with my elbows.

For this woman, the activity imperative pressed on, in spite of the increased pace of the physiological imperative, and in fact brought her through this period into a long period of remission.

Just such knowledge of the capricious behavior of the disease provides a psychological strategy to counter the dread: hope for remission or, at least, temporary relief. Often this is expressed in theories of causation, the hope that a remission can be correlated with something the arthritic can control, such as diet. [Symptom-control efforts may be based on conventional medical treatment or folk remedies; several examples are given, including acupuncture. Wiener discusses several other aspects of the hope strategy.]

Social strategies of covering-up and keeping-up

Another means of dealing with the problem of battling imperatives is to develop social strategies to assist one in *normalizing* life, i.e. suppressing the physiological imperative and proceeding with the activity imperative *as if* normal. The principal strategies employed are covering-up and keeping-up, which in turn generate problems of their own.

Covering-up, concealing disability and/or pain, while not a behavioral phenomenon peculiar to arthritics, is nevertheless an important component of their repertoire. Variations of the following quotes appear throughout the interviews: "If anyone asks me how I am, I say fine." "When I walk, I walk as normally as possible – if I walked like I felt like walking, I'd look like I should be in a wheelchair." Covering-up is not a denial of the disease, in the psychological sense of the word. As described by Davis: "it is the rejection by the patient of the handicap as his total identity. In effect, it is the rejection of the social significance of the handicap and not rejection of the handicap *per se*" (1973: 18). To explain, unsuccessful covering-up invites the risk of interrupted interaction with offers of help, or with questions ("skiing accident?") . . . Interaction, so interrupted, impedes the arthritic's ability to view himself as he would prefer to be viewed by others.

There are various conditions under which covering-up is impeded. An arthritic who is subject to sudden attacks, such as a freezing of the back and the resultant immobility, is a case in point. This woman had such an attack while visiting her home town, found she could only walk at a creeping pace, some of the time only backwards:

> People on the street would ask if they could help . . . the embarrassment was worse than the pain. I thought they would all think I was crazy or drunk.

Visibility – use of a cane or crutches, wincing when arising from a chair or getting out of a car – is another impediment to covering-up . . .

If covering-up is successful, a price may be paid, for the strategy drains already depleted energy: "Do you know the stress you put your body to trying to walk straight so people won't see you can't walk?" There is increased awareness of pain and stiffness once within the confines of the home and increased strain on tolerating. Patients report that after situations in which they "toughed it out", they give in to their fatigue and nervousness, dumping their irritability upon close family members.

Armed with their repertoire for covering-up, and lulled by their good days, arthritics struggle to keep the activity imperative ahead in the race, through efforts at *keeping-up* – keeping-up with what they perceive to be normal activities (preparing a holiday meal for the family, maintaining a job, participating in a family hike). They may carry through the moment successfully and then suffer increased pain and fatigue; the risk is taken precisely because of the uncertainty that such a price will in fact be extracted. Keeping-up efforts may also continue in spite of their seeming irrationality to an outsider, in order to maintain a self-image. To illustrate, one woman, who reported a period of relief as a guest of her daughter, where she was not allowed to use her hands to so much as open a car door, suffered another painful onset when she cleaned her sink and bathrub the first day home, because "I hate dirt" . . .

Some arthritics engage in excessive keeping-up – supernormalizing – to prove a capacity, to deny incapacity or to recapture a former identity. Pain-free and energetic days invite frenetic activity, or catching-up, for the above reasons. The result is often (but uncertain again) that time is lost through increased pain and/or decreased energy the next day . . .

A successful repertoire for covering-up and keeping-up may at times turn out to be a mixed blessing. Relationships generally remain normal, but when the arthritic cannot get by, it is harder to *justify inaction* to others. Again this is related to the variable uncertainty – they cannot legitimize their abnormality because sometimes they are normal, and other times, although hurting, they are covering-up or keeping-up. This problem is increased when others have stakes in the arthritic's remaining active, as was the case with a young mother whose condition worsened when she tried to keep athletic pace with her husband and son: "My husband really doesn't understand. He is very healthy and he thinks there is some magic formula that I'm not following – if I would just exercise, or have people over." . . .

Paradoxically, patients who are presenting a normal image to the world are nevertheless perplexed when they are not taken seriously by others. There is a longing for understanding, for a sensitivity from others, that goes beyond justifying inaction. An arthritic may be proud that "nobody knows" and yet wish that "somebody cared". The same patient can boast of a mastery of covering-up, "If I went around looking like I feel no one would want to be with me" and still say, "I don't think anyone has any idea how much pain I have." . . .

The social strategy of pacing

Weaving in and out of the normalization repertoire is the governor of the activity imperative, *pacing* – identifying which activities one is able to do, how often, under what circumstances. The import-ance of this strategy lies in the fact that these are the activities which allow one to view oneself as normal.

Arthritics know it takes them longer to complete everyday tasks. For example, they learn to allow extra time just to get dressed, since putting on hose or tying shoe laces can be agonizing-ly painful. To quote one patient, "I dress a little, lie down and cry a little and dress a little more." They decide if they can only work a three day week, or do housework for an hour; they know if they shop they may not be able to cook. Housework is not spon-taneous, but planned around periods of respite. During remission, the arthritic may have resumed activities, or assumed new ones (for example, work, recreation, lodge and church), and then be forced by a flare-up into cancelling some or all of these. This all ties in with the variable uncertainty again; pacing is not a static decision, but must fluctuate with a monitoring of the physiological imperative. Along with pacing decisions run all the problems mentioned earlier related to justifying inaction.

Decisions on activities (which ones, how often) are also affected by the time lost in the rest required between activities. Rest is prescribed, but not always honored . . . Since covering-up and keeping-up have become an integral part of the arthritic's mechanism for coping, many prefer to rest and then make a fresh assessment of the physiological imperative rather than suffer the embarrassment of cancelling plans.

RE-NORMALIZING: THE ADJUSTMENT TO REDUCED ACTIVITY

Re-normalizing, i.e. lowering expectations and developing a new set of norms for action, is directly related to the frequency and duration of flare-up. Reif (1973) describes this process.

> Over the course of time, sick persons revise their expectations regarding what constitutes a normal or acceptable level of activity. That is, standards for performance are set in accordance with what is reasonable and possible, given limited capacity to cope with certain pursuits, at certain points in the illness. Bringing expectations into line with abilities is one strategy for coping with an otherwise untenable situation.

For the arthritic, this means settling for half a window being clean when the arm starts to hurt in the middle of the cleaning, or, as one patient put it, "Sometimes I cannot open a jar; I'll bang it on the sink, and finally say damn it, put it away and have something else." . . .

Increased frequency and duration of flare-ups will spiral re-normalization into lower and lower expectations. New coping mechanisms replace old mechanisms for tolerating uncertainty . . . If the flare-ups and the embarrassment of cancelling become too frequent, there may be a resultant change in life-style, such as a reduction in working hours or retirement, a move to a retirement home or the acquisition of a boarder-helper. Frequent cancelling of church or recreational activities, inability to visit or entertain friends ends in withdrawal into a narrowed social world . . .

Eliciting help

Part of the step downward, of re-normalization, is accepting help. Arthritics may have to *elicit help* from others – to dress them, cook and/or shop for them, help them carry out tasks at home and at work. If they live alone they may have to ask a neighbor for help with zippers and buttons. Once the need to ask extends beyond the immediate family, the act is weighed for importance. For example, one may consider asking a neighbor to unscrew the cork from a wine bottle and decide to forgo the wine, but, when pain and stiffness make public transportation a forbidding prospect, one will ask a friend to be driven to the clinic.

Eliciting help places increased strain on tolerating the uncertainty, for it reinforces the dread of possible dependency. As perhaps the most extreme illustration, one woman stood without moving for two hours, when her back froze while visiting a friend in a convalescent home. She would not ask for help in spite of the easy accessibility of assistance, and waited until she could walk home, one mincing step at a time. Throughout her interview ran her fear of "being a burden".

The hesitation in eliciting help also stems from the fear that others may not be responsive . . . Eliciting help decreases the arthritic's potential for covering-up and keeping-up. A case in point is the woman who took a leave of absence from work because she could no longer perform to her own satisfaction – she could not lift the heavy robes on her saleswoman job and could not stand having other workers do it for her: "after all they're being paid the same thing as I". Deprived of her strategies for normalizing, she could no longer view herself as she wished to be viewed by her co-workers, as self-sufficient and capable. Lastly, awkward and/or embarrassing situations of eliciting help may occur, which only serve to highlight dependency. One such case was reported by a man who was forced to ask a stranger in a public toilet to zip him up; his fingers are closed to the palms of his hands, and he had left his trusty button-hook home. He could laugh in retrospect, "You have to be careful who you ask."

Since eliciting help is a tacit acknowledgement of the gain that the physiological imperative is making on the activity imperative, an additional weight on tolerating stems from the identity problems which arthritics suffer when their eliciting of help results in a role-reversal . . . Male arthritics who have lost their dexterity must rely on wives to carry heavy objects, open garage doors, etc. Women frequently complained of their diminished roles as homemaker in variations of the following quote:

> I like being a housewife and keeping the house immaculate. The house is my responsibility, and now my husband (children) have to do much of the work.

Dependent as it is on duration and frequency of flare-ups, role-reversal may result in a permanent change in the household's division of labor. Helping out has now become a new job. In these cases, tolerating the uncertainty has lessened and dependency need no longer be a dread – it is all too clearly a reality.

BALANCING THE OPTIONS

In tolerating the uncertainty, the arthritic is ultimately engaged in a precarious balancing of options – options somewhat limited because of already reduced resources of mobility, skill, strength and energy. Indeed, a balancing is involved in all of the pacing decisions (weighing the potential benefit of acupuncture against the climb up two flights of stairs "that will just about kill me", the potential withdrawal from church activity against the loss of social interaction). The options are constantly presenting themselves, each to be met with an *ad hoc* response: whether to keep up and suffer the increased pain and fatigue; whether to cover-up and risk inability to justify inaction when needed; whether to elicit help and risk loss of normalizing, whether to re-normalize and decrease the need for covering-up and keeping-up. Furthermore, as explained earlier, there exists a constant balancing of the hope of relief and/or remission against the dread of progression.

At the same time another very worrisome balancing is going on. Since all of the patients in this study were being treated at a clinic, all were on a strict drug regimen. With no cure available, the drugs hopefully provide symptom control and help the arthritic normalize. Patients with long histories of frequent flare-ups had undergone sequential trials of potent anti-rheumatic drugs, all of which can have adverse side effects. Some people had difficulty in recalling the sequence of these trials; frequently they were not told what was in their injections and did not ask. For them, the balancing was weighted in favor of relief at any cost: "When you're hurting like that you have to do something." . . .

Balancing decisions are therefore constantly being reassessed. One must decide what one's options are: one must decide between them by calculating consequences; one must pace the consequences whatever . . . they actually turn out to be; and one cannot rest easily or for long on previous definitions and decisions about options. Thus, about balancing – there is at best only temporary certainty. This, too, the arthritic must learn to live with.

IMPLICATIONS

To reiterate the self-evident proposition with which this paper began, all of life is uncertain. Living requires coming to terms with that uncertainty in much the same manner as described herein – by balancing options and making choices. Thus, arthritics were found in this study to be dealing with a universal aspect of the human condition, but in *exaggerated form and with severely limited options*. Further research could enlarge the scope of the framework presented in this paper, by theoretically sampling under different conditions, for example in another culture. The heuristic value of substantive theory is that such "new theory" is not viewed as conflicting or invalidating, but rather as an extended explanation which can be incorporated into extant theory (see Strauss, 1970, on the possibilities of this relationship between new theory and extant theory). Equally important is the consideration of the crucial variables of tolerating the uncertainty as they apply to other chronic illnesses, where they appear in different combinations and where uncertainty takes on varying degrees of significance. It is in this regard that the presentation of substantive theory, developed through systematic analysis of qualitative data, makes a contribution: not only in its practical use in the substantive area being examined, but in its application and adjustment to other situations with sufficient exactitude to guide thinking, understanding and further research.

Consider the normalization strategy of covering-up. Some arthritics can choose to employ this strategy because of the invisibility of pain, but for the individual with ulcerative colitis the uncertainty of the constant possibility of external evidence of diarrhea may vitiate against this strategy. The relationship between uncertainty and covering-up for persons with ulcerative colitis more closely resembles the experience of those arthritics who are subject to sudden attacks, and those with decreased dexterity and/or visible deformity. [Omitted here is a section in which further examples are given illustrating that, while the concepts developed in this paper are equally applicable to other medical conditions involving pain management, the *relationships* between the concepts may differ considerably.] Space does not allow more than this brief glimpse at the applicability of these concepts. What is clear is that we are just beginning to grasp their implications as a key to understanding and explaining interaction that pertains to persons with chronic illness.

Regardless of the burden of tolerating the uncertainty, no one would suggest that persons so afflicted would choose the certitude of invalidism, and the attendant extreme dependency and lessened social contact. Nor are individuals with chronic illness asking for approbation for how they balance their remaining options. Rather, what they *are* asking, is for some comprehension on the part of those around them, and on the part of health professionals, of their situation *vis-à-vis* the general human condition . . .

22

Additional Studies

Chapters 10 to 21 provide a range of examples of different approaches to research, but nevertheless some basic aspects of research methods cannot be illustrated from these twelve reports. The purpose of this chapter is to give brief summaries of five additional studies; the reasons for the inclusion of each study will become evident as it is discussed. The first three are examples of field research using qualitative data, and these supplement the four reports included as Chapters 11, 19, 20 and 21.

Jacobs on symbolic bureaucracy

This is a participant-observation study of a social-welfare agency (Jacobs, 1969). As the author was employed by the agency he was a 'complete participant' but it is not evident whether the research was covert. Data-collection techniques are not described in detail, but it is fairly clear that Jacobs used observation, eavesdropping, situated conversations, and documents (the 'rule-books' of the agency).

For present purposes, the most important feature of the study is Jacobs's theorising. The data are used to *test* Weber's theory of bureaucracy, as modified by Blau; the procedure is to examine the workings of the social-welfare agency to test the extent to which it exhibits the characteristics suggested by the theory – specialization, hierarchy of authority, rules and impersonality. Jacobs argues that these characteristics only *appear* to be present. While this is how the agency may be viewed by an outsider, they are not features of the way the work is actually organised – hence the term "symbolic bureaucracy". The precise content of Jacobs's conclusions need not concern us here; the main point is that an existing theory has been tested using qualitative data, and a substantial reformulation of the theory is proposed.

On another level, it is worth noting that the process of field-work is not described adequately in the report, and that no 'raw' data (extracts from conversations or field-notes) are offered as evidence. For reasons such as this, the validity of Jacobs's argument is, strictly speaking, dubious (although readers with direct experience of work in other bureaucratic agencies will perhaps agree with the general thrust of his findings).

Cressey on the violation of financial trust

In this article Cressey (1950) gives only a brief account of his field methods. The study is based on all trust violators confined in one US prison; sample size is not stated in the article (but from other information it is seventy-three).[1] Data collection was by interview, though the exact procedure varied depending on the co-operation of the inmate (Cressey, 1950: 740–1). The details of empirical procedures need not, however, concern us unduly here; the study is included in this chapter mainly as an example of data analysis, since Cressey is quite explicit on this aspect of the research.

The purpose of the study was to construct a theory of trust violation; Cressey's aim was to "[determine] whether a definable sequence of events is *always* present when trust violation is present" (1950: 739, emphasis added). He therefore used the principle of analytic induction to guide the data analysis, and he eventually identifies a three-factor sequence describing a universal process leading to trust violation. In brief, this sequence is (1) the existence of a non-shareable problem, (2) an awareness that the problem can be resolved by violation of trust, and (3) verbal rationalisations about the behaviour (see Cressey, 1950: 742 for full details). It should be noted that a trust violator is defined by Cressey as one who *initially* takes on a position of trust in good faith (which excludes many individuals convicted of embezzlement and forgery).

In most respects Cressey's research is very similar to that of Becker on marijuana users (Chapter 11), yet the two research

reports are written in quite different ways. Becker presents a great
deal of data in support of his conclusions, but says nothing about
his analysis of the data; Cressey gives no data at all in the report,
but describes clearly the process of data analysis. The three-stage
sequence was arrived at through progressive refinement of initial
hunches. Four previous hypotheses were tested out against the
data; at each stage there were negative cases which provided the
information necessary for further refinement (1950: 741–2). This is
a useful account of how, by trial and error, the qualitative data
analyst builds theory from evidence (see Chapter 8).

Becker on the dance musician

The purpose of this study was to describe the culture of dance
musicians, who are regarded as a deviant group (Becker, 1951).
The "dance musician" is defined as "someone who plays popular
music for money". Becker was himself a working musician, so
access to the group and field-relations were unproblematic. This is
therefore an example of participant-observation, though it is not
clear whether Becker's 'complete' participant role was wholly
covert. He states that he took extensive notes "on the job" and at
the job market. The results are presented under three headings,
which taken together constitute the main features of the dance
musicians' distinctive life-style: the musician's attitude to
"squares" (non-musicians) is analysed, and a strong element of
isolation and self-segregation is found.

Becker's sampling is a mixture of accidental and theoretical
sampling (see Chapter 8). Clearly, he had only minimal control
over who else might be in the band on any occasion, or who he
might meet at the job market in the union offices; once at any
location, however, he would have some element of control over
who to talk to, and how to 'steer' the conversation. As is usual in
this kind of research, each of Becker's respondents would have
provided a different amount of information, ranging from extensive details to one utterance or one observed piece of behaviour,
and it is not really appropriate to think in terms of sample size (cf.
Smith, Chapter 20).

The working universe is (probably) dance musicians in Chicago (and perhaps in two other towns where Becker played subsequent-ly, though he did no formal research there); the date of the research is not stated, but is presumably in the late 1940s. The extent to which Becker's sample can be taken as representative of this working universe is, however, not clear.

Berelson and Salter on prejudice against minority groups

This study is a content analysis of popular magazine fiction. Berelson and Salter (1946) set out to answer one basic question – are minority groups treated differently from majority groups in magazine fiction? Clearly, their interest in this question stemmed from concern about prejudice and discrimination against minority groups, but there appears to be no explicit theory to be tested. The purpose of the research is to describe the differentials in treatment given to the majority and minority groups.

The operationalisation will be described only briefly here[2]. The authors first selected eight of the most widely read US magazines (e.g. the *Saturday Evening Post*), from each of two years (1937 and 1943) they selected four issues of each magazine, and the first, third and fifth short stories were then included in the sample. The sample was 185 short stories, which involved a total of 889 characters. Most of the analysis is concerned with these 889 characters, though in one section (on whether the relationship between ethnic groups was overtly discussed) Berelson and Salter revert to the 185 stories. The study therefore acts as an example of changes in the *unit* of analysis, for both the character and the story are used as units in the presentation of results.

Berelson and Salter demonstrate quite convincingly that minor-ity groups are treated relatively badly in magazine short stories, compared with the "American" majority; for example, they appear more often in minor roles, are more likely to be dis-approved of, are of lower socio-economic status, and so on. These findings apply both to "American minorities" (e.g. Jews, blacks) and "foreigners" (e.g. Italians, Poles) when they are compared with the "Americans". The authors' conclusions are that "[even] here in . . . fiction fashioned of sweetness and light . . . [there is] a subtle discrimination against minorities and foreigners".

Breed on suicide and occupational mobility

As the basis for this research, Breed (1963) studied suicides in New Orleans in the period 1954–9 and compared their patterns of occupational mobility with a control group selected from the general population. For present purposes, it is Breed's approach to *sampling* which deserves special attention, and his findings will not concern us here. Breed first selected a group of suicides to study; the 103 victims were white, male, aged 20 to 60, and had lived in New Orleans for at least six months. Thus, in defining the working universe, Breed effectively controlled the variables of race, sex, age range and length of residence; attempted suicides and 'murder-suicides' (e.g. a father who deliberately kills his wife and children, and then himself) were excluded. The rationale for narrowing down the special universe in this way is spelled out (Breed, 1963: 180–1); as the size of the group is only 103, it was not necessary to reduce it further, so the sample (or study group) is the whole of this working universe. For each member of the sample, interviews were carried out with relatives to establish the occupational history of the victim; in most cases, several different interviews were undertaken, and this enabled details to be checked thoroughly.

The procedure for establishing a control group from the general population is quite complicated, and is not altogether clearly explained. Interviewers were sent to the block where each victim had lived, the object being to obtain two interviews from two different respondents who lived at least five doors away. These two respondents were then asked to give information about one living male each; these males became members of the control group of size 206, all whites, and in the age range 20–60. It appears that the interviewers were instructed to ask the respondent to nominate a male relative who lived in the neighbourhood and who satisfied the relevant criteria. It is not possible to work out the full details of the control-group selection from Breed's account, and indeed it ought to be stressed that the procedure used is more complex than is usual in control-group studies (see Chapter 4). Nevertheless, Breed's intention is clear; each person in the study group was to be *matched* by two individuals in the control group, not only on sex, race, age group and residence in New Orleans (controlled for the whole study), but also on area of residence, and perhaps on actual age and social class (Breed, 1963: 181). This is, therefore, in principle, an example of a *retrospective matched control-group design* – although in practive it is difficult to see how successful the matching was.

Appendix: Glossary of Terms

Techniques for data collection have not been discussed in any detail in this book and this glossary is intended mainly for the beginning student who is unfamiliar with terminology. Most of the headings deal with specific methods of data collection; a selection of other headings has also been included to clarify certain general terms used in the literature on research methods. The reader is reminded that many other general terms are explained in Chapters 1–9. The definitions given here are brief; they may be followed up by consulting the specific sources cited, but for most of the headings further details will be found in any standard textbook on research methods. References to the material presented in this book are shown simply by citing chapter numbers. Terms which are defined elsewhere in the glossary are italicised.

Case study   This term normally denotes a detailed study of *one* person, or a family or an 'event' such as a political demonstration (Mitchell, 1968: 26). Sometimes a researcher will take several case studies and discuss their similarities and differences. 'Typical' case studies are also used to illustrate broad statistical patterns, e.g. a poverty survey with descriptions of typical low-income families.

Comparative studies   Generally refers to research which involves comparing elements of two or more societies and analysing their similarities and differences: also called 'cross-cultural' studies (see Marsh, 1967). The term 'comparative' is sometimes used to denote the study of different groups within the same society.

Concepts and indicators   Many of the theoretical concepts used in sociology (e.g. social status, conformity, alienation, authority) are images of reality, abstractions which are not observable directly. To investigate a proposition like 'people who have no children are more likely to be enthusiasts for violent change', we must define empirical indicators for the concepts. The process of developing an indicator and testing its validity is often called 'operationalising' a concept; sometimes this is done through the use of an existing *scale*. See Chapter 3.

Content analysis   Systematic (usually statistical) analysis of the content of communications, generally applied to the mass media – newspapers, magazines, television, and so on. (See Holsti, 1969.)

Demographic data and records of past events   Sociologists often use demographic data and other official statistical material (e.g. criminal statistics). They also use records of past events, like public archives and administrative records of organisations (e.g. coroners' files). While these are rich sources of data, the main methodological problem is that the material is collected for some administrative purpose and not with the sociologist in mind. Collections of newspapers and other products of mass media are also important records of the past (see *content analysis*).

Empiricism, empirical   'Empiricism' is generally used in a derogatory sense and denotes research which is lacking in theoretical orientation, or research which does not make explicit the theory which guides its procedures (Mitchell, 1968: 67). Not to be confused with 'empirical', which is a more general term referring to any research involving the collection of new data (in contrast to 'library research'). Most empirical research in contemporary sociology is soundly based on theory.

Experiments   The two common forms are laboratory experiments and field experiments (Tripodi *et al.*, 1969: 22–23). In both cases the researcher is concerned primarily with measuring the effect of the experimental conditions which he creates. Laboratory experiments are often used to study group dynamics, e.g. a reconstruction of a jury situation with a bogus juryman 'planted' and instructed to maintain the defendant's innocence, against all evidence. An example of a field experiment would be to introduce a new system of policing political demonstrations and measure the effect on police–public relations.

Field-work   In the literature on qualitative research methods many writers use the terms field-work and field-reserch interchangeably with *participant-obervation*, as discussed below. This usage should be distinguished from that of research based on more structured methods such as a *social survey* based on a *questionnaire*, where the term field-work has been used (in Chapters 1–6) to denote the practical problems involved in data-gathering.

Grounded theory   A term introduced by Glaser and Strauss (1967) meaning methods for carrying out field-work in such a way that theory is systematically generated from the data as part of the ongoing research process. Hence theory is said to be 'grounded' in data. This is in contrast to the more traditional approach where data are collected in order to test an existing theory. See Glaser and Strauss (1967), Schatzman and Strauss (1973) and Chapters 7 and 8.

Interviews   There are many different kinds of interviews. In a 'standardised' interview both the question and the permissible range of answers are predetermined – see *questionnaires*. By contrast, in 'unstructured' interviews, neither the questions nor the form of the answers are set out in advance: 'focused', 'depth' and 'non-directive' are different varieties of unstructured interviews. Many interviews fall between the two extremes, and include some questions which are standardised and some sections which are unstructured (Selltiz *et al.*, 1976: ch. 9 and appendix B).

Life history   A particular type of *case study*, where the emphasis is on reconstructing the whole life history of an individual. (See Denzin, 1970: ch. 10.)

Methodology Principally, this term refers to the study of the logical basis of a discipline, and in this usage it can be equated with the term 'philosophy of science' (Mitchell, 1968: 118). However, most writers use the term methodology more loosely to mean the study of 'methods of doing sociology', including techniques of collecting and analysing data.

Participant-observation This is a term originally applied to the research technique where the researcher becomes as much as possible a member of the group he is studying, and participates fully in the activities of the group. In the most extreme form the observer's research aims are not known to the group, but naturally there are considerable ethical objections to such 'spying' (Mitchell, 1968: 129–30). Today, participant-observation is used more generally to refer to *field-work* where the observer (whose role as a researcher is usually known) is involved in continuing social interaction with the subjects of the study. In this situation many techniques for data collection will be used, including conversations and the use of documentary evidence. Thus the data are not confined to observations in the strict sense. See McCall and Simmons (1969), Schatzman and Strauss (1973) and Chapters 7 and 8. An example could be research in a large hospital. The co-operation of the authorities would be needed. The researcher would observe staff and patients, and talk with them ('situational conversations'); he might also use documents such as the hospital's administrative records, and certain members of staff might act as key 'informants' because they have special knowledge of the phenomenon being studied. The researcher can therefore check data from one source against that from others – thus using the principle of *triangulation* (see Chapter 7).

Projective and other indirect methods A range of techniques developed mainly by psychologists and social psychologists, where the individual's responses to (say) a questionnaire are not taken at face value; some underlying dimension, which will not be known to the respondent, is being measured (Selltiz *et al.*, 1976: ch. 10). It could be argued that many *scales* used by sociologists are partly projective, e.g. scales measuring alienation or authoritarianism (Miller, 1970).

Questionnaires Questionnaires may be administered to respondents by interviewers or may be 'self-completed'. The two situations require different approaches to questionnaire design, as in the latter case the questions should be self-explanatory. See Selltiz *et al.* (1976: ch. 9 and appendix B) on the design of questionnaires and the wording of questions. One major distinction is between questions which are 'fixed-choice' (e.g. How long have you lived at this address? Less than a year/1–2 years/Over 2 years?) and 'open-ended' (e.g. What do you think of the protest marches?).

Replication Repetition of a research study using the same procedures but on a different sample or in a different setting. Replication is important because a proposition which is confirmed at one time and in one place will not necessarily hold at other times and places. Testing and retesting a proposition at different times and in different places provides more conclusive results.

Sampling The selection of *units* for study. The most important approach is statistical (or probability) sampling, which aims to provide a representative cross-section of a 'population' (Selltiz *et al.* 1976: appendix A). The term 'population' has a general meaning here – it can denote a population of people, but equally well a population like 'all primary schools in city A'. The representativeness of a sample can be ensured, in principle, by random selection – as in a simple lottery system (see Chapter 4). One common problem, however, is 'non-response'; a researcher may use the electoral register to select a representative sample of adults from suburb X, but 20 per cent may refuse to be interviewed. See Chapter 4 on the practical problems of representative sampling.

Sociologists often use other (non-probability) approaches to sampling. Samples selected completely unsystematically (e.g. interviewing the first ten people you meet) are generally unsatisfactory. But sampling can be theoretically directed – for example, we may select cases which provide the most critical test of a theory. It is also very important to point out that certain kinds of sociological research preclude the sampling of individual units from a population; for example, in a study of friendship networks in a school classroom we would include *all* the children in the class (see Chapter 4).

Scales and indexes   Sociologists often use *questionnaire* techniques to measure attitudes, personality dimensions, social status, alienation, and so on. In most cases this involves a set of questionnaire items which has become 'standard', in the sense of being used in a large number of studies; see Miller (1970) for a useful summary. Normally, a scaling method involves combining an individual's responses on the set of items (questions) according to a given procedure; the result is the individual's 'score' on that scale. Despite the large number of standard scales available, the researcher will often need to construct his own scale and will therefore design a set of items for inclusion in his questionnaire; most books on research methods deal with this topic – see, for example, Selltiz *et al.* (1976: ch.12).

Sometimes individual persons are rated on scales using other kinds of data (such as observations). Also, some indexes are devised for different units of analysis, for example census districts or whole countries. Naturally, these indexes are based on appropriate data-collection methods, rather than questionnaires; an example is the ranking of suburbs of a city according to the socio-economic characteristics of the population.

Secondary analysis   Research based on the re-analysis of empirical data already collected for a previous study.

Simple observation   This technique is characterised by *lack* of social interaction between the researcher and the participants in the events being studied. In general, the technique is most applicable to public situations, e.g. behaviour in bars or restaurants.

Social survey   The systematic collection of facts about people living in a specific area (Mitchell, 1968: 189). The earliest examples were surveys of living conditions, usually with the aim of demonstrating the need for reform. Today, social surveys are widely used by government and administrators as well as market researchers and social scientists. Normally, the procedure is to select a *representative sample* of people to be surveyed (rather than the whole population) and these 'respondents' are *interviewed* with the help of *questionnaires* (Moser and Kalton, 1971).

Sociometry The term sociometry (or sociometrics) is used in two different senses. Miller (1970: 163) regards any *scale* used by sociologists as a 'sociometric scale'. Some writers, however, use this term in the very specific sense of the collection of data on a small group, with the purpose of describing the group structure (Northway, 1967). An example would be the description of friendship networks in a class of schoolchildren, based on a questionnaire about who the children would like (or not like) as companions for certain activities. Results are often drawn up as a diagram with the most popular individuals at the centre, and arrows indicating friendship choices.

Triangulation A term used by Denzin (1970) to describe an important **methodolo-gical** principle. It means the use of two or more different methods in studying the same phenomenon – the point is that no *one* method is infallible, so the use of several methods gives more conclusive results. For example, to study interaction processes in a prison one might use participant-observation, questionnaires, and focused interviews.

Unit The individual element which is the basis for *sampling, data collection,* or *data analysis*. In most *social surveys,* and indeed for social research generally, the unit is the individual person. Examples of other units are the family (for a survey of family income), the individual advertisement (for a content analysis of advertising), the locality (in an analysis of crime rates) and the society (for *comparative studies*). In some research the unit for sampling may be different from the unit of data collection or the unit of data analysis. See Chapter 4 for further details.

Unobtrusive methods The data-collection techniques most often used by social researchers (*interviews, questionnaires* and *participant-observation*) are all poten-tially 'reactive' methods – there is a possibility that the data collected are to some extent distorted by the very process of research. For example, the presence of a participant-observer in a school classroom may make the children behave different-ly from usual because they see him as a member of the teaching staff. Unobtrusive methods is a term used to characterise methods which are non-reactive. Techniques include the use of *demographic data* and *records of past events, content analysis* and *simple observation* (see Webb *et al.*, 1966).

Variable A variable is any known characteristic which varies between the individuals in a *sample*. A 'distribution' is simply a description of the variable for the sample. For example the statement '55 per cent of the sample were Catholic and 45 per cent Protestant' would show the distribution of the variable 'religion'. Any *indicator* is a variable; the separate terms are maintained because 'indicator' makes it clear that a *concept* is being measured. In the analysis of statistical relationships between two variables a distinction is usually drawn between the 'independent' and 'dependent' variable – the former is seen as influencing the latter. For example, 'the degree of cohesiveness of family life (dependent) depends on religious affiliation (independent)'. See Chapter 5.

Notes

Chapter 2

1. In this discussion of the validity of arguments presented in research reports, the term 'validity' is used in a broad sense. This usage should not be confused with the narrower issue of measurement validity, which is taken up in Chapter 3. The terms 'internal empirical validity' and 'internal theoretical validity' are used in this book to refer to validity in the broader sense.
2. It is clear from Garabedian (1963: 143, n. 12), Schrag (1959: 178, n. 2) and other material in these two articles that Schrag, Garabedian and Wheeler, together with others, were members of the same research group. A series of linked studies were carried out by this group in the mid-1950s; these studies were probably undertaken in the same prison, and may to some extent have used a common data-base. The results are given in a series of University of Washington Ph.D. theses. Schrag's was the earliest – 1950, and Wheeler's and Garabedian's theses were two of a series finalised during 1956–9. It appears that Garabedian and Wheeler were two of Schrag's graduate students.
3. This aspect of the study could have been improved fairly easily at the sampling stage. Obviously, one solution would have been to take a bigger sample, thus increasing the numbers in all the categories considered. But even *given* a sample size of 380 it would have been better to select a representative sample of (say) 125 from each career stage (3 × 125 = 375). This sampling method could have been implemented using prison records on intake date, length of sentence and time to parole.
4. Testing the difference between 67 per cent ($n = 12$) and 30 per cent ($n = 20$) for formal statistical significance we find chi-square = 2.74, which is not significant at the 5 per cent level (1 degree of freedom, Yates correction used).

Chapter 3

1. In this chapter references to 'validity' are generally to be construed in the narrower sense of measurement validity.

2. In the original study (Neal and Rettig, 1967), there were twelve items on powerlessness; each was contrasted with an opposing statement, and respondents were asked to choose which of each pair of statements was preferred. Here, five of the twelve items have been selected, and the example has been modified for the purposes of simplicity. See Miller (1970: 316–26) for a summary of questionnaire items designed to measure powerlessness and other dimensions of alienation.
3. As far as I know, no sociologist has yet been able to produce a theory in this ideal form. The often-quoted Durkheim theory of suicide may appear to be deductive at the theoretical level, but it is still operationalisable only after translating into a data-language (Hughes, 1976: 55). Also see Ford (1975) on "gold-star" theories.

Chapter 4

1. This example is formally correct, but does not provide a good illustration of the advantages of cluster sampling. For a standard example see Moser and Kalton (1971: 100). Cluster sampling is one of the most commonly used sampling techniques for large-scale social surveys of the general population, as it is a comparatively economical method where interviewer-administered questionnaires are used.
2. This is a poor example, but snowball sampling can be very useful for studying populations which are deviant or clandestine, where a sampling frame is impossible to obtain. (See, for example, Goode, Chapter 13.)
3. The term 'group' is used here in a general sense, and normally refers to an aggregate of individual persons or other units rather than a social group as such (although the latter usage is not excluded).
4. It should be recognised that, as there are so many different sampling designs, this chapter cannot be fully comprehensive; there are, therefore, some studies in which the sampling procedures are more complex than (or simply different from) those outlined above. In sociology three fairly common situations of this kind can be distinguished. First, the use of different or more complex kinds of representative sampling, such as 'area sampling', and second the use of longitudinal or panel designs for 'over-time' studies (Moser and Kalton, 1971: ch. 6). The third situation is the use of several samples (or 'levels' of sampling) within one study, and in sociology this approach is sufficiently common to be worthy of special attention. A researcher will sometimes select a 'sub-sample' from within a main sample, and study the sub-sample more intensively (for example, see Moser and Kalton, 1971: ch. 6, on multi-phase samples). In other cases, such as 'community studies', research may involve two or more samples which are separate but which usually have some relationship to each other (for example, Wild, 1974). The question of deciphering book-length studies such as that of Wild will be discussed in Chapter 9. It is, however, appropriate to point out here that the material in Chapter 4 gives a good basis for analysing the sampling in *most* sociological research; for example, in a 'community study' which involves several samples, each is likely to be selected by a fairly simple method.

Chapter 5

1. Many other authors give a treatment of levels of measurement which is more detailed than that offered here. This is not intended to be a comprehensive analysis of the topic; the distinctions made between the four levels are simply the most useful for the purposes of this book. Silvey (1975) offers a similar analysis.
2. It is often possible (and is sometimes sensible too) to calculate mean values for ordinal variables, such as 'enthusiasm for violent change' measured as 0,1,2,3. The circumstances under which such mean values are permissible, however, raises quite difficult problems of measurement theory which are outside the scope of this book.
3. In Chapter 2 Garabedian's interpretation of the results was, of course, criticised. However, there was nothing wrong with the *procedure* of data analysis itself; the point of criticism was that the sample was too small to permit reliable interpretation of the results.

Chapter 6

1. It may be of interest to refer briefly to Douglas's book on theories of suicide, where arrow diagrams are used for part of the analysis (Douglas, 1967: part 2).
2. Readers interested in these aspects of the study should refer to the original article; see also the other references to the project given in the conclusion to Chapter 15.
3. Admittedly, even after a close reading of the report one cannot be quite sure that this interpretation of Goode's theorising is correct, since Goode does not make this aspect of the study clear. In the analysis given here, however, it is assumed to be a theory-building study, and this allows a number of important points to be made about deciphering theory-building studies generally.

Chapter 7

1. These four roles incorporate a distinction between *covert* and *overt* participant-observation, which is the terminology used by many other writers.

Chapter 8

1. Lofland's analysis of Sykes and Matza's work acts as a good example for present purposes. In the original article, however, Sykes and Matza (1957) do not demonstrate how the concept of "neutralization" techniques and the five categories are built upon evidence, since no data are given.
2. Of course, Becker argues that his findings are of general applicability and Goode does not, but this is because of the nature of the results, not the sample selection.

3. Becker (1958) has suggested that tables of "quasi-statistics" can be presented in reports, as summaries of certain kinds of participant-observation data. The version of Becker's article reprinted in McCall and Simmons (1969: 245–54) includes further details; the use of quasi-statistics seems to be a valuable technique, though it has not been applied very often.

Chapter 9

1. I have omitted from this analysis the various accounts of the logic of 'scientific procedure' in sociology since, in general, they do not use research reports as examples; Riley (1963), which is an exception, is included. In my view the principal defect of much of the writing on scientific procedure, including that of Wallace (1971), is that it is too abstract and suffers from lack of examples.
2. The 'advanced statistical techniques' referred to here may be techniques of either *descriptive* or *inferential* statistics. There is, in fact, no common agreement within statistics textbooks on whether certain multivariate techniques, such as factor analysis or path analysis, are descriptive or inferential, though there is little doubt that the sociology student will find them difficult to grasp.
3. Although Mullins's eight theory groups are defined for American sociology, I have taken them as applicable to sociology as a whole.

Chapter 22

1. Information given in Cressey's later book based on the same research (1953:25).
2. Berelson and Salter's study is, in fact, an excellent example to use as an exercise in deciphering research reports. It could not be considered for inclusion in Part Two for various reasons, including length; it has been reprinted in Straus and Nelson (1968) and in Cohen and Young (1973).

References

Abell, P. (1971) *Model Building in Sociology*, London, Weidenfeld & Nicolson.

Anderson, T. R. and Zelditch, M. (1968) *A Basic Course in Statistics*, New York, Holt, Rinehart & Winston.

Banks, O. (1971) *The Sociology of Education*, London, Batsford.

Barnes, J. A. (1979) *Who Should Know What?*, Harmondsworth, Penguin.

Becker, H. S. (1951) The professional dance musician and his audience, *American Journal of Sociology*, 57: 136–43.

Becker, H. S. (1958) Problems of inference and proof in participant observation, *American Sociological Review*, 23: 652–60.

Becker, H. S. (1963) *Outsiders*, New York, Free Press.

Becker, H. S. (1970) *Sociological Work*, Chicago, Aldine.

Bell, C. and Newby, H. (eds) (1977) *Doing Sociological Research*, London, Allen & Unwin.

Berelson, B. and Salter, P. J. (1946) Majority and minority Americans: an analysis of magazine fiction, *Public Opinion Quarterly*, 10: 168–90.

Berger, P. L. (1971) Sociology and freedom, *American Sociologist*, 6: 1–5.

Blalock, H. M. (1972) *Social Statistics*, New York, McGraw-Hill.

Blau, P. M. and Duncan, O. D. (1967) *The American Occupational Structure*, New York, Wiley.

Blum, R. H. and Associates (1969) *Students and Drugs*, San Francisco: Jossey-Bass.

Breed, W. (1963) Occupational mobility and suicide amongst white males, *American Sociological Review*, 28: 179-88.

Broom, L. and Lancaster Jones, F. (1969) Career mobility in three societies: Australia, Italy and the United States, *American Sociological Review*, 34: 650–8.

Broom, L., Lancaster Jones, F. and Zubrzycki, J. (1965) An occupational classification of the Australian workforce, *Australian and New Zealand Journal of Sociology*, 1 (October): supplement.

Broom, L., Lancaster Jones, F. and Zubrzycki, J. (1968) Social stratification in Australia, in J. A. Jackson (ed.), *Social Stratification*, Cambridge University Press, pp. 212–33.

Broom, L., Lancaster Jones, F. and Zubrzycki, J. (1976) *Opportunity and Attainment in Australia*, Canberra, Australian National University Press.

Broom, L. and Selznick, P. (1968) *Sociology*, New York, Harper & Row.

Brown, G. W. (1973) Some thoughts on grounded theory, *Sociology*, 7: 1–16.

Bulmer, M. (ed.) (1977) *Sociological Research Methods*, London, Macmillan.

Cain, M. (1970) On the beat: interactions and relations in rural and urban police forces, in S. Cohen (ed.), *Images of Deviance*, Harmondsworth, Penguin, pp. 62–74.

Campbell, D. T. and Stanley, J. C. (1963) *Experimental and Quasi-Experimental Designs for Research*, Chicago, Rand McNally.

Chappell, D. and Wilson, P. R. (1969) *The Police and the Public in Australia and New Zealand*, University of Queensland Press.

Clemmer, D. (1958) *The Prison Community*, New York, Holt, Rinehart & Winston.

Cohen, A. K. (1966) *Deviance and Control*, Englewood Cliffs, N.J., Prentice-Hall.

Cohen, S. and Young, J. (eds) (1973) *The Manufacture of News*, London, Constable.

Coleman, J. S. (1961) *The Adolescent Society*, New York, Free Press.

Congalton, A. A. (1953) Social grading of occupations in New Zealand, *British Journal of Sociology*, 4: 45–9.

Cressey, D. R. (1950) The criminal violation of financial trust, *American Sociological Review*, 15: 738–43.

Cressey, D. R. (1953) *Other People's Money*, Belmont, Calif., Wadsworth.

Dahrendorf, R. (1959) *Class and Class Conflict in Industrial Society*, Stanford University Press.

Dahrendorf, R. (1964) Recent changes in the class structure of European societies, *Daedalus*, Winter: 225–70.

Davis, J. A. and Jacobs, A. M. (1968) Tabular presentation, in *International Encyclopedia of the Social Sciences, Vol. 15*, New York, Macmillan and Free Press, pp. 497–509.

Davis, M. Z. (1973) *Living with Multiple Sclerosis: A Social Psychological Analysis*, Springfield, Illinois, C. C. Thomas.

Dean, J. P., Eichhorn, R. L. and Dean, L. R. (1967) Observation and interviewing, in J. T. Doby (ed.), *An Introduction to Social Research*, New York, Appleton, pp. 274–304.

Denzin, N. K. (1970) *The Research Act*, Chicago, Aldine.

Douglas, J. D. (1967) *The Social Meanings of Suicide*, Princeton University Press.

Douglas, J. W. B. (1964) *The Home and the School*, London, MacGibbon & Kee.

Dowse, R. E. and Brier, A. (1968) Political mobilisation: a case-study, *International Review of Community Development*, 19–20: 327–40.

Dowse, R. E. and Hughes, J. A. (1971) The family, the school, and the political socialisation process, *Sociology*, 5: 21–45.

Easton, D. and Dennis, J. (1969) The child's acquisition of regime norms, *American Political Science Review*, 61: 25–38.

Federal Bureau of Narcotics (1965) *Living Death: The Truth about Drug Addiction*, Washington, US Government Printing Office.

Fletcher, C. (1974) *Beneath the Surface*, London, Routledge & Kegan Paul.

Floud, J. E., Halsey, A. H. and Martin F. M. (1957) *Social Class and Educational Opportunity*, London, Heinemann.

Ford, J. (1975) *Paradigms and Fairy Tales: An Introduction to the Science of Meanings*, 2 vols, London, Routledge & Kegan Paul.

Freeman, L. C. (1965) *Elementary Applied Statistics*, New York, Wiley.

Freire, P. (1972) *Pedagogy of the Oppressed*, Harmondsworth, Penguin.

Garabedian, P. G. (1963) Social roles and processes of socialization in the prison community, *Social Problems*, 11: 139–52.

Garfinkel, H. (1967) *Studies in Ethnomethodology*, Englewood Cliffs, N.J, Prentice-Hall.

Glaser, B. G. and Strauss, A. L. (1967) *The Discovery of Grounded Theory*, Chicago, Aldine.

Golden, M. P. (ed.) (1976) *The Research Experience*, Itasca, Illinois : Peacock.

Hall, J. and Jones, D. C. (1950) The social grading of occupations, *British Journal of Sociology*, I: 31–55.

Hammond, P. E. (ed.) (1964) *Sociologists at Work*, New York, Basic Books.

Holly, D. N. (1965) Profiting from a comprehensive school, *British Journal of Sociology*, 16: 150–7.

Holsti, O. R. (1969) *Content Analysis for the Social Sciences and Humanities*, Reading, Mass., Addison-Wesley.

Homans, G. C. (1964) Contemporary theory in sociology, in R. E. L. Faris (ed.), *Handbook of Modern Sociology*, Chicago, Rand McNally, pp. 951–770.

Homans, G. C. (1967) *The Nature of Social Science*, New York, Harcourt Brace & World.

Hughes, J. (1976) *Sociological Analysis: Methods of Discovery*, London, Nelson.

Hyman, H. (1955) *Survey Design and Analysis*, New York, Free Press.

Hyman, H. (1959) *Political Socialization*, New York, Free Press.

Jackson, B. (1964) *Streaming: An Education System in Miniature*, London, Routledge & Kegan Paul.

Jacobs, J. (1969) Symbolic bureaucracy: a case-study of a social welfare agency, *Social Forces*, 47: 413–22.

Kahl, J. A. and Davis, J. A. (1955) A comparison of indexes of socio-economic status, *American Sociological Review*, 20: 317–25.

Kalton, G. (1966) *Introduction to Statistical Ideas for Social Scientists*, London, Chapman & Hall.

Knop, E. (1967) Suggestions to aid the student in systematic interpretation and analysis of empirical sociological journal presentations, *American Sociologist*, 2: 90–2.

Labovitz, S. and Hagedorn, R. (1971) *Introduction to Social Research*, New York, McGraw-Hill.

Lacey, C. (1970) *Hightown Grammar: The School as a Social System*, Manchester University Press.

Lacey, C. (1976) The problems of sociological fieldwork: a review of the methodology of Hightown Grammar, in M. Shipman (ed.), *The Organisation and Impact of Social Resarch*, London, Routledge & Kegan Paul, pp. 63–8.

Lazarsfeld, P. F. and Rosenberg, M. (eds) (1955) *The Language of Social Research*, New York, Free Press.

Lindesmith, A. R. (1947) *Opiate Addiction*, Bloomington, Principia Press.

Lofland, J. (1971) *Analyzing Social Settings*, Belmont, Calif., Wadsworth.

Lopreato, J. (1965) Social mobility in Italy, *American Journal of Sociology*, 71: 311–14.

McCall, G. J. and Simmons, J. L. (eds) (1969) *Issues in Participant Observation*, Reading, Mass., Addison-Wesley.

Mackay, R. W. (1973) Conceptions of children and models of socialization, in P. Dreitzel (ed.), *Recent Sociology, No. 5*, London, Macmillan, pp. 27–43.

MacQueen, D. R. (ed.) (1973) *Understanding Sociology Through Research*, Reading, Mass., Addison-Wesley.

Mann, M. (1981) Socio-logic, *Sociology*, 15 (4) (forthcoming).

Marsh, R. K. (1967) *Comparative Sociology*, New York, Harcourt Brace & World.

Mead, G. H. (1934) *Mind, Self and Society,* University of Chicago Press.

Merton, R. K. (1957) *Social Theory and Social Structure*, New York, Free Press.

Merton, R. K. (1968) *On Theoretical Sociology*, New York, Free Press.

Milbrath, L. W. (1965) *Political Participation*, Chicago, Rand McNally.

Miller, D. C. (1970) *Handbook of Research Design and Social Measurement*, New York, McKay.

Mills, C. W. (1959) *The Sociological Imagination*, New York, Oxford University Press.

Mitchell, G. D. (ed.) (1968) *A Dictionary of Sociology*, London, Routledge & Kegan Paul.

Moser, C. A. and Kalton, G. (1971) *Survey Methods in Social Investigation*, London, Heinemann.

Mullins, N. (1973) *Theories and Theory Groups in Contemporary Sociology*, New York, Harper & Row.

Nash, R. (1973) Clique formation among primary and secondary school children *British Journal of Sociology,* 24: 303-13.

Neal, A. G. and Rettig, S. (1967) On the multidimensionality of alienation, *American Sociological Review*, 32: 54–64.

North, C. C. and Hatt, P. K. (1947) Jobs and occupations: a popular evaluation, *Opinion News*, 9: 3–13.

Northway, M. L. (1967) *A Primer of Sociometry*, University of Toronto Press.

Oppenheim, A. N. (1966) *Questionnaire Design and Attitude Measurement*, London, Heinemann.

Phillips, B. S. (1966) *Social Research: Strategy and Tactics*, New York, Macmillan.

Reif, L. (1973) Managing a life with chronic disease, *American Journal of Nursing*, 73: 262.

Reiss, A. J. Jr (1971) *The Police and the Public*, London, Heinemann.

Riesman, D., Glazer, N. and Denney, R. (1950) *The Lonely Crowd*, New Haven, Conn., Yale University Press.

Riley, M. W. (1963) *Sociological Research: A Case Approach*, New York, Harcourt Brace & World.

Rose, G. (1979) Counter-predictive research outcomes: some methodological issues, in Jean I. Martin (ed.), *Counter-predictive Research Outcomes*, Canberra, Department of Sociology, Research School of Social Sciences, Australian National University, pp. 129–80.

Rosenberg, M. (1968) *The Logic of Survey Analysis*, New York, Basic Books.

Runcie, J. F. (1976) *Experiencing Social Research*, Homeward, Illinois, Dorsey.

Schatzman, L. and Strauss, A. L. (1973) *Field Research: Strategies for a Natural Sociology*, Englewood Cliffs, N.J., Prentice-Hall.

Schrag, C. (1959) Social role, social position and social structure, *Proceedings of the American Correctional Association*, 1959: 178–88.

Schrag, C. (1961) Some foundations for a theory of corrections, in D. R. Cressey (ed.), *The Prison: Studies in Institutional Organization and Change*, New York, Holt, Rinehart & Winston, pp. 309–57.

Seeman, M. (1959) On the meaning of alienation, *American Sociological Review*, 24: 783–91.

Selltiz, C., Wrightsman, L. S. and Cook, S. W. (1976) *Research Methods in Social Relations*, New York, Holt, Rinehart & Winston.

Shipman, M. (1972) *The Limitations of Social Research*, London, Longman.

Shipman, M. (ed.) (1976) *The Organisation and Impact of Social Research*, London, Routledge & Kegan Paul.

Silvey, J. (1975) *Deciphering Data*, London, Longman.

Sjoberg, G. and Nett, R. (1968) *A Methodology for Social Research*, New York, Harper & Row.

Smith, H. W. (1975) *Strategies of Social Research: The Methodological Imagination*, Englewood Cliffs, N.J., Prentice-Hall.

Stinchcombe, A. L. (1968) *Constructing Social Theories*, New York, Harcourt Brace & World.

Straus, M. A. and Nelson J. I. (1968) *Sociological Analysis: An Empirical Approach Through Replication*, New York, Harper & Row.

Strauss, A. L. (1970) Discovering new theory from previous theory, in T. Shibutani (ed.), *Human Nature and Collective Behavior*, Englewood Cliffs, N.J., Prentice-Hall, pp. 46–53.

Sykes, G. M. (1958) *The Society of Captives*, Princeton University Press.

Sykes, G. M. and Matza, D. (1957) Techniques of neutralization: a theory of delinquency, *American Sociological Review*, 22: 664–70.

Tripodi, T., Fellin, P. and Meyer, H. J. (1969) *The Assessment of Social Research*, Itasca, Illinois, Peacock.

Turner, R. H. (1953) The quest for universals in sociological research, *American Sociological Review*, 18: 604–11.

Tyler, S. A. (ed.) (1969) *Cognitive Anthropology*, New York, Holt, Rinehart & Winston.

Voelcker, P. M. W. (1962) The teenage slant, in C. H. Rolph (ed.), *The Police and the Public*, London, Heinemann, pp. 80–95.

Wakeford, J. (1968) *The Strategy of Social Enquiry*, London, Macmillan.

Wallace, W. L. (1971) *The Logic of Science in Sociology*, Chicago, Aldine.

Webb, E. J., Campbell, D. T., Schwartz, R. D. and Sechrest, L. (1966) *Unobtrusive Measures*, Chicago, Rand McNally.

Weeks, D. R. (1972) *A Glossary of Sociological Concepts*, Milton Keynes, Open University Press.

Westergaard, J. and Resler, H. (1975) *Class in a Capitalist Society: A Study of Contemporary Britain*, London, Heinemann.

Wheeler, S. (1961) Socialization in correctional communities, *American Sociological Review*, 26: 697–712.

Whyte, W. F. (1955) *Street Corner Society*, University of Chicago Press.

Wilson, T. P. (1970) Conceptions of interaction and forms of sociological explanation, *American Sociological Review*, 35: 697–710.

Wiseman, J. P. and Aron, M. S. 1970 *Field Projects for Sociology Students*, New York, Harper & Row.

Worsley, P. *et al.* (1977) *Introducing Sociology*, Harmondsworth, Penguin.

Wright, E. O. and Peronne, L. (1977) Marxist class categories and income inequality, *American Sociological Review,* 42: 32–55.

Yablonsky, L. (1967) *The Violent Gang*, Harmondsworth, Penguin.

Young, J. (1970) The role of the police as amplifiers of deviancy, negotiators of reality and translators of fantasy, in S. Cohen (ed.), *Images of Deviance*, Harmondsworth, Penguin, pp. 27–61.

Zetterberg, H. L. (1963) *On Theory and Verification in Sociology*, Totowa, N.J., Bedminster Press.

Selected research reports (see Chapter 9)

Brown, G. W., Bhrolchain, M. N. and Harris, T. (1975) Social class and psychiatric disturbance among women in an urban population, *Sociology*, 9: 225–54.

Crawford, M. P. (1972) Retirement and role-playing, *Sociology*, 6: 217–36.

Davidson, C. and Gaitz, C. M. (1974) Are the poor different? A comparison of work behavior and attitudes among the urban poor and non-poor, *Social Problems,* 22: 229–45.

Frease, D. E. (1973) Schools and delinquency: some intervening processes, *Pacific Sociological Review*, 16: 426–48.

Gerbner, G. (1964) Ideological perspectives and political tendencies in news reporting, *Journalism Quarterly*, 41: 495–508.

Goldthorpe, J. H., Lockwood, D., Bechhofer, F. and Platt, J. (1969) *The Affluent Worker in the Class Structure*, Cambridge University Press.

Hargreaves, D. H. (1967) *Social Relations in a Secondary School*, London, Routledge & Kegan Paul.

Moorhouse, H. F. (1976) Attitudes to class and class relationships in Britain, Sociology, 10: 469–96.

Pearlin, L. I. (1962) Alienation from work: a study of nursing personnel, *American Sociological Review*, 27: 314–26.

Polsky, H. W. (1962) *Cottage Six*, New York, Wiley.

Simon, R. J. (1974) An assessment of racial awareness, preference and self-identity among white and adopted non-white children, *Social Problems*, 22: 43–57.

Spates, J. L. (1976) Counterculture and dominant cultural values: a cross-national analysis of the underground press and dominant culture magazines, *American Sociological Review*, 41: 868–83.

Villemez, W. J. (1975) Gemeinschaft, non-economic distinctions and the migrant worker, *Pacific Sociological Review*, 18: 463–82.

Wild, R. A. (1974) *Bradstow: A Study of Status, Class and Power in a Small Australian Town*, Sydney, Angus & Robertson.

Index

This index includes only authors of studies in Part Two; for a full list of authors see the References (pp. 314–19). Entries followed by (*ex*) refer to Exercises.

322   *Index*